Privacy and Cybersecurity Law

Jon M. Garon
Professor of Law
Nova Southeastern University
Shepard Broad College of Law

A SHORT & HAPPY GUIDE® SERIES

444 Cedar Street, Suite 700
St. Paul, MN 55101
1-877-888-1330

Printed in the United States of America

ISBN: 978-1-68467-983-6

Table of Contents

A Short & Happy Guide to Privacy and Cybersecurity Law

CHAPTER 1

Introduction

A. The Modern Meaning of Privacy

Privacy is "the right to be let alone," but it is also much, much more. Privacy is one of the fundamental human rights enumerated in the United Nations Universal Declaration of Human Rights. It protects individuals from improper surveillance and searches by the government, from interference with personal choices of marriage and contraception, from unauthorized exposure of personal information to the public, and from misuse of information by employers, lenders, and insurance companies. Although privacy is a fundamental right, it is also a qualified right, meaning that the right to privacy must be balanced against competing fundamental rights. For example, privacy rights are often juxtaposed against free speech interests. The protections against governmental searches and seizures are balanced against the state's police power and its ability to establish probable cause sufficient to obtain a search warrant.

Because privacy covers such a wide range of activities, privacy often means very different things to different people. The kind of information considered appropriate to share and the kind of information deemed personal varies within cultures and eras, and among individuals. Although privacy is recognized as a fundamental right by the United Nations, the meaning of that right differs significantly among the different governments of the world. This guide will largely limit itself to privacy laws in the United States.

Privacy laws of various kinds have existed throughout legal history. Roman law recognized a form of attorney-client privilege. Canon law recognized clergy-penitent confidentiality. Colonial America inherited its initial privacy laws from British law, which included a prohibition on eavesdropping for the purpose of making slanderous and mischievous tales as a form of nuisance.

Privacy laws operate using two different approaches. Some privacy laws stop a party from obtaining restricted information. Other privacy laws stop a party from using information for unauthorized purposes. The same law may do both.

For example, attorney-client privilege stops the prosecution in a criminal proceeding from compelling an attorney to reveal confidential information about the attorney's client to the prosecutor. In this way, the policy blocks the prosecutor from obtaining information. At the same time, the attorney-client privilege rules limit an attorney's right to use information obtained from a client. The attorney cannot disclose the privileged information to the prosecutor, even if the attorney would like to do so, and the attorney cannot use the privileged information in other matters if it would be detrimental to the client.

In contrast, the laws governing health care privacy prohibit a hospital from revealing patient information unless approved by the patient or as part of the treatment, billing, or health care operations obligations of the hospital. These laws stop the health care organization from using information it has obtained from its patients. However, the health privacy laws do not stop a newspaper from publishing the health information about a star athlete that the newspaper may have obtained through various interviews.

Privacy laws are also drafted to target specific constituencies, such as the government, employers, commercial enterprises, or the general public. For example, the constitutional Bill of Rights and many state and federal statutes focus on stopping the government from intruding on the privacy of U.S. citizens. Many federal and state regulations focus on the use or misuse of information by commercial enterprises, including lenders and financial services companies, insurance companies, health care organizations, and media companies.

Some of the laws focus on pre-existing confidential relationships between parties, such as the role of a member of the clergy with a congregant, an attorney with a client, or a doctor with a patient. In addition, there are also common law privacy rules that focus on the private conduct between parties.

Many of the laws focus on how commercial businesses collect, process, utilize, and sell the personal information of their visitors, customers, clients, and patients. The laws sometimes vary on how they describe the enterprise covered by the law. Whenever a company is regulated by the privacy law, that regulation extends to both the legal entity and to the employees and management of a company. If a company is restricted from disclosing the personal information of its customers, then every owner, manager, executive, and employee of that company is also restricted from the disclosure of the personal information for any purposes prohibited by the law.

Health privacy laws tend to specify the doctors, medical workers, and administrators separately. This is because a hospital extends privileges to doctors but does not necessarily employ those physicians. Many of the medical services provided in a hospital are contracted to medical groups that are not employed by the hospital.

To be sure everyone with access to medical records is covered by the privacy laws, the privacy regulations point out each person and each entity in the patient care, billing, coding, and insurance process are covered by similar data privacy and security obligations.

B. Privacy and Its Origins

1. Constitutional U.S. Privacy

The strongest aspects of privacy in the United States arose in response to the British occupation of the Colonies. The quartering of troops in private homes and other acts of Royal intrusion leading up to the Revolutionary War highlighted the need to protect the public from the unlimited power of the government. These lessons led directly to the constitutional protection against those governmental intrusions embodied in the constitutional Bill of Rights.

The Fourth Amendment was drafted to protect "against unreasonable searches and seizures," requiring warrants that are issued only after probable cause is established. In the warrant, there must be particularity with regard to the place to be searched and the items or persons seized.

The Fifth Amendment has two clauses that each provide forms of privacy protection. The first protects a criminal defendant from being "compelled in any criminal case to be a witness against himself" and the other assures that no person can be "deprived of life, liberty, or property, without due process of law."

The First Amendment's protections of speech, religion, and association are also forms of privacy. Any government that can require permits to own a printing press or insist on approval before publication of a book, newspaper, or pamphlet can intrude very directly on the privacy of the author. Similarly, the relationship between a person and his or her God is potentially among the most intimate of relationships. The First Amendment protects against significant intrusions into these zones of privacy.

The Ninth Amendment reserved all rights not specifically granted to the federal government to the people. The Ninth Amendment also made clear that the absence of a statement in the Constitution protecting of a particular right did not mean the right no longer existed.

The scope and effect of the Bill of Rights was greatly expanded with the adoption of the Post-Civil War Amendments. The Thirteenth Amendment abolished slavery and the Fifteenth Amendment gave black men the right to vote.

The Fourteenth Amendment was the most sweeping of the Reconstruction amendments. It provides, in part, that "[n]o state shall make or enforce any law which shall abridge the privileges or immunities of citizens of the United States; nor shall any state deprive any person of life, liberty, or property, without due process of law; nor deny to any person within its jurisdiction the equal protection of the laws." The Fourteenth Amendment was slowly applied by the Supreme Court to extend the Bill of Rights to the States and to ground privacy rights as a constitutional protection in certain instances. Although the Fourteenth Amendment was enacted in 1868, much of its impact was not truly felt for another century.

In *Katz v. United States* (1967), the Supreme Court reversed its 1928 ruling on wiretaps by finding that the Fourth Amendment created a reasonable expectation of privacy and that expectation of privacy applied to electronic searches as well as physical searches. Because of the reasonable expectation of privacy, the government could overcome that expectation only if it met the legal requirements to obtain a search warrant. Importantly, the Court also shifted the focus of privacy from places like the home to the privacy of the person. In his concurrence, Justice John Marshall Harlan summarized and reframed the constitutional protection of privacy embodied in the Fourth Amendment by explaining "the rule that has emerged from prior decisions is that there is a twofold requirement, first that a person have exhibited an actual (subjective) expectation of privacy and, second, that the expectation be one that society is prepared to recognize as 'reasonable.' " Justice Harlan's formulation of the reasonable expectation of privacy provided the modern framework for understanding the role of the Bill of Rights in protecting citizens from governmental intrusions. While some constitutional cases vary from this formulation to focus on places being searched, the two-pronged approach focusing on the subjective expectation of privacy and its general, normative acceptance in the public provides the most flexible tool to adapt constitutional provisions to modern technology and new forms of surveillance.

2. Decisional Privacy, Autonomy, and Personal Choice

An offshoot of the jurisprudence regarding the government's ability to use wiretaps and other forms of surveillance has been the ability of the government to criminalize certain types of behavior. These cases represent the intersection between privacy law and more general aspects of civil liberties, but historically, they have often been articulated by the Supreme Court as decisions focusing on private conduct that is outside the scope of a state's power to police. The free expression cases under the First Amendment represent an example of a specifically enumerated constitutional right to keep the government out of the private decision-making of the individual. Most of these examples, however, are not as explicitly embodied in the Bill of Rights.

The first of the decisional privacy cases was *Griswold v. Connecticut* (1965), where the Supreme Court struck down a Connecticut law criminalizing the use of contraceptives as a violation of "marital privacy." The Court explained that "specific guarantees in the Bill of Rights have penumbras, formed by emanations from those guarantees that help give them life and substance. Various guarantees create zones of privacy." The Court found that the intimacy and sanctity of marriage involved a "right of privacy older than the Bill of Rights," even though the specific right was not embodied in the Constitution. In addition to marriage, the Supreme Court also acknowledged that procreation, contraception, child rearing and education, and family relationships were all protected by a constitutional conception of privacy that restricted governmental intrusion.

These cases were followed by *Roe v. Wade* (1973), a seminal case regarding the right to abortion. The appellants in the case articulated the right to choose abortion "in the concept of personal 'liberty' embodied in the Fourteenth Amendment's Due Process Clause; or in personal marital, familial, and sexual privacy said to be protected by the Bill of Rights or its penumbras" as pronounced in *Griswold v. Connecticut*. The *Roe* Court focused on the privacy rights of the woman to make personal decisions about maintaining or terminating a pregnancy. The Court, however, also made clear that the right of privacy, "is not absolute and is subject to some limitations; and that at some point the state interests as to protection of health, medical standards, and prenatal life, become dominant."

In *Lawrence v. Texas* (2003), the Court used the precedent of *Griswold* and the language of Fourteenth Amendment liberty to extend the protections against government intrusion into anti-homosexuality sodomy laws and laws regulating consensual sexual activities.

Privacy scholars including Professors Daniel Solove and Paul Secunda have summarized this sphere of privacy as "decisional privacy" because it focuses on the government's incursion into the private affairs of the individual. Decisional privacy represents the protection of personal autonomy and can be framed as a part of the liberty protected by the Fourteenth Amendment as well as within the scope of the unspecified rights protected by the Ninth Amendment. The various doctrinal approaches are often narrowly drawn, but the practical implications are clear that private, personal choices regarding marriage, sex, and family are constitutionally protected.

The Supreme Court decision of *Obergefell v. Hodges* (2015), providing constitutional protection for same-sex marriage, highlights the liberty aspects of *Lawrence* rather than its privacy protections. The dissent in *Obergefell* objects, in part, because the state recognition of marriage is a public act, the very opposite of a right protected by privacy. The *Obergefell* decision helps separate out fundamental rights based on the liberty rights embodied in the Fourteenth Amendment and the right to private decision making associated with *Griswold*.

Decisional autonomy can be understood to represent the line of Supreme Court decisions that are most heavily associated with *Griswold* and *Lawrence*, including the decisions relied upon in *Griswold* and the decisions that followed *Lawrence*. It represents a small but important part of privacy centered on the individual's right to be free from the government's intrusion into personal life choices of religion, marriage, sex, and parenting. In most areas, decisional privacy focuses on the non-public aspects of a person's relationship and the right of that person to keep the government out of the decision-making process.

3. Common Law Privacy

Privacy laws continued to develop in the nineteenth century through common law development, state statute and congressional action. The growth of the United States saw greater urbanization and the birth of the industrial revolution, each of which changed the social dynamic in the country. These changes made privacy a more significant legal right. In the 1830s New York and other states began to recognize physician-patient privilege. In 1872, Congress passed a law prohibiting the opening of first class mail by the postal service unless it did so in compliance with the Fourth Amendment.

Although there were a number of different state and federal laws recognizing that certain types of information should not be shared, the Harvard publication of "The Right to Privacy" by Samuel Warren and Louis Brandeis in 1890 transformed a very disparate set of state and federal policies into a modern legal field to address the coming technological age.

In their article, Warren and Brandeis argued that from time to time it became necessary to define new legal protections out of the common law. Focusing on the industrial revolution sweeping post-Civil War America, they wrote "[r]ecent inventions and business methods call attention to the next step which must be taken for the protection of the person, and for securing to the individual . . . the right 'to be let alone.' " They highlighted concerns about "numerous mechanical devices threaten[ing] to make good the prediction that 'what is whispered in the closet shall be proclaimed from the house-tops.' "

Warren and Brandeis build their argument regarding the preexisting law of privacy by pointing to the Fifth Amendment protections against self-incrimination and the federal and state copyright laws. Those copyright laws gave authors and artists absolute control of their pre-published expression in addition to significant control of the exploitation of their published works. Arguing that there must be a reason the pre-publication legal protections were so much stronger than the post-publication protections, Warren and Brandeis proposed several theories. They argued that copyright demonstrated the common law's interest in protecting the privacy of the unpublished thoughts for the author, irrespective of whether the works would eventually be destined to be published as literary works or remain private as correspondence. They further argued that the common law approach to breach of confidence and the trade regulations involving trade secrets featured examples of the law reinforcing privacy as a theme under the common law.

The Warren and Brandeis article served both to enhance the legal standing of the trade secrets, breach of confidence, and copyright laws on which the arguments were based and to develop a direct common law or statutory protection for invasions of privacy. By statute and court decisions, the arguments of Warren and Brandeis eventually created a substantial body of legal support.

Although the New York Court of Appeals was unwilling to recognize the right of privacy as articulated by Warren and Brandeis, the Supreme Court of Georgia did so in *Pavesich v. New England Life Ins. Co.* (1905). A photograph of the plaintiff was used in an advertisement for life insurance without his consent. The Georgia Supreme Court embraced the arguments of Warren and Brandeis, finding that the common law has protected the right of a person to seek seclusion from public life, and one has a right to control the publicity surrounding one's activities.

> Liberty includes the right to live as one will, so long as that will does not interfere with the rights of another or of the public. One may desire to live a life of seclusion; another may desire to live a life of publicity; still another may wish to live a life of privacy as to certain matters and

> of publicity as to others. One may wish to live a life of toil where his work is of a nature that keeps him constantly before the public gaze; while another may wish to live a life of research and contemplation, only moving before the public at such times and under such circumstances as may be necessary to his actual existence. Each is entitled to a liberty of choice as to his manner of life, and neither an individual nor the public has a right to arbitrarily take away from him his liberty.

The public agreed with the approach taken by the Georgia courts rather than by the New York courts. Within two years of its Court of Appeals decision, the State of New York enacted the first statutory right of publicity that included both a civil tort and a criminal misdemeanor for its violation.

The national trend continued. The Restatement of the Law of Torts § 867 provided that "[a] person who unreasonably and seriously interferes with another's interest in not having his affairs known to others or his likeness exhibited to the public is liable to the other." The tort was distinct from either trespass or defamation and did not require a confidential relationship to be breached.

4. *Privacy in the Twentieth Century*

Seventy years following the Warren and Brandeis article, another seminal law review article on the topic was published. William Prosser, Dean and Professor of Law at University of California School of Law, Berkeley, revisited the transformation of the common law and attempted to bring order and structure to the doctrine that was missing a formal prima facie approach to the law.

While critical of Warren and Brandeis, Prosser notes that only three states had rejected the right of privacy at the time of his 1960 article. Prosser then categorized the body of law into four distinct causes of action underlying the right to privacy in an attempt to articulate the standards for each. By 1977, Prosser's revised understanding of the Law of Privacy was adopted into the Restatement (Second) of the Law of Torts § 652A:

> (1) One who invades the right of privacy of another is subject to liability for the resulting harm to the interests of the other.
>
> (2) The right of privacy is invaded by
>
> > (a) unreasonable intrusion upon the seclusion of another;
> >
> > (b) appropriation of the other's name or likeness;
> >
> > (c) unreasonable publicity given to the other's private life; or
> >
> > (d) publicity that unreasonably places the other in a false light before the public.

The first two of Prosser's four causes of action were those recognized by the Georgia Supreme Court, while the tort of giving unreasonable publicity to another's private life and the tort of false light were both expansions of the common law right under common law development.

Each of the four types of tort privacy have continued to develop. In addition, as discussed below, the development of the First Amendment has added a significant limitation on these common law rules, often contrasting the right to speak and the right to be left alone.

C. Privacy in the Twenty-First Century

Just as the industrial revolution presaged the development of Warren and Brandeis' "The Law of Privacy," in 1890, the changes to society triggered by the growth of the Information Age brought with them a different form of the right to be let alone. These demands were based on the ability of technology to identify, track, and collate data through increasingly sophisticated databases, analytics, and artificial intelligence.

1. Federal Sectoral Privacy

American society is still in the relatively early stages of the information age. The growth of the computer industry, the Internet, mobile communications, and data networks have led to social media, smart machines, robotics, and many other changes that all rely on massive amounts of individuals' information to operate.

These technologies have triggered new responses through the development of state and federal statutes as well as by common law doctrines. Beginning in the 1970s, Congress enacted a series of laws to promote privacy of personal information and data in specific industries or economic sectors:

- The Federal Privacy Act to protect against the misuse of federally collected public data;
- Family Educational Rights and Privacy Act to protect student records;
- Fair Credit Reporting Act to protect against the abuse and exploitation of consumer credit information;
- Video Privacy Protection Act and Cable Communications Policy Acts to stop the public disclosure of a person's media consumption history;
- Gramm-Leach-Bliley Act, also known as the Financial Modernization Act of 1999, to require notice about the sharing of a financial institution's consumer data;

- Health Insurance Portability and Accountability Act, which includes the HIPAA Privacy Rule and the HIPAA Security Rule, to establish obligations for medical industry protection of personal and protected health information; and
- Children's Online Privacy Protection Act (COPPA) to limit the collection and use of personal information regarding children under the age of 13.

The concerns raised by these federal statutes and the kind of data consumption in the information age is less frequently about the intrusion into one's seclusion through the newspapers to the public and more about the use or misuse of data collected about one's movements and purchases being sold to data brokers for inappropriate purposes.

As laws have evolved at both the state and federal level, the focus has been, first, to provide the consumer notice of the uses for which data are being collected and, second, to establish standards to assure that the data being collected are not stolen and used for fraudulent or illegal purposes. These laws are still in their developmental stages. They include mandatory privacy notices and mandatory data breach disclosure requirements.

Some states, such as California, require that every business enterprise doing business with California residents have a posted privacy policy. Both state and federal regulations require that a company follow its posted privacy policies. This combination of state and federal regulations combined make posted privacy policies mandatory for most U.S. businesses. Multinational companies must also comply with regulations that are based on their European customers or the storage of data in European countries.

Some states, such as Illinois, have passed laws specifically requiring additional consumer consent to the collection of biometric data, including fingerprints, DNA, facial characteristics, retinal patterns, voice patterns, and similar identifiers.

The twentieth century protections for intrusions into seclusion continue to apply to the modern data misuse situations as well. Unfortunately, the rights and remedies of twentieth century torts may not always fit twenty-first century conduct. Instead of relying on a slow evolution of the common law, the state and federal governments have enacted laws focused on areas where the exploitation of private information was most likely to cause economic or personal harm.

This approach is known as "sectoral privacy" because each industry or economic sector has its own laws. These laws vary considerably. Banks, for example, are required merely to notify consumers of their data privacy practices. Customers have very limited choices about accepting or rejecting the privacy terms offered. In contrast, health care organizations are severely restricted in how they share certain health information about patients, and they face severe fines for failure to protect the health information of their patients. Other industry sectors fall somewhere in the middle of these two regulatory sectors.

Under the various state and federal statutes, sectoral information privacy has expanded beyond confidentiality to also include the obligation to maintain the integrity of the information, and in some cases, to require the correction of inaccurate data. In some sectors, the right to collect personal identifiable information includes the obligation to secure that data and to ensure that it is accurate.

2. Personal Information Under Data Privacy Laws

The personal identifiable information covered by privacy laws varies as greatly as do the types of privacy regulations. There is no single definition of personal information because the definition is specific to each statute. The U.S. Department of Labor provides this summary as useful guidance:

> Personal Identifiable Information (PII) is defined as . . . [a]ny representation of information that permits the identity of an individual to whom the information applies to be reasonably inferred by either direct or indirect means. Further, PII is defined as information: (i) that directly identifies an individual (e.g., name, address, Social Security number or other identifying number or code, telephone number, email address, etc.) or (ii) by which an agency intends to identify specific individuals in conjunction with other data elements, i.e., indirect identification. (These data elements may include a combination of gender, race, birth date, geographic indicator, and other descriptors).

These individual pieces of information are common in many of the sectoral privacy laws. There are also significant exceptions to treating these items of information as private. For example, the Family Educational Rights and Privacy Act (FERPA) regulations have an exception for "directory information," meaning information that a school or district might publish. Schools once regularly published directories so that parents and students could contact each other. The directory information usually includes the name, address, telephone listing, age, grade level, participation in officially recognized activities and sports, and dates of attendance. This allows a school to promote its athletic teams and publicize the success of its students without seeking permission before every press release and yearbook is published or before its website is updated.

The rules are very different under COPPA for information collected about children under 13 by organizations that are not schools or do not fall within FERPA. Personal information under COPPA includes the following:

- First and last name;
- A home or other physical address including street name and name of a city or town;
- Online contact information;
- A screen or user name that functions as online contact information;
- A telephone number;
- A Social Security number;
- A persistent identifier that can be used to recognize a user over time and across different websites or online services;
- A photograph, video, or audio file, where such file contains a child's image or voice;
- Geolocation information sufficient to identify street name and name of a city or town; or
- Information concerning the child or the parents of that child that the operator collects online from the child and combines with an identifier described above.

In practice, this means that an elementary school could publish photos from a play put on by its students (and capture the pictures with the student names) on its website because that is directory information under FERPA, but the Cub Scouts or Brownies (Girl Scouts) would need the permission of each parent to publish the same photos and captions. Although the personal information is the same, the governing law defines the scope of the laws and the exceptions differently.

To identify whether information is protected by a privacy law, the company or organization (enterprise) seeking to use that information must generally answer four questions:

1. What regulations apply to the enterprise?
2. What is the information the enterprise wishes to use?
3. How did the enterprise acquire the information?
4. How will the enterprise use the information?

By following the answers provided by these four questions, an enterprise will know the extent to which it can use the information it has collected. An enterprise is free to use and sell any information that is not protected under one of the sectoral privacy laws or otherwise protected by confidentiality, contract, or trade secret law. If the enterprise is governed by one or more data privacy laws, then it must obtain permission to sell or disclose that information unless the sale or disclosure falls within a specific exception to the privacy under the law. In some cases, the right to sell or disclose the information requires the consent of the person identified by the information.

Finally, because the enterprise has the obligation not to sell or disclose the personal information, the enterprise also has a duty to protect the information from accidental disclosures, theft, and third-party publication of the information. The duty to protect the collected personal information from disclosure requires sufficient security to keep the information from loss or theft. As a result, the law of privacy also extends into the law of cybersecurity.

3. The Modern Meaning of Cybersecurity

Because commercial businesses are required to follow their posted privacy policies and the policies in many sectors are governed by specific privacy laws related to the collection, protection, and use of the personally identifying information, modern privacy law also entails substantial cybersecurity.

Protecting the personal identifiable information means protecting the systems that store, transmit, and utilize the information. This applies to the computers, mobile devices, networks, routers, servers, and other systems, whether connected to the Internet or which operate separately. It requires that software is up to date so that all known vulnerabilities, flaws, or errors in the software are corrected promptly. It requires that systems use passwords and other means to keep unauthorized individuals out of enterprise systems, and anticipate the techniques used by potential intruders.

Cybersecurity can be thought of as the reasonable duties that an enterprise must undertake to assure that the information it has collected is not misused by individuals within the enterprise or by outside third parties. Cybersecurity requirements outline the steps needed to assure the continued confidentiality, integrity, and availability of the data.

Based on the HIPAA Security Rule, cybersecurity is often organized into three separate spheres: physical, technical, and administrative safeguards. Physical safeguards relate to the physical assets involved in a facility and its information networks. If a thief steals a laptop from a car, that theft may result in the potential disclosure of thousands or millions of protected health care or financial records. If disgruntled employees can remove servers from a company's business center, the theft could involve millions of dollars in financial accounts. So, the physical safeguarding of buildings and equipment is a necessary first step in any cybersecurity plan.

Technical safeguards are often the steps most commonly described as cybersecurity. Technical safeguards may include the use of encryption, firewalls, multi-factor authentication techniques, penetration testing, network logs to monitor traffic, and other technological solutions to make it more difficult for unauthorized individuals to access data stored on the systems. Up-to-date technology is essential to stop hackers and other intruders from introducing software that can damage, steal, or open an enterprise's systems to theft, destruction, or ransom.

Administrative safeguards are the third feature of an effective cybersecurity plan. These are the policies and practices that assure an enterprise operates its cybersecurity policy in a strategic and effective manner. Administrative safeguards require that cybersecurity is a top priority within the enterprise, receiving sufficient funding and staffing to carry out the objectives. Administrative safeguards establish the policies that require up-to-date software upgrades needed to eliminate known vulnerabilities; train all personnel on the best practices regarding authentication; keep access of sensitive information to the smallest group of employees needed to use that information; require procedures for the termination of personnel so that accounts are closed promptly; and take other steps so that the physical and technological safeguards are followed carefully and risks are mitigated to the greatest extent possible.

For an enterprise to have a successful cybersecurity system, it must know what information it has collected, where it is stored, and how it is used. The enterprise must then establish policies and procedures to physically protect its assets, use appropriate technology to protect its systems, train its employees, and continually update and upgrade its efforts as a core competency of the organization. If a company does this, then it can respond to the inevitable challenges it will face.

For example, since laptops are often lost or stolen, it would be better not to use laptops for the storage of certain data, such as medical and financial records. Where laptops are permitted, personnel should be trained not to leave laptops on the seats of cars that are visible to the public. More importantly, the enterprise should encrypt all its laptops so that when one is stolen, the data cannot be easily accessed. In addition, the enterprise should include remote data-wiping for laptops and mobile devices, so that the stolen data can be removed remotely. Taken together, these technological and physical safeguards help minimize and mitigate the risk. The example highlights that an enterprise must combine administrative policies, training, technological measures, and physical measures to achieve cybersecurity.

Cybersecurity should also be scaled appropriately for the size of the enterprise and the nature of the risks involved. A small business will do best by simply avoiding the collection of unnecessary personal identifiable information. By reducing the amount of information it retains, the small business will also reduce its exposure to loss. A hospital, in contrast, must collect a substantial amount of information governed by HIPAA, which includes the most exacting federal regulations on data privacy and security. Each enterprise must respond to its particular situation.

D. A Practical Approach to Understanding Privacy Law

Information privacy, decisional privacy, protections from governmental surveillance, and common law privacy each share common roots, and they may all come into play in certain situations. When approaching a conflict over privacy, the analysis generally starts by identifying the parties to the conflict. If it is a state or federal criminal proceeding against a person, then we must first look at what constitutional or statutory limitations restrict the power of the government to collect information regarding the defendant. Even on identical facts, the government may face fewer restrictions if the case involves a civil or administrative action against the defendant.

If the conflict involves the public disclosure of personal identifiable information by a commercial or nonprofit enterprise, then the conflict will likely be governed by the laws passed for that particular industry. The plaintiff in such a conflict will be much more likely to have legal protection if the disclosure involved a health care organization or lender because those laws are much more protective than other sectors. If the disclosure occurred through a data breach, then other state laws might also offer some protection to the individuals whose data were inappropriately disclosed. If the information was disclosed by a newspaper, then the common law rights to privacy might still apply. In each situation, there are exceptions to the rights of privacy.

For example, in 2014, malicious software was secretly inserted into the software of Sony Pictures. The software went undiscovered for at least two months. During that time, the software allowed hackers to copy significant amounts of data from Sony. On the day the hackers went public, they published unreleased movies, email correspondence, financial records, and other data. The hackers used the name "Guardians of Peace." The hackers demanded that Sony stop the release of a forthcoming movie, *The Interview*, which featured a farcical and comedic depiction of North Korean leader Kim Jong-un. Although North Korea claimed it was not responsible for the Sony data breach, it did label the release of the film as an "act of war." The terrorist threats accompanying the data breach hack initially led to the cancellation of the film's release, but concerns over international censorship led to the film being released on a small scale.

Correspondence in the leaked emails led Sony Pictures co-chairwoman, Amy Pascal, to resign over published content relating to an upcoming meeting with then-President Barack Obama as potentially racist. Former employees of the studio sued for the release of their personal identifiable information, including Social Security numbers and health care information. Actor Charlie Sheen's HIV positive medical status was captured by the hackers and may have led to his decision to make his diagnoses public.

These examples highlight the continued relevance of the common law protections into the intrusion of privacy, the statutory protections to protect against disclosure of protectible identifiable information, and the consequence of cybersecurity failures. Criminal charges were never filed in the incident despite investigations by the FBI and other agencies. Nonetheless, those criminal statutes governed how the FBI operated to try to obtain information about the attack and what laws limit its investigative efforts.

Ultimately, Sony was reported to have settled the lawsuits for approximately $15 million dollars. The impact on revenue from *The Interview* cannot easily be calculated. (The publicity might have actually increased its long-term return.) In addition to the jobs lost and relationships damaged by the public disclosure by Sony, the company's initial "investigation and remediation costs" were also listed as $15 million.

While these sums are significant, the breach did not involve customer data. In comparison, Sony suffered an estimated $171 million in costs for a breach of its PlayStation Network in 2011.

While the attack against Sony was highly unfortunate, it illustrates how each of the areas of privacy law can shape the consequence for a single event. Each chapter below will explore how these areas of law and practice have developed and how best to understand them in the context of this rapidly changing field.

Key Takeaways from This Chapter:

Privacy laws have existed as part of law throughout history, but they have grown in scope as notions of privacy and the technology to invade privacy have changed.

Privacy is not mentioned by name in the Constitution, but it is found within the penumbra of many constitutional rights, including the First Amendment, Fourth Amendment, Fifth Amendment, Ninth Amendment, and Fourteenth Amendment.

Privacy is a broad concept, closely tied to personal liberty, that limits the use of personal information in four areas:

- the government's ability to collect information about its citizens for criminal prosecutions
- the government's ability to criminalize certain intimate, personal choices, regarding marriage, sex, abortion, and procreation
- how the press and public can disclose certain types of personal information, and
- how enterprises can sell and distribute the information they collect about their customers.

Although privacy is a fundamental right, it is not an absolute right and in each of the areas protected by privacy law, the privacy interests must also be balanced against other governmental interests.

Since information is collected and stored by enterprises in their computer systems and networks, there is an obligation to maintain cybersecurity to protect the information so that it is not misused by the individuals within the organization or disclosed to the public by hackers and thieves.

Things to Know:

Privacy is a very old legal protection, but it has changed significantly in the twenty-first century as new technologies require updated rules to protect from unwanted use of private information.

Privacy protections include statutory and constitutional protections against the government taking legal actions against citizens, restrictions on how businesses use of information they collect about their customers, and how individuals share information about their neighbors.

Privacy in the United States is changing as laws that once focused on specific sectors of the economy are being supplemented with state laws that cover much more personal information.

While privacy is a fundamental right, there are many fundamental rights including the right of free speech, requiring courts and lawmakers to balance these interests.

Things to Think About:

The right of privacy was never described in the Constitution, but as many as five of the Amendments in the Bill of Rights provided forms of privacy protection. Why did the framers fail to speak directly to privacy as a right?

Why did Justice Harlan ground the right of privacy in an expectation that the privacy interest be "one that society is prepared to recognize as 'reasonable'"? What would the difference be if the reasonable privacy interests were only those identified under the law?

To what extent does decisional privacy, including marital privacy and sexual privacy have the same basis as protections from government searches or behavior advertising? Would these be better understood under a single theory or by separating out these rights using different terms?

Why are there many different definitions of personal information? Should some identifiers be excluded from the list of personal information? How do the state and federal regulations make the definition important to enforcement?

CHAPTER 2

Constitutional Protections of Privacy Under the Fourth Amendment

A. Introduction

The constitutional right to be free of government intrusion can be understood most clearly through the language of the Fourth Amendment and the laws developed because of those rights. The Fourth Amendment provides the "right of the people to be secure in their person, houses, papers, and effects, against unreasonable searches and seizures." Similar protections were incorporated into state constitutions as well. The new Americans were still reeling from the abusive conduct of the British royal government, so they did not want to recreate the same potential for abuse in the new state or federal governments.

The Fourth Amendment requires the government to obtain a warrant to search a person's home, car, or similar location based on probable cause. Probable cause for a search warrant requires that the facts and circumstances provide the basis for a reasonable person to believe that a crime was committed at the place to be searched, or that evidence of a crime exists at the location. A search warrant must both specify the place where the search will be conducted and the items to be seized.

The consequence of violating the Fourth Amendment results in the information obtained being excluded from use in the trial against the accused. Known as the "Exclusionary Rule," the policy discourages unlawful police practices because it frustrates the purpose for violating the constitutional rights of the target.

There are a number of exceptions to the warrant requirement. The warrantless search will be lawful if the police are given consent to the search by the person whose property they wish to search, if the items to be searched are in plain view, or if there are exigent circumstances. Exigent circumstances may exist if there is an imminent danger to a person, imminent risk of destruction of the items to be seized, or threat of a suspect's imminent escape.

The warrant requirement may be quite similar to the rules of common law trespass and the common law prohibition against eavesdropping. In *Silverman v. U.S.* (1961), the court used the trespass analogy to find that using a "spike microphone" to attach an audio pickup through a wall onto the building's heating duct violated the Fourth Amendment. The Supreme Court returned to the analogy of trespass as recently as 2012 in *U.S. v. Jones*. Nonetheless, the trespass rules are merely an analogy. The exceptions to allowing a warrantless search may have little to do with the exceptions to common law trespass, so the use of the analogy may be overstated. And even some cases involving a trespass did not result in a Fourth Amendment violation.

In addition, trespass is not relevant in other situations. Professor Orin Kerr explains that cases going back to the nineteenth century invoked the Fourth Amendment to require a warrant before a court could order a party to turn over a document. In *Boyd v. U.S.*

(1886), the Supreme Court found that the order to turn over documents was the equivalent of a search and subject to the warrant requirement.

B. Electronic Surveillance Under the Fourth Amendment

While every search and seizure is an intrusion on privacy, the general application of search and seizure law falls within the disciplines of criminal law and criminal procedure. Electronic surveillance, however, has implications well beyond the specific enforcement of criminal laws and represents an important element of information privacy policy.

1. *Olmstead v. U.S.*

The Supreme Court first wrestled with the consequences of modern technology in *Olmstead v. U.S.* (1928). *Olmstead* involved the use of a wiretap to observe and break up a major bootlegging operation during the height of prohibition. Ninety-one defendants were indicted for violation of the National Prohibition Act. Roy Olmstead was joined by eight other defendants challenging the introduction of the wiretap evidence.

Olmstead argued that the use of a wiretap to listen in on the telephone calls in his home (and the office of his attorney) violated both his Fourth Amendment and Fifth Amendment rights. The wiretaps were placed on the telephone wires at the telephone poles and switching stations. At least five homes were tapped as part of an investigation lasting seven months.

The Supreme Court determined there was no trespass since the taps were not placed directly on the homes. The Court also rejected an analogy of the phone lines to sealed first-class mail. Although the Court acknowledged that "the unlawful rifling by a government agent of a sealed letter is a search and seizure of the sender's papers or effects," the government does not have a similar "care of telegraph or telephone messages." The Court, therefore, rejected the application of the Fourth Amendment to what was overheard on the telephone lines, even though the police could only hear the content of the phone calls through their invasive acts.

In his dissent, Justice Brandeis wrote that it was "immaterial where the physical connection with the telephone wires was made." Instead, he highlighted the pernicious nature of the invasion of privacy:

> The evil incident to invasion of the privacy of the telephone is far greater than that involved in tampering with the mails. Whenever a telephone line is tapped, the privacy of the persons at both ends of the line is invaded, and all conversations between them upon any subject, and although proper, confidential, and privileged, may be overheard. Moreover, the tapping of one man's telephone line involves the tapping of the telephone of every other person whom he may call, or who may call him. As a means of espionage, writs of assistance and general warrants are but puny instruments of tyranny and oppression when compared with wire tapping.

Justice Brandeis returned to the themes of his law review article, "The Right to Privacy," by explaining what the right to be let alone means in the context of constitutional protections:

> The makers of our Constitution undertook to secure conditions favorable to the pursuit of happiness. They recognized the significance of man's spiritual nature, of his feelings and of his intellect. They knew that only a part of the pain, pleasure and satisfactions of life are to be found in material things. They sought to protect Americans in their beliefs, their thoughts, their emotions

> and their sensations. They conferred, as against the government, the right to be let alone-the most comprehensive of rights and the right most valued by civilized men. To protect, that right, every unjustifiable intrusion by the government upon the privacy of the individual, whatever the means employed, must be deemed a violation of the Fourth Amendment. And the use, as evidence in a criminal proceeding, of facts ascertained by such intrusion must be deemed a violation of the Fifth.

Although Justice Brandeis' opinion was only in the dissent, it became the touchstone of American Fourth Amendment thinking both through legislative enactment and constitutional interpretation.

2. *Communications Act of 1934*

The public was not satisfied with the decision in *Olmstead*, which took a significant step backward in the protections from unlawful searches and seizures or of the treatment of wiretaps of a person's home as the same as overhearing a conversation held in public. Radio, telephone, and telegraph technology were undergoing rapid development in the 1920s and the nature of these technologies was transforming society. Congressional hearings were held, and legislation intended to overrule *Olmstead* was introduced in Congress.

In response to the changes in both radio and telephony, Congress updated the Radio Act of 1927 by passing the Communications Act of 1934, a sweeping new law to regulate both telephony and radio. Section 605 of the new law provided, in part, that "no person not being authorized by the sender shall intercept any communication and divulge or publish the existence, contents, substance, purport, effect, or meaning of such intercepted communication to any person."

Congress did not specifically identify *Olmstead* when writing this provision. Nonetheless, the provision of the new law clearly barred the wiretapping and interception of telegraphs and telephone calls in the same way that Congress had barred intercepting first class mail.

There was significant conflict whether § 605 was intended to apply to law enforcement. The Supreme Court answered this question three years later, in *Nardone v. United States* (1937). The Supreme Court held that the broad language of § 605 applied to law enforcement as well as other persons. Since the law was not drafted as an evidentiary rule, it did not include an exception for a search based on a warrant. Instead it created an absolute prohibition against wiretaps.

The FBI and other law enforcement agencies did not accept this blanket prohibition on wiretaps. Instead, the police and FBI continued to conduct warrantless wiretaps in certain situations. The Justice Department used wiretaps, arguing that the law was violated only if a party both intercepted and divulged the communication. Using the information learned from intercepting a wiretap, the Justice Department reasoned, did not violate the statute if the wiretap was not also used publicly. Instead, the FBI used the information learned from the wiretaps to identify evidence that could be used in court, to interrogate witnesses, and to anticipate criminal conduct.

These practices were heavily used to stop espionage during World War II and to counteract organized crime in the 1950s. Numerous investigations beginning in the 1960s substantiated concerns that the FBI also used wiretaps extensively for political purposes and for other illegal activities. The courts were split on how to handle challenges to the FBI wiretaps, but as time went on, the Supreme Court and lower courts extended *Nardone* to stop many of these practices.

Even before the passage of the Communications Act, many states had laws limiting the use of wiretaps and regulations about telegraph and telephone communications. The Communications Act preempted all the state laws regarding radio and telephone communications. Although the federal law barred states from approving wiretaps, in many states the law was not followed. Instead, some states allowed wiretaps when approved by warrants, court orders, or subpoenas. The state courts were aware that their procedures were in direct violation of federal law, but the dislike for the absolute ban on wiretaps encouraged some jurisdictions to ignore the federal law.

In addition, many of the listening devices developed in the 1950s and 1960s were not connected to telephone wires. Instead, wired and wireless technologies were created to listen in on telephone calls and private conversations using microphone "bugs" placed in lamps, desks, showerheads, picture frames, cigarette lighters, and pens. The technology of surveillance had vastly outpaced the laws regulating these activities.

In the thirty years since *Olmstead*, the technology of eavesdropping had progressed radically, and the use of electronic surveillance had expanded significantly.

3. Wiretap Act (1968)

The efforts in Congress to update the wiretap laws took over three decades to pass. The law was shaped by the efforts among legislators and the significant expansion of privacy protection that occurred with the 1967 decision in *Katz v. U.S.* (1967). *Katz* adopted the dissenting position of *Olmstead*, holding that a right to privacy extended well beyond physical trespass and would be recognized if the party claiming the privacy right had a subjective expectation in that privacy and the expectation was objectively reasonable.

After *Katz*, § 605 of the Communications Act was no longer consistent with the Fourth Amendment and statutory revisions were essential. Passed as Title III to the Omnibus Crime Control and Safe Streets Act of 1968, the "Wiretap Act" established a warrant requirement for the use of electronic surveillance. Under the new law, which remains in place today with only a few amendments, the Wiretap Act prohibits the interception of both oral and wire communications, but also provides a mechanism for seeking a court order to issue a wiretap or electronic surveillance.

The law expanded the general prohibition against intercepting telephone or telegraph communications into a much broader prohibition against any surveillance of oral or wire communication. By doing so, the law was expanded to cover all the eavesdropping devices that had been proliferating during the 1950s and 1960s.

In 1986, the law was expanded from wire and oral to all electronic communications. In 1998, it was also expanded to cover email and other forms of stored electronic communications. Then, in the wake of the September 11th terrorist attacks on the United States, it was amended through the USA PATRIOT Act and subsequent revisions to those laws. These changes, however, have been relatively minor, and the modern law governing electronic surveillance was established with the 1968 Wiretap Act.

The Wiretap Act represented a significant step forward to reconcile the statutory law of surveillance with the expanded constitutional protections of the Fourth Amendment. It provided law enforcement an effective tool to fight crime and civil rights advocates a powerful mechanism to reign in the illegal use of wiretaps by state and federal governments. It prohibits the interception, disclosure, use, or procurement of another person to intercept or attempt to intercept the communications unless there is an exception to the court order requirement, or a court order is granted.

There are exceptions to the prohibition on eavesdropping. For example, the law exempts the various business operations involved in the telephone and communications industry from the prohibition, provided the surveillance was necessary for the provision of the communications services. Similarly, a law enforcement officer may disclose information obtained in authorized wiretapping to another law enforcement officer or during testimony, provided the use or disclosure "is appropriate to the proper performance of the official duties of the officer making or receiving the disclosure."

In addition, the law allows that either party to a communication may consent to having that conversation monitored or recorded. Some state laws, in contrast, allow for the recording of conversations only if all parties to the conversation consent to it being recorded.

The most significant part of the law, however, is the regulations regarding the issuance of a court order. Section 2518 creates a statutory system for issuing wiretap orders. To be eligible to request a wiretap or other form of electronic surveillance, the government must swear out a request to a judge that it is investigating a criminal felony, establish that the government has probable cause the crime has occurred or will occur, and identify particular communications concerning that crime that the government seeks to obtain.

The statute lists specific predicate offenses for which a wiretap is available. For crimes not on the list, access to wiretaps and electronic surveillance are not permitted. The list of predicate crimes has grown since the initial adoption of the Wiretap Act, making it less of a limit on law enforcement than it once had been.

The documentation requirement for the court order are substantial.

> Each application shall include the following information:
>
> (a) the identity of the investigative or law enforcement officer making the application, and the officer authorizing the application;
>
> (b) a full and complete statement of the facts and circumstances relied upon by the applicant, to justify his belief that an order should be issued, including (i) details as to the particular offense that has been, is being, or is about to be committed, (ii) except as provided in subsection (11), a particular description of the nature and location of the facilities from which or the place where the communication is to be intercepted, (iii) a particular description of the type of communications sought to be intercepted, (iv) the identity of the person, if known, committing the offense and whose communications are to be intercepted;
>
> (c) a full and complete statement as to whether or not other investigative procedures have been tried and failed or why they reasonably appear to be unlikely to succeed if tried or to be too dangerous;
>
> (d) a statement of the period of time for which the interception is required to be maintained. If the nature of the investigation is such that the authorization for interception should not automatically terminate when the described type of communication has been first obtained, a particular description of facts establishing probable cause to believe that additional communications of the same type will occur thereafter;

(e) a full and complete statement of the facts concerning all previous applications known to the individual authorizing and making the application, made to any judge for authorization to intercept, or for approval of interceptions of, wire, oral, or electronic communications involving any of the same persons, facilities or places specified in the application, and the action taken by the judge on each such application; and

(f) where the application is for the extension of an order, a statement setting forth the results thus far obtained from the interception, or a reasonable explanation of the failure to obtain such results.

The warrant issued by a judge may last up to thirty days. If the investigation needs additional time, then a new warrant must be requested, and the judge must be updated on the effectiveness of the surveillance during the time of the previous warrant.

Like other warrants for probable cause, there are also provisions for exigent circumstances. Section 2517 provides the basis for an emergency order. It requires that the investigating officer "reasonably determines that an emergency situation exists," that involves immediate danger of death or serious physical injury to any person; a conspiracy "threatening the national security interest;" or an emergency involving "conspiratorial activities characteristic of organized crime." Even if the emergency exists, the investigating officer must act only if the officer believes there are sufficient grounds for a warrant to have been issued. The court order must be filed within forty-eight hours of the emergency surveillance, and if the warrant is denied, then the information gathered will be considered to have been in violation of Title III and it cannot be used.

Like the Communications Act before it, the Wiretap Act preempts state law. The law establishes federal minimum requirements for protection of electronic communications. States have the option to add additional privacy protections. Unlike the Communications Act, the broad nature of the statute, the changes to the Fourth Amendment jurisprudence by the courts, and the public understanding of the prior abuses of wiretaps have changed the practices at both the state and federal levels of law enforcement.

4. Additional Amendments to the Wiretap Act

Since the adoption of the Wiretap Act in 1968, there has been a continued expansion of electronic communications involving home computers, the Internet, mobile devices, and cloud-based or online storage. Various laws have updated the Wiretap Act to account for these changes but also to address the growing threat of international and domestic terrorism.

The Electronic Communications Privacy Act and the Stored Wire Electronic Communications Act are two laws commonly known together as the Electronic Communications Privacy Act of 1986 (ECPA). They were passed to expand the scope of legal protection to all electronic communications, including email and private content posted to computer networks. The ECPA expanded the scope of the law to the evolving modern communications. The law provides civil and criminal penalties for intentional, unauthorized interception of private electronic communications. It expands the warrant requirement under the Wiretap Act to nonverbal communications, such as emails, texts, and visual communications.

In addition to its expansion of electronic communications protected under the warrant requirements of the ECPA, it also added two additional titles, each with a lower form of legal protection.

Title II of the ECPA, the Stored Communications Act, provides civil and criminal protection from intercepting, copying, or otherwise accessing stored communications such as emails, bulletin board messages, or private communications stored on cloud-based systems. Unlike communications protected under the Wiretap Act, emails and other communications stored on a remote system such as an ISP's server can be obtained by law enforcement using a court order under § 2703(d) that does not require probable cause. Instead, the investigating officer must provide "specific and articulable facts showing that there are reasonable grounds to believe that the contents of a wire or electronic communication, or the records or other information sought, are relevant and material to an ongoing criminal investigation." These standards fall significantly below the warrant requirements for a wiretap or surveillance of email correspondence.

A warrant is still required for email on a person's home computer, for email and similar communications in transit, and for unopened email stored for 180 days or less on a remote computer. But if the email is stored on a remote computer and opened, or the email on the remote computer has been left unopened for more than 180 days, then the § 2703(d) court order is sufficient for the court to issue its order.

Title III of the ECPA refers to "pen registers and trap and trace" investigations. These dialed number recorder devices provide information about the origin and destination of a communication but do not provide any content. The information is quite similar to the contents of a telephone bill that lists the calls and call duration for the preceding month.

In *Smith v. Maryland* (1979), the Supreme Court held that trap and trace information can be considered a third-party business record. Such records are not private information and do not receive any protection from the Fourth Amendment. An investigating officer can obtain a court order provided the government has certified the pen register's use is relevant to an ongoing criminal investigation. This is the lowest standard for issuing a court order.

The Wiretap Act was also substantially amended following the September 11, 2001, terrorist attacks. The USA PATRIOT Act (Uniting and Strengthening America by Providing Appropriate Tools Required to Intercept and Obstruct Terrorism Act of 2001) and its amendments in 2005, 2006, and 2011 have greatly expanded the power of the government to conduct surveillance and operate without public oversight.

Most of the legislation added by the USA PATRIOT Act focus on foreign intelligence gathering within the United States. These laws allowed for expanded surveillance unrelated to specific criminal investigations. The law also significantly expanded anti-money laundering statutes by adding additional obligations on banks and financial institutions.

The USA PATRIOT Act expanded the list of predicate crimes under investigation for purposes of obtaining a wiretap to include terrorist and computer crimes. The law also expanded the stored communication provisions to include voice mail and audiovisual records, not just email messages. In addition, it extended the pen register definition to include the ability to cover non-telephone electronic communications through electronic tracking devices.

C. The Reasonable Expectation of Privacy

1. *Katz v. United States (1967)*

The *Olmstead* decision became increasingly difficult for the Supreme Court to uphold in the decades that followed the decision. Neither the courts nor the public were satisfied with the legal distinction between a spike microphone that unconstitutionally tapped physically into an adjoining room and a parabolic microphone that could constitutionally eavesdrop into a room from across the street.

Cases arising in the 1960s sometimes involved the use of court ordered warrants to approve electronic surveillance. The courts varied in how they required law enforcement to establish the probable cause and specificity needed to use electronic surveillance. These cases approved recording devices under circumstances needed to obtain search warrants, illustrating the approach being debated in Congress.

By 1967, the Supreme Court was ready to reassess the law of surveillance. In *Katz v. United States*, the petitioner, Charles Katz, was a professional bookmaker or gambler. FBI agents observed him placing bets. The FBI rented a room next to Katz and began listening in to his phone calls made from his apartment. They also observed him using a bank of three telephone booths, each of which was made of glass and wood, and which closed with a folding door. Without a warrant, the FBI taped microphones to the outside of two telephone booths regularly used by Katz and marked the third telephone booth out of order. As the Ninth Circuit noted in upholding the conviction, "[t]he microphones were attached to the outside of the telephone booths with tape. There was no physical penetration inside of the booths. The microphones were activated only while appellant was approaching and actually in the booth."

The FBI obtained a warrant to search Katz's apartment. When Katz met with the FBI agents following a search of his apartment, he asked "why he could not have his records back. He stated without them he was out of business and that he had been a handicapper and a better most of his life. He suggested that if he got his records back he would continue to bet."

In the Supreme Court opinion, the Court never mentions Katz by name. Instead, the Court objects to both the petitioner and respondent's characterization of the phone booths. The Court rejects a focus on the physical telephone booth as subject to trespass while being used. The Court also rejected the notion that there are private places and public places. It explained that the "effort to decide whether or not a given 'area,' viewed in the abstract, is 'constitutionally protected' deflects attention from the problem . . . . For the Fourth Amendment protects people, not places." The Court moved from the location of a private communication to the nature of the communicator's intent:

> [W]hat [petitioner] sought to exclude when he entered the booth was not the intruding eye—it was the uninvited ear. He did not shed his right to do so simply because he made his calls from a place where he might be seen. No less than an individual in a business office, in a friend's apartment, or in a taxicab, a person in a telephone booth may rely upon the protection of the Fourth Amendment. One who occupies it, shuts the door behind him, and pays the toll that permits him to place a call is surely entitled to assume that the words he utters into the mouthpiece will not be broadcast to the world. To read the Constitution more narrowly is to ignore the vital role that the public telephone has come to play in private communication. . . .
>
> [W]e have expressly held that the Fourth Amendment governs not only the seizure of tangible items, but extends as well to the recording of oral statements overheard without any 'technical trespass under . . . local property law.' Once this much is acknowledged, and once it is recognized that the Fourth Amendment protects people—and not simply 'areas'—against unreasonable searches and seizures it becomes clear that the reach of that Amendment cannot turn upon

the presence or absence of a physical intrusion into any given enclosure.

The *Katz* Court rejected the contention of the government that the search was permissible because the government had sufficient probable cause that it could have obtained a warrant or that there were other exceptions that would permit the recordings to be used at trial.

The majority opinion, however, did not provide the government or the lower courts a roadmap for future decisions. Instead, Justice Harlan's concurrence provided the summary essential to the future shape of the Fourth Amendment:

> My understanding of the rule that has emerged from prior decisions is that there is a twofold requirement, first that a person have exhibited an actual (subjective) expectation of privacy and, second, that the expectation be one that society is prepared to recognize as 'reasonable.' Thus a man's home is, for most purposes, a place where he expects privacy, but objects, activities, or statements that he exposes to the 'plain view' of outsiders are not 'protected' because no intention to keep them to himself has been exhibited. On the other hand, conversations in the open would not be protected against being overheard, for the expectation of privacy under the circumstances would be unreasonable.

The outline and examples in *Katz* served as the blueprint to revise and pass the Wiretap Act the following year. Harlan's concurrence was noted in *Terry v. Ohio* (1968) the following year.

2. *Smith v. Maryland (1979)*

Over the ensuing decade, additional cases helped shaped the understanding of *Katz* and the scope of the Fourth Amendment. In

Smith v. Maryland (1979), the Court summarized a decade of decisions applying *Katz*.

> Consistently with *Katz*, this Court uniformly has held that the application of the Fourth Amendment depends on whether the person invoking its protection can claim a "justifiable," a "reasonable," or a "legitimate expectation of privacy" that has been invaded by government action. This inquiry, as Mr. Justice Harlan aptly noted in his *Katz* concurrence, normally embraces two discrete questions. The first is whether the individual, by his conduct, has "exhibited an actual (subjective) expectation of privacy," whether, in the words of the *Katz* majority, the individual has shown that "he seeks to preserve [something] as private." The second question is whether the individual's subjective expectation of privacy is "one that society is prepared to recognize as 'reasonable,' "—whether, in the words of the *Katz* majority, the individual's expectation, viewed objectively, is "justifiable" under the circumstances.

The *Smith v. Maryland* summary of the *Katz* Fourth Amendment understanding provides a clear, two-prong analysis that there is both the subjective expectation of privacy and that the expectation of privacy is based on a reasonable understanding of social norms.

Although the social norms for privacy have changed significantly in the ensuing decades, this formulation provides the framework for modern courts and legislators.

D. Pervasive Surveillance Under the Fourth Amendment

The Supreme Court has decided more than 150 Fourth Amendment decisions since *Katz*, helping shape and define the constitutional law of criminal procedure. In the past decade, however, changes to the nature of surveillance technology have pushed the Supreme Court to focus on electronic surveillance and changing technologies once again. Today, these technologies include facial recognition, biometric screens for fingerprints, retinal patterns, or DNA, artificial intelligence, license plate cameras, cell phone passwords, social media accounts, and GPS tracking information captured by mobile devices, by device apps, and by content aggregators. The government has the ability to use these technologies and many more. In addition, the government can purchase DNA databases and customer information that are commercially collected and sold by industry.

Against this backdrop, the Supreme Court, again, addressed the scope of *Katz* and electronic surveillance in a series of cases.

1. *U.S. v. Jones (2012)*

The first of the modern surveillance cases is *U.S. v. Jones* (2012), though in many ways, it reflects a jurisprudence that predates *Katz*. In *Jones*, the FBI obtained a warrant to attach a tracking device on a suspect's wife's car within ten days within the District of Columbia. Unfortunately, when the FBI placed the tracking device, it was on the eleventh day and they attached it while the car was parked in Maryland rather than the District of Columbia. As a result, the search was conducted without a valid warrant. The scope of the surveillance was significant. "Over the next 28 days . . . the device established the vehicle's location within 50 to 100 feet, and communicated that location by cellular phone to a Government computer. It relayed more than 2,000 pages of data over the 4-week period." The Supreme Court found that the placement of the GPS tracking device constituted a search and because there was no exception to the warrant requirement, the search was invalid.

The Supreme Court avoided the most significant political issues involved with the ability to use technology to create blanket surveillance for weeks at a time. Instead, the Supreme Court opinion focused on the physical trespass of the Maryland parking lot and suspect's car to place the tracking device. The Court affirmed *Katz* yet again, but emphasized that *Katz* expanded the scope of the Fourth Amendment when it held that the constitutional right protects people, not places.

Instead, the Court held "that the Government's installation of a GPS device on a target's vehicle, and its use of that device to monitor the vehicle's movements, constitutes a 'search.' " The Court emphasized the importance of the trespass doctrine as a corollary to *Katz*. Quoting *Kyllo v. U.S.* (2001) extensively, the *Jones* Court explained that "we must "assur[e] preservation of that degree of privacy against government that existed when the Fourth Amendment was adopted." . . . [F]or most of our history the Fourth Amendment was understood to embody a particular concern for government trespass upon the areas ("persons, houses, papers, and effects") it enumerates.

In *Kyllo*, the Court had prohibited the use of heat-sensing technology to read into a private home and gauge the energy usage and likelihood of growing marijuana plants. Though not a physical search, the Court had found that the use of the technology to read the thermal energy on the walls was a search. In *Kyllo*, however, the private home was protected because it continued to meet the *Katz* formulation that "a Fourth Amendment search occurs when the government violates a subjective expectation of privacy that society recognizes as reasonable."

Kyllo gave examples of searches of homes that fell inside and outside the Fourth Amendment. A search, for purposes of the Fourth Amendment, does not occur in a house unless "the individual manifested a subjective expectation of privacy in the object of the challenged search, and society is willing to recognize that expectation as reasonable." The Court pointed out that the use of a pen register in a private home does not turn the use of a pen register into a search under the Fourth Amendment and that aerial surveillance of private homes does not transform the fly-over into a search.

In *Jones*, the Court extended its arguments even further. It held that the *Katz* test for an expectation of privacy was in addition to the line of cases emphasizing trespass of the persons, houses, papers, and effects listed in the Constitution.

Although not a majority opinion, five different justices in *Jones* raised concerns regarding the growing reach of surveillance technology. They were less focused on the manner by which the tracking device was attached to the car. One raised concerns that the reliance on trespass harkened back to *Olmstead* and the arbitrary line-drawing that occurred between different types of listening devices. The other concurrence focused on the relative ease of the government to conduct large-scale surveillance of its citizens, increasingly through the use of documents not protected by the Fourth Amendment because these documents were third-party records and like pen registers, could be obtained without probable cause. The facts described by the concurrence came before the court six years later.

2. Riley v. California (2014)

Two years after *Jones*, the Supreme Court addressed the power of the police to search a cell phone, even if incident to an arrest. The Supreme Court rejected the arguments that a cell phone is personal property which can be searched incident to arrest or that there is a high risk of the destruction of evidence on the cell phone. The Court explained that mobile devices "place vast quantities of personal information literally in the hands of individuals . . . and hold instead that officers must generally secure a warrant before conducting such a search." The police do have the power to seize a cell phone while making an arrest to prevent the destruction of evidence and hold the phone to permit time to secure a warrant. As the Court notes, "once law enforcement officers have secured a cell phone, there is no longer any risk that the arrestee himself will be able to delete incriminating data from the phone."

While the Court in *Riley* treated the cell phone warrant requirement as an extension of cases regarding searches incident to arrest, it also acknowledged the unique types of information that a cell phone can hold. Returning to concerns raised in a concurrence in *Jones*, the *Riley* Court acknowledged that "[d]ata on a cell phone can also reveal where a person has been. Historic location information is a standard feature on many smart phones and can reconstruct someone's specific movements down to the minute, not only around town but also within a particular building." In addition to movement, the Court raised concerns about the private content exposed on a cell phone.

> The storage capacity of cell phones has several interrelated consequences for privacy. First, a cell phone collects in one place many distinct types of information—an address, a note, a prescription, a bank statement, a video—that reveal much more in combination than any isolated record. Second, a cell phone's capacity allows even just one type of information to convey far more than previously possible. The sum of an individual's private life can be reconstructed through a thousand photographs labeled with dates, locations, and descriptions; the same cannot be said of a photograph or two of loved ones tucked into a wallet. Third, the data on a phone can date back to the purchase of the phone, or even earlier. . . .

> An Internet search and browsing history, for example, can be found on an Internet-enabled phone and could reveal an individual's private interests or concerns—perhaps a search for certain symptoms of disease, coupled with frequent visits to WebMD. . . . Mobile application software on a cell phone, or "apps," offer a range of tools for managing detailed information about all aspects of a person's life. There are apps for Democratic Party news and Republican Party news; apps for alcohol, drug, and gambling addictions; apps for sharing prayer requests; apps for tracking pregnancy symptoms; apps for planning your budget; apps for every conceivable hobby or pastime; apps for improving your romantic life. There are popular apps for buying or selling just about anything, and the records of such transactions may be accessible on the phone indefinitely.

The Court reminds the parties that once secured, the cell phones and mobile devices are subject to searches provided a proper warrant is issued. *Riley* highlights the transition of the Court back from the historical approach taken in *Jones* to an approach that reflects the nature of current technology on traditional Fourth Amendment jurisprudence.

3. Carpenter v. U.S. (2018)

Privacy advocates had been disappointed by *Jones* because its reliance on trespass sidestepped the important issues regarding the use of public data for individual surveillance. They found support in *Riley* and the Court's characterization of the content available on a cell phone. In *Carpenter v. U.S.* (2018), the Supreme Court returned to the concerns over the government's ability to access a large database and track and an individual's movement.

In *Carpenter*, the government collected cell site location information (CSLI) of a suspect from two wireless telephone companies. The two companies "produced (CSLI) for petitioner Timothy Carpenter's phone, and the Government was able to obtain 12,898 location points cataloging Carpenter's movements over 127 days—an average of 101 data points per day."

The government obtained these records through a court order issued pursuant to the Stored Communications Act. The government can compel disclosure of the telecommunication records "when it 'offers specific and articulable facts showing that there are reasonable grounds to believe' that the records sought 'are relevant and material to an ongoing criminal investigation.' " This standard is significantly lower than the probable cause standard required for a search warrant.

Using the CSLI, the government was able to track the precise movements of the suspects over the previous month. The government, of course, noted that it had properly followed the statutory provisions of the Wiretap Act for stored communications. In addition, the government relied on the third-party doctrine first developed for bank records in *U.S. v. Miller* (1976) and extended to pen registers in *Smith v. Maryland* (1979). The third-party record rule provides that a person does not have a reasonable expectation of privacy in that person's records or documents kept by a bank, telephone company, or other party since such records are made for the purpose of the third party. Even though the documents may be protected under privacy laws and treated confidentially, they are not subject to Fourth Amendment protections from subpoena.

CSLI are clearly third-party records. They are business records created and maintained by the wireless carriers as part of the cell tower operation. CSLI is essential to the operation and functioning of cell phones as they move in and out of range of each cell tower. They are also a very effective tracking device to pinpoint the location of a cell phone at any moment in time. The *Carpenter* Court recognized that "historical cell-site records present even greater privacy concerns than the GPS monitoring of a vehicle."

Despite the relevance of the third-party doctrine and the statutory procedures of the Stored Communications Act, the Court instead determined that CSLI requests were searches, requiring a warrant upon a showing of probable cause. As a result, the Court took a significant step beyond *Jones* to require that pervasive tracking of a suspect be conducted only following a search warrant. The Court did not specifically go further. It did not, for example, prohibit the tracking of a particular app that provides the government specific geolocation data as requiring a warrant. Nonetheless, the combination of *Jones* and *Carpenter* strongly suggest that any form of technology used to track an individual for prolonged periods of time requires a warrant.

At the same time, the Court made efforts to restrict the scope of its decision in *Carpenter*.

> Our decision today is a narrow one. We do not express a view on matters not before us: real-time CSLI or "tower dumps" (a download of information on all the devices that connected to a particular cell site during a particular interval). We do not disturb the application of *Smith* and *Miller* or call into question conventional surveillance techniques and tools, such as security cameras. Nor do we address other business records that might incidentally reveal location information. Further, our opinion does not consider other collection techniques involving foreign affairs or national security.

The trilogy of *Jones*, *Riley*, and *Carpenter* have followed the pattern established by *Katz* to look at people, not places, and the consequence of governmental searches rather than the methods. These three cases are also likely to provide the government and courts a blueprint on how to anticipate the development of the Fourth Amendment as the technologies for surveillance continue to improve.

Key Takeaways from This Chapter:

The constitutional protection of the Fourth Amendment restricts state and federal law enforcement from conducting searches and seizures without warrants establishing probable cause. Under *Olmstead v. U.S.*, the Supreme Court did not originally recognize wiretaps and other forms of electronic surveillance as a search subject to the warrant requirement.

Congress responded to *Olmstead* with § 605 of the Communications Act making wiretapping illegal. Although the law lasted for thirty years, law enforcement increasingly avoided the law by using equipment that did not require a physical intrusion into the location being tapped or simply by ignoring the law.

In 1967, the Supreme Court reversed *Olmstead*, with *Katz v. U.S.*, which expanded the scope of the Fourth Amendment. Under *Katz*, the Fourth Amendment protected people, not places. Under *Katz*, when an individual has a subjective expectation of privacy, and the expectation of privacy is one that society is prepared to recognize as reasonable, then the official intrusion into that private sphere generally qualifies as a search and requires a warrant supported by probable cause.

Katz was followed in 1968 with the Wiretap Act that established very specific requirements for surveillance of oral and wire communications. As technology evolved, the law added additional protections for all electronic communications. Different types of electronic communications receive different levels of court scrutiny regarding the issuance of a requested court order.

In a series of recent cases, the Supreme Court has followed *Katz*, expanding Fourth Amendment privacy protection to cell phones and to technologies used to track individuals both with and without the necessity of a particular device. *Carpenter* imposed a warrant requirement for cell phone location information, overruling the statutory subpoena provisions of the Wiretap Act.

Things to Know:

The rules of the Fourth Amendment are much broader than those described here regarding electronic surveillance.

The search warrant requirement has many exceptions, including consent and exigent circumstances. Those exceptions apply in electronic surveillance situations as well as the other forms of police searches.

Not every government request for electronic records is a search. The Stored Communication Act still allows for computer records to be disclosed with a less exacting court order for emails and similar records. The third-party doctrine for bank records and telephone records also continues to remain good law.

The police may secure a cell phone while conducting an arrest, but they may not search the contents of the cell phone without a court order.

Things to Think About:

Technology continues to evolve. Watches, sneakers, purses, and other devices may be equipped with cell phone or wireless technology. To what extent do the provisions of the Wiretap Act and the decisions of *Jones*, *Riley*, and *Carpenter* apply to those devices?

In addition to electronic surveillance, the government and private companies collect significant amounts of consumer information and biometric information. To what extent do the policies about collecting surveillance information apply to a person's DNA or physical identity tracked using facial recognition technology? Do the existing statutes and court decisions provide an appropriate balance, or does new legislation need to be added?

CHAPTER 3

Contours of Privacy, Publicity, and Free Speech Rights

A. The Right to Be Let Alone

1. *The Right to Privacy, Harvard Law Review (1890)*

The common law approach to privacy in the United States can be traced directly to the 1890 publication by Samuel Warren and Louis Brandeis of "The Right to Privacy" in the Harvard Law Review. Of the two, Samuel Warren was more likely the instigator of the article, because he and his family were part of the social elite in Boston, and they often objected to what Henry James termed the "newspaperization" of society and what the New York Times described as the "kodaking" of the press. Society columns in the Saturday Evening Gazette and other papers detailed the lives of Warren, his family, and their social class. Brandeis, in contrast, was less directly impacted by the imposition of paparazzi, but he was keenly aware of the constitutional and structural concerns at the heart of the call for a doctrine surrounding privacy. Warren's experience represented the need for privacy among the elite and Brandeis' outsider status represented the need for privacy protection from the powerless.

In their law review article, Warren and Brandeis went out of their way to establish a right of privacy as already existing through precedents in property law, copyright law, constitutional law, and other fields. They grounded their analysis in a phrase from the treatise on torts written by Judge Thomas Cooley regarding the right "to be let alone." The treatise provided the following:

> Personal Immunity. The right to one's person may be said to be a right of complete immunity: to be let alone. The corresponding duty is, not to inflict an injury, and not, within such proximity as might render it successful, to attempt the infliction of an injury.

Cooley also explained that tort law held actionable the interference with a person's right to develop and maintain a good reputation. He wrote that "evil-minded or thoughtless persons, by inventions or insinuations to [a person's] discredit, prevent his acquiring a good repute, they thereby invade his right, and he should have the appropriate redress." This harm is exactly the type then being suffered by Warren and his family through the gossip columns. Moreover, the right to develop one's good reputation must be more than to be free from defamation, or else there would be no independent right.

The change in society during the period also gave rise to many other areas where new legal norms were changing. Photography, for example, had been transformed as improvements in the technology allowed for cameras to go from taking very slow and highly arranged photographs to nearly instantaneous pictures. The telegraph was enabling instantaneous communications across the continent. Motion pictures and wireless communications were under development and often reported in the press. These various forms of mass communications allowed newspapers, magazines, and other publishers far greater reach than ever before in history.

Demographically, the country was also in a time of upheaval. The United States was still recovering from a devastating civil war and experiencing a massive immigration wave transforming the population. By 1890, the continent had been largely settled, and the frontier society had shifted into the beginnings of the industrial age. The demographic changes and technological shifts also changed the economy. Large commercial manufacturers and retailers were changing how products were manufactured, advertised, and sold. Warren and Brandeis highlighted these concerns by describing both "recent inventions and business methods" as triggering the need to rearticulate and reframe the right to privacy.

One example used by Warren and Brandeis involved the "unauthorized circulation of portraits of private persons." Actress Marion Manola had sued her theatrical producer for using an unauthorized photograph as the poster for her appearance. At the time of the article's publication, a lower New York court had entered a preliminary injunction for Manola. The photograph was not defamatory, but its use without authorization for a commercial purpose was not authorized, so the court enjoined its further publication.

Another example described in the article was described in the 1769 British case of *Millar v. Taylor* as the "right to keep one's own sentiments." Despite the influence of the press, a person has a right to judge whether to make one's opinions "public or commit them only to the sight of his friends."

Warren and Brandeis argued that these and many other cases were all better understood as comprising a single tort that could be described as an invasion of privacy. These cases were often difficult and strained under the law of property, contract, copyright, defamation, or assault, but could be reconciled under the jurisprudential approach described by the rubric of privacy. They were not inventing a new tort; they were explaining the shape of the tort that had been hidden within the other types of analysis.

2. *Adoption of the Right to Privacy*

The Warren and Brandeis article had immediate public impact. Professor Dorothy Glancy described the influence through reviews in magazines such as the Atlantic Monthly and The Spectator. The Spectator, for example, noted that "[c]ultivated Americans begin so keenly to hate the system of excessive publicity, which they themselves have been mainly instrumental in producing, that they are discussing ways and means of restricting it by legal penalties."

Although there were a number of lower court decisions that aligned with the privacy tort described by the article, the Michigan Supreme Court rejected the article in 1899. Following that decision, in *Roberson v. Rochester Folding Box Company* (1902), New York's Court of Appeals issued the most significant early opinion on privacy. In *Roberson*, a divided New York Court of Appeals rejected the approach advocated by Warren and Brandeis. The lawsuit sought to enjoin the use of a photograph of Roberson, a very young woman, from being used in an advertising campaign for the Franklin Mills Company to advertise flour. Her image was used without her consent on posters and brochures with the tag line, "Flour of the Family." She claimed to be humiliated by the campaign, suffering damages of $15,000. The majority opinion found no basis for finding a new cause of action in tort law and specifically rejected the analysis of the Warren and Brandeis article. Since the photographic likeness was not defamatory, there was no legal recourse.

The dissent, however, quoted Warren and Brandeis to embrace the new proposition embodying the right to privacy:

> The right to life has come to mean the right to enjoy life—the right to be let alone; the right to liberty secures

> the exercise of extensive civil privileges; and the term 'property' has grown to comprise every form of possession, intangible as well as tangible.' Instantaneous photography is a modern invention, and affords the means of securing a portraiture of an individual's face and form in invitum their owner. While, so far forth as it merely does that, although a species of aggression, I concede it to be an irremediable and irrepressible feature of the social evolution. But if it is to be permitted that the portraiture may be put to commercial or other uses for gain by the publication of prints therefrom, then an act of invasion of the individual's privacy results, possibly more formidable and more painful in its consequences than an actual bodily assault might be.

In contrast to the dissent, the majority refused to recognize any need to evolve the common law in this regard. Instead, the opinion suggested that any revisions to the law be contemplated elsewhere.

> The legislative body could very well interfere and arbitrarily provide that no one should be permitted for his own selfish purpose to use the picture or the name of another for advertising purposes without his consent. In such event no embarrassment would result to the general body of the law, for the rule would be applicable only to cases provided for by the statute.

Following *Roberson*, there was a public outcry against the decision. Judge O'Brien actually wrote his own law review article entitled "The Right of Privacy" in the 1902 Columbia Law Review to defend his concurrence in the decision. His article, however, did not change public sentiment. Instead, in response to *Roberson*, the New York legislature enacted Sections 50 and 51 of the New York Civil Rights Law. This created the first statutory protection for the right to privacy in the country. In its 1903 law, New York provided both civil and criminal protections against interference with a person's right of publicity.

> An act to prevent the unauthorized use of the name or picture of any person for the purposes of trade (passed April 6, 1903).
>
> Section 1. A person, firm or corporation that uses for advertising purposes, or for purposes of trade, the name, portrait or picture of any living person without having first obtained the written consent of such person, or, if a minor, of his or her parent or guardian, is guilty of a misdemeanor.
>
> Sec. 2. Any person whose name, portrait or picture is used within this state for advertising purposes or for the purposes of trade without the written consent first obtained as above provided may maintain an equitable action in the Supreme Court of this state against the person, firm or corporation so using his name, portrait or picture, to prevent and restrain the use thereof; and may also sue and recover damages for any injuries sustained by reason of such use, and if the defendant shall have knowingly used such person's name, portrait, or picture in such manner as is forbidden or declared to be unlawful by this act, the jury, in its discretion, may award exemplary damages.

Although the law has since been updated numerous times, it remains the New York framework for the law of privacy.

The experience in New York informed the rest of the country that the public expected protections from the increasingly intrusive modern rule. This context became clear when Georgia became the first state to recognize the right to privacy as a matter of common law. In *Pavesich v. New England Life Ins. Co.* (1905), an advertisement for life insurance featured a person whose photograph was reproduced without consent.

The Georgia Supreme Court learned from experience in New York, relying both on the Warren and Brandies article and the public's demand for legal protections. The *Pavesich* Court began its opinion in the manner as had Warren and Brandeis:

> The question therefore to be determined is whether an individual has a right of privacy which he can enforce, and which the courts will protect against invasion. It is to be conceded that prior to 1890 every adjudicated case, both in this country and in England, which might be said to have involved a right of privacy, was not based upon the existence of such right, but was founded upon a supposed right of property, or a breach of trust or confidence, or the like, and that therefore a claim to a right of privacy, independent of a property or contractual right, or some right of a similar nature, had, up to that time, never been recognized in terms in any decision.

Pavesich recounts many of the precedents described by Warren and Brandeis and adds many more. It grounds the right of privacy in natural law, making an even more strident argument that the rights of privacy are innate and inviolate. The opinion describes the case of Marion Manola and the public outcry against the decision in *Roberson*. Although the opinion recognized the need to balance the right of privacy against other common law and constitutional rights, the Court treats the unauthorized commercial exploitation of a person's photograph as a rather straight-forward example of an invasion of privacy.

Despite the outcome of the case, the *Pavesich* Court wrestled with the scope of the right that it had newly recognized. Among the leading concerns, the opinion noted the tension with the rights of free speech.

> The stumbling block which many have encountered in the way of a recognition of the existence of a right of privacy has been that the recognition of such right would inevitably tend to curtail the liberty of speech and of the press. . . .
>
> The right of privacy is unquestionably limited by the right to speak and print. It may be said that to give liberty of speech and of the press such wide scope as has been indicated would impose a very serious limitation upon the right of privacy, but, if it does, it is due to the fact that the law considers that the welfare of the public is better subserved by maintaining the liberty of speech and of the press than by allowing an individual to assert his right of privacy in such a way as to interfere with the free expression of one's sentiments, and the publication of every matter in which the public may be legitimately interested.

The decision in *Pavesich* established the basis for the development of the right of privacy nationally. It was not universally embraced, and some commentators viewed the law as an intrusion on common law principles. Nonetheless, *Pavesich* firmly embedded the arguments of Warren and Brandeis into the common law throughout the United States.

B. The Four Privacy Torts

In 1960, Dean William Prosser published a law review article entitled "Privacy" which successfully reframed the growing development of privacy law. Prosser had very strong opinions about the appropriateness of privacy rights and influenced the development of privacy law through his characterizations.

At the heart of Prosser's approach was his assertion that "[t]he law of privacy comprises four distinct kinds of invasion of four different interests of the plaintiff, which are tied together by the common name, but otherwise have almost nothing in common except that each represents an interference with the right of the plaintiff, in the phrase coined by Judge Cooley, 'to be let alone.' "

Prosser described four different torts that together comprised the law of privacy. Prosser then served as the reporter for the Restatement (Second) of Torts, bringing his analysis of more than three hundred privacy cases into a proposed, unified framework. His approach was largely incorporated into Restatement (Second) of the Law of Torts § 652A through four different causes of action with for different prima facie cases:

(a) unreasonable intrusion upon the seclusion of another;

(b) appropriation of the other's name or likeness;

(c) unreasonable publicity given to the other's private life; or

(d) publicity that unreasonably places the other in a false light before the public.

This section of the Restatement had a profound effect on the law. Even by 1960, when Prosser wrote his article, more than thirty jurisdictions had recognized privacy through the common law or through statutory adoption. Today, the vast majority of jurisdictions recognize the privacy torts, and they nearly all use the Restatement's version of the torts or a close approximation.

The formulations in the Restatement (Second) of Torts for the privacy violation of *Intrusion Upon Seclusion* is:

> *Intrusion Upon Seclusion*: One who intentionally intrudes, physically or otherwise, upon the solitude or seclusion of another or his private affairs or concerns, is subject to liability to the other for invasion of his privacy, if the intrusion would be highly offensive to a reasonable person.

This tort most closely resembles the right to be let alone. It makes actionable the direct invasion of one's space, such as by breaking into one's home or office to rifle through one's papers. It could be used to bring a tort claim against a stalker or someone who has used access to a computer or mobile device to spy on another person.

To establish a *prima facie* case for intrusion upon seclusion, the plaintiff must prove (1) a highly offensive intrusion by the defendant, (2) *mens rea* (intentional, knowledgeable, reckless, or negligent), (3) causing the plaintiff's privacy to be violated and (4) causing measurable harm. The *mens rea* may vary by jurisdiction.

The formulations in the Restatement (Second) of Torts for the privacy violation of *Public Disclosure of Private Facts* is:

> *Public Disclosure of Private Facts*: One who gives publicity to a matter concerning the private life of another is subject to liability to the other for invasion of his privacy, if the matter publicized is of a kind that (a) would be highly offensive to a reasonable person, and (b) is not of legitimate concern to the public.

This tort most closely reflects the legal recourse for Samuel Warren's complaints about the society pages and hordes of photographers dogging public figures. The information disclosed must be unknown to the public and the type of information that the public has no public interest in learning.

To establish a *prima facie* case for public disclosure of private facts, the plaintiff must prove (1) a publication, such as in a newspaper, (2) of private facts unknown to the general public, (3) that a reasonable person would find highly offensive to be publicized, (4) which are not newsworthy, meaning the public has no legitimate interest in the information, (5) made by the defendant, (6) with a minimum *mens rea* (intentional, knowledgeable, reckless, or negligent).

The formulations in the Restatement (Second) of Torts for the privacy violation of *False Light* is:

> *Publicity Placing Person in False Light*: One who gives publicity to a matter concerning another that places the other before the public in a false light is subject to liability to the other for invasion of his privacy, if (a) the false light in which the other was placed would be highly offensive to a reasonable person, and (b) the actor had knowledge of or acted in reckless disregard as to the falsity of the publicized matter and the false light in which the other would be placed.

False light is the invasion of privacy most closely associated with defamation. Like defamation, the tort requires that the defendant publish a false statement to one or more third parties, causing injury to the plaintiff. The statement must be one that harms the reputation of the plaintiff. The defamatory statement has been described as exposing a person to hatred, ridicule or contempt, or to lowering a person in the esteem of the person's peers. It can also cause a person to be shunned or injured in trade or business. Like defamation, the constitutional protections for free speech require "actual malice," meaning the *mens rea* of intentional, knowing, or reckless conduct.

False light represents those non-defamatory untrue statements that also have the consequence to hold a person to ridicule, contempt, or to lower a person in the opinion of one's peers. The leading case of *Spahn v. Julian Messner, Inc.* (1967) provides an excellent illustration. Warren Spahn was a Cy Young award-winning, left-handed baseball pitcher with the Milwaukee Braves. The author of a children's book about Spahn conducted virtually no research, instead inventing most of the facts about the book's subject, including the false statement that Spahn had earned a Bronze Star. Spahn successfully sued to enjoin the book which created a complementary but false and embarrassing account of his personal story. The book's facts were not libelous, but the cumulative effect was to harm Spahn's reputation.

The Supreme Court has held that false light is subject to the same constitutional protections for speech as is defamation, but when intentional falsehoods are made about a person that harm the individual, those falsehoods remain actionable.

False light is sometimes viewed as a means to assert a claim of defamation using a less harmful statement. As a result, at least ten states have questioned or rejected the appropriateness of a false light claim. In these jurisdictions, for a statement to be false and harmful, it must meet all the elements of a claim for defamation.

The formulations in the Restatement (Second) of Torts for the privacy violation of *Appropriation of Name or Likeness* is:

> *Appropriation of Name or Likeness*: One who appropriates to his own use or benefit the name or likeness of another is subject to liability to the other for invasion of his privacy.

To prove a *prima facie* case of appropriation of plaintiff's name or likeness, the plaintiff must establish (1) a commercial publication or exploitation, (2) by the defendant, (3) of the plaintiff's name, likeness or other attribute of identity, (4) with *mens rea* (intentionally, knowingly, or recklessly), (5) without authorization.

In addition to names and photographs, a person's catchphrase, voice, and player statistics have been used to establish "likeness." The commercial exploitation generally means the use to sell a good or service or to advertise the sale of a good or service. Newsworthy publications and fictionalizations using real persons are generally excluded from the category of commercial appropriation, although there have been some states where the tort has been applied more broadly.

Like false light, the law of commercial appropriation is subject to concerns about the First Amendment, so even where there is a direct commercial use, the law generally recognizes some accommodation for free speech concerns analogous to fair use in the copyright and trademark areas. This tension occurs, for example, with parody products, such as bobble-head dolls depicting politicians. Because the product is itself a form of speech, the rights to control one's commercial identity is limited by the free speech rights of the manufacturer of the toy. A politician would not be able to enjoin the sale of the bobble-head.

In many jurisdictions, this tort has evolved into a property right under the label of the "right of publicity." The interest has many attributes that are more akin to property rights. For example, a person is free to assign one's publicity rights, and they are sometimes central to complex marketing and financing arrangements. In some states, the rights of publicity have also been extended to last many years following the death of the person holding the right.

Each of the four privacy torts have many nuances that distinguish one doctrine from the next. Courts struggle to balance the privacy interests with the public's right to information, free speech rights, and similar issues. In addition, Dean Prosser was not an advocate for broad privacy rights, and the Restatement reflects his very narrow view of privacy, an approach that has shaped the development of privacy law in the United States.

Critics of the Restatement approach to privacy note that these rights are highly constrained and provide the bare minimum of protections. Unlike property rights which are robust under the common law and by statute, the intangible rights are written in a very distrustful manner, proving only the smallest amount of protection in the most outrageous of circumstances. Because they are so restricted, they have not been expanded to the twenty-first century concerns regarding data privacy and corporate tracking of consumers.

Precisely because Dean Prosser formulated the common law privacy torts to be very narrow, they do not serve to cover the problems with tracking, data mining, publication of a person's behaviors, or other concerns that have arisen in the information age. The definition of the right to publicity excludes its use for concern about commercializing a consumer's data or DNA information. Those causes of action, if they are to be recognized in the law, will require statutory protections.

Had Prosser shared the opinions of Warren and Brandeis, the Restatement would likely have had a much more generous interpretation of common law privacy. Instead, the common law right to be let alone has a very narrow set of situations where it is helpful to protect the interests first summarized in 1890.

C. Constraints of Privacy Through the First Amendment

As highlighted by the *prima facie* case for each of the privacy rights, there are serious tensions between the right of privacy and the First Amendment rights to freedom of speech and press. These concerns were first raised by the Georgia Supreme Court in *Pavesich v. New England Life Ins. Co.* (1905), the first court to recognize the common law privacy tort. Although the *Pavesich* Court acknowledged both federal and state free speech rights, the U.S. Supreme Court first recognized the application of the Fourteenth Amendment to the First Amendment in *Gitlow v. New York* (1925). Following *Gitlow*, all decisions involving state privacy laws had to take the federal First Amendment into account.

With limited exceptions, there is no First Amendment right to violate the property rights of a private person. The limited exceptions apply to privately owned public spaces, such as company towns and shopping malls. Even when the public square has been privatized, only a minority of jurisdictions recognize any rights to assemble, petition, or speak publicly. The Supreme Court has rejected this right under the federal constitution, though it has upheld the rights of individual states to interpret the state constitution to extend the right.

Property rights associated with keeping someone from physically intruding or using technology to intrude are not limited by the First Amendment claims of the intruder. There is only a limited First Amendment right to violate property rights, the privacy tort of intrusion into seclusion has no First Amendment restrictions.

The privacy torts regarding public disclosure of private facts and false light invasion of privacy both have significant limitations based upon the First Amendment. The most important jurisprudence addressing the scope of privacy is the defamation case of *New York Times v. Sullivan* (1964) and the line of cases that followed it.

Applying the First Amendment to state common law torts regarding libelous publications, the Supreme Court established that for public officials, liability cannot exist without proof of "actual malice," the *mens rea* establishing actual knowledge of the falsity of the statements or reckless disregard as to the falsity of the libelous statements. Subsequent cases extended this rule to public figures as well. The risk of censorship will be minimized sufficiently to withstand First Amendment scrutiny only by requiring that a plaintiff establish every element of the *prima facie* case, such as the falsity of the statements and the knowledge or reckless conduct of the defendant. Even in cases involving private individuals, the plaintiff must prove the defendant was at least negligent in defamation cases.

The Supreme Court further extended the constitutional limitations on privacy in the case of *Cox Broadcasting Co. v. Cohn* (1975). Although personal information might be highly offensive to an ordinary person if broadcast to the public, a truthful broadcast is protected by the First Amendment if it is a matter of "legitimate concern to the public." For matters of public concern, truth serves as a defense to a claim for invasion of privacy. Not everything broadcasted is a matter of public concern, however, and intimate aspects of a person's life cannot automatically be broadcasted. Very few cases, however, provide examples of clear invasions of privacy due to unwanted publicity.

One such case which found the plaintiff could establish the cause of action despite the constitutional limitations was *Diaz v. Oakland Tribune, Inc.* (1983). In *Diaz*, the defendant newspaper ran a short article about the plaintiff, the student body president, noting that she was a transsexual, having been born as male. The story regarding Diaz' sexual identity ran in a column months after the coverage about possible misuse of school funds had concluded and had nothing to do with thc original story. The Court of Appeals found there was no newsworthy connection between the unwanted disclosure and the news coverage. The case provides an excellent illustration on the types of newspaper items that are outside of First Amendment protection.

In *Cox*, the Supreme Court also explained that "[s]tates may not impose sanctions for the publication of truthful information contained in official court records open to public inspection." For example, state laws protecting rape victims from being named in the news have been struck down despite the unwanted publicity that can result from being a victim of such a crime.

The Supreme Court also addressed the constitutional limitations of the false light privacy tort. In *Time, Inc. v. Hill* (1967), the Supreme Court extended *New York Times v. Sullivan* to privacy torts that were actionable under New York privacy statutes, saying "that the constitutional protections for speech and press preclude the application of the New York statute to redress false reports of matters of public interest in the absence of proof that the defendant published the report with knowledge of its falsity or in reckless disregard of the truth." All false light actions, therefore, are included in the sphere of *New York Times v. Sullivan*.

Ten years later, the Supreme Court provided guidance on the intersection between First Amendment rights of broadcasters and the privacy right associated with commercial misappropriation in *Zacchini v. Scripps-Howard Broadcasting Co.* (1977). Hugo Zacchini performed as a "human cannonball," shooting himself from a cannon into a net 200 feet away. A freelance reporter for Scripps-Howard Broadcasting Co. captured the fifteen second act on video, even after Zacchini had asked the reporter not to film the performance. The Supreme Court found that the right of "publicity" was recognized and enforceable under Ohio's right of privacy statute. The Supreme Court noted that [i]t is also abundantly clear that *Time, Inc. v. Hill* did not involve a performer, a person with a name having commercial value, or any claim to a "right of publicity." The Supreme Court than explained the relationship between the two torts:

> "The interest protected" in permitting recovery for placing the plaintiff in a false light "is clearly that of reputation, with the same overtones of mental distress as

> in defamation." [Quoting Prosser.] By contrast, the State's interest in permitting a "right of publicity" is in protecting the proprietary interest of the individual in his act in part to encourage such entertainment. . . .
>
> Second, the two torts differ in the degree to which they intrude on dissemination of information to the public. In "false light" cases, the only way to protect the interests involved is to attempt to minimize publication of the damaging matter, while in "right of publicity" cases, the only question is who gets to do the publishing. An entertainer such as petitioner usually has no objection to the widespread publication of his act as long as he gets the commercial benefit of such publication. Indeed, in the present case, petitioner did not seek to enjoin the broadcast of his act; he simply sought compensation for the broadcast in the form of damages.

The Supreme Court clarified the scope of *Time v. Hill* and also made clear that the First Amendment is not harmed by the right to commercially exploit one's name, likeness, or performance. As the Court notes, "neither the public nor respondent will be deprived of the benefit of petitioner's performance as long as his commercial stake in his act is appropriately recognized. Petitioner does not seek to enjoin the broadcast of his performance; he simply wants to be paid for it."

By limiting publicity rights to the narrow commercial realm, many of the First Amendment concerns are addressed. Where the right of publicity is limited to the sales of goods or services or the advertisements for goods and services, the speech implications are reduced. Courts have established a number of approaches to address the use of a commercial appropriation of a name or likeness in music, books, films, and other communicative works. Courts will sometimes treat the titles and advertising for such work differently from the use of a person's name or likeness within the work itself. The approaches vary greatly, but in general, there can only be a cause of action if the unauthorized use is unrelated to the communicative work, essentially taking advantage of the commercial power of the plaintiff in a manner that is not tied to any need to use the name or likeness as part of the work's expression.

Other than intrusion into seclusion, the privacy torts have important limitations placed on them by the Supreme Court to accommodate First Amendment Interests. Together, these constitutional limitations highlight the ongoing availability of common law privacy protections, but they also serve to limit the right of privacy to those situations where the public interest has not been implicated. Wherever a publication involves a matter of public concern, privacy interests are diminished or disregarded in favor of the public's access to the information.

Key Takeaways from This Chapter:

In 1890, Samuel Warren and Louis Brandeis wrote "The Right to Privacy," which collected examples of privacy concerns in ancient law and British law that were framed in contract law, property law, copyright law, and other doctrines, but all of which demonstrated a general legal concern for the "right to be let alone." Their law review article redefined how the courts and legislatures understood the nature of privacy.

The article and the public demand for a privacy tort was driven by the changes in technology for publications, photography, and mass communication as well as the growing industrialization and urbanization of the country.

Based directly on the Warren and Brandeis article, the right to privacy was first established by statute in New York in 1903 and by case law in Georgia in 1905. Since then it has been adopted widely.

In the Restatement (Second) of Torts, the right to be let alone was redefined to represent four discrete torts, each with its own requirements.

The common law privacy torts are very narrowly defined and provide relief only in very specific situations. Because they are so restricted, they have not been expanded to the twenty-first century concerns regarding data privacy and corporate tracking of consumers.

Beginning with *New York Times v. Sullivan*, the Supreme Court has restricted privacy causes of action for the privacy torts regarding public disclosure of private facts and false light invasion of privacy. The First Amendment concerns require that plaintiff establish the defendant's *mens rea* and prove every element of the claim.

The privacy tort regarding commercial appropriation of one's name or likeness has largely transformed into a property right, known as the right of publicity. The attributes are largely the same, but some state statutes allow it to extend beyond the life of the individual and be commercially transferred.

Things to Know:

Privacy is a relatively young legal doctrine that has been largely shaped by the Warren and Brandeis article of 1890 and the William Prosser article of 1960. Prosser's narrow view of privacy became the official view of the Restatement (Second) of Torts, which has defined and limited the growth of common law privacy.

The growth of First Amendment protections which began with *New York Times v. Sullivan* further limited the growth of privacy protection. Although privacy has been considered a constitutional right with regard to decisional privacy, it has been required to be subservient to free speech in Supreme Court jurisprudence.

Things to Think About:

The greatest success of the right to privacy has been the expansion of the right of publicity. The right to protect commercial exploitation resulted in New York's first statute and the first State Supreme Court recognition in Georgia. Even in the U.S. Supreme Court, *Zacchini* has been one of the very few cases where the Court was willing to allow interests other than First Amendment interests to prevail.

How would privacy law differ if the Restatement (Second) of Torts had not broken the right of privacy into four very narrow sub-categories? Would Warren and Brandeis' understanding of privacy fare better at addressing concerns over data tracking, behavioral advertising, and other online invasions of privacy than the version of the Restatement?

The Constitution does not create a hierarchy of rights. If both privacy and free speech are recognized as fundamental rights protected by the Fourteenth Amendment, to what extent has the Court struck the right balance between the rights?

If the balance of privacy protection and other constitutional protections needs to be adjusted, what is the most effective way to make that adjustment?

CHAPTER 4

Workplace Privacy

The common law of privacy provides only narrow protections from surveillance and observation. The Restatement's privacy torts do not generally apply to the workplace relationships. Instead, a series of state and federal labor regulations have developed to protect individual employees from conduct deemed inappropriate for the employment relationship.

Workplace privacy is just one of many areas of law that are specially regulated. These include laws to eliminate discrimination and harassment, to promote equal treatment of workers, to assure public safety, and to address wages and compensation. This chapter will focus only on the workplace privacy concerns. Consumer laws, health care laws, and financial regulations which apply to other forms of data privacy often cover employees as part of their more general privacy obligations. In addition to being prospective employees or current employees, the workers employed at most companies are also protected by the consumer laws, financial disclosure regulations, and health care laws that also apply to those businesses.

A. Introduction of Labor and Employment Laws

The U.S. Department of Labor reports that it administers and enforces more than 180 federal laws related to employment relationships. In addition to these, there are many supplemental state laws, and many regulations at the state and federal level which interpret these laws and add additional requirements. The Department of Labor enforces the Fair Labor Standards Act to assure compliance with minimum wage laws, wage and hour classifications, overtime laws, pension or welfare benefit plans, and other compensation requirements.

State law governs the insurance provided for worker injuries through state Worker Compensation laws, while health insurance is regulated through the Comprehensive Omnibus Budget Reconciliation Act of 1985 (COBRA). Additional health care laws are governed by the Family and Medical Leave Act (FMLA) and the health care portability requirements on group plans under the Health Insurance Portability and Accountability Act (HIPAA).

The Occupational Safety and Health Administration (OSHA) administers the Occupational Safety and Health Act to assure that health and safety conditions comply with the standards and regulations promulgated by the agency. There are more specific laws governing farming, trucking, and many other industries. In addition, employers have a general duty to provide their employees with work and a workplace free from recognized, serious hazards.

These are just a few of the many laws governing the employment relationship. Most of these laws do not directly relate to privacy regulations, but some have specific privacy obligations. Laws such as HIPAA include privacy and data security provisions. Other privacy and data security laws, such as the Fair Credit Reporting Act (FCRA), are not primarily employment laws, but they have provisions that apply to the pre-employment setting and employment relationships. The same is true under state law.

Despite the myriad of laws, most of the relationship between the employee and employer is based on the contractual agreement among the parties. For ten to fifteen percent of the workforce, the contract is formed through the collective bargaining process in which the employee is represented by a union. For the non-unionized workforce, the agreement is negotiated privately between the employer and employee.

B. Background Screening of Employees and Applicants

Privacy protections begin even before an employment relationship is started. Employers are increasingly tempted to use social media and online tools to explore the candidates for job openings. An employer is free to use publicly available information, but there may be risks associated with doing so because the employer is put in a position of collecting information that cannot be legally used in the hiring process.

Beyond public information, employers typically use background investigations and criminal checks as part of the hiring process. These sometimes also include credit checks for potential employees. In addition, there are more intrusive tests that employers require for some positions, including drug and alcohol testing, fingerprinting, medical testing, and even polygraph and honesty testing. These more intrusive requirements are subject to legal restrictions and permitted only in certain situations.

These screenings and tests are used by employers both at the pre-employment step and throughout the employment relationship. They are sometimes used at the hiring stage as conditions of employment, or they may be conducted on current employees as part of the employment retention or employment promotion process. The legal protections from excessive privacy intrusions will not vary based upon when during the employment relationship the testing was conducted.

1. Discrimination in Pre-Employment Screening

For all but the smallest organizations, an enterprise begins the hiring process by creating the job description and then advertising or promoting the availability of that opening to the public. As the applications for the position come in, the hiring party begins by screening the applicants. Those who make it past the initial screening will be invited to interview for the position. Depending on the nature of the position and needs of the employer, there may be additional testing requirements, the submission of work samples by the candidate, or a review of the candidate's portfolio. The finalists will likely be subject to a background check and additional interviews and screenings before the offer is made. Each of these steps involves an increasing level of personal disclosure by the candidate.

While employers are seeking to hire the best fit for their organization, they are prohibited from discriminating in their hiring on the basis of protected categories such as age, race, gender, religion, veteran status, and disability status. Many states also protect job candidates from discrimination based on marital status, sexual preference, and sexual identity.

Because it is illegal to discriminate based on these factors, a potential employer is prohibited from inquiring about these issues. For example, job forms cannot ask for the name of an applicant's spouse or the gender of the spouse without intruding into the privacy of the candidates. The application cannot inquire about participation in religious activities, pregnancy, or any other questions that would enable the employer to use the information in a discriminatory fashion.

2. *Social Media in Pre-Employment Screening*

The use of social media in hiring is not illegal, but because of the discrimination concerns, the misuse of the information is actionable. Nonetheless, employers almost all take advantage of social media to screen potential candidates. Companies are concerned that if adverse material information about a potential hire is readily available on the Internet and overlooked, then the company could be subject to public embarrassment and potential liability. To avoid such risks, employers will screen out those candidates who post inappropriate photographs, drug use, discriminatory comments, false qualifications, confidential information, or disparaging comments about their current employer.

At the same time, the information on social media can disclose a candidate's religious affiliation, age, gender, sexual preference, veteran's status, disabilities, and other attributes that cannot be legally used in the decision to hire the person, set pay, or determine the terms and conditions of employment. The online information may not be used to discriminate without violating the Federal Equal Employment Opportunity Laws (including Title VII of the Civil Rights Act of 1964; the Equal Pay Act of 1963; the Age Discrimination in Employment Act of 1967; the Americans with Disabilities Act of 1990; the Rehabilitation Act of 1973; and the Civil Rights Act of 1991) along with additional state laws.

To avoid the misuse of the publicly available online information, an enterprise's HR department can mitigate the problem by having the online screening process be separated from any hiring decisions. The staff members involved in the screening should not be the same team involved in any interviewing and should be kept separate from any hiring or compensation decisions. The separation between the online screening staff and the rest of the employment process should be well documented. Unless a person is screened out of the applicant pool due to the candidate's online posts, those involved with hiring should be unaware of anything posted online.

Generally, non-public information posted to social media cannot be used in an employment setting. Employers should not have access to the private accounts of the candidates. Candidates should not be asked to provide their private account information. At least ten states have enacted legislation barring employers or potential employers from demanding the sign-on information by job candidates or employees. Except in very unique situations, employers should never ask for their employees' passwords or other sign-on information. These practices may also violate the Computer Fraud and Abuse Act, which makes unauthorized access to a computer system a federal crime.

To learn more about the online presence of potential candidates, some employers have instead used the technique of "shoulder surfing" to look over the shoulder of their job candidates and employees. When shoulder surfing, a person does not disclose his or her password, but he or she does open their account and provide full access to the content on the account. This technique increases the likelihood that the employer will learn information that is not permitted to be used in the employment setting. It is highly intrusive, and it is much easier for a job candidate to identify particular information that could lead to illegal, adverse hiring decisions. As a result, it is a practice that employers should avoid.

3. *Drug Testing*

Drug testing job candidates and employees is a common practice for large organizations, for enterprises that rely on heavy machinery, businesses involved in transportation, and similar organizations. Federal law permits drug testing, but the use of drug tests must be conducted in a manner that respects the employee's rights to privacy and includes protections from discrimination. The law recognizes that the collection of the urine or blood sample is an invasion of privacy that must be justified to be reasonable. Using viewers to assure the sample comes directly from the participant further increases the invasion of privacy.

Drug testing may reveal confidential medical conditions as well as disclose an employee's conduct when not at work. The process of drug testing often includes a requirement that the person being screened provide a list of drugs being ingested. An employer cannot require a list of legally prescribed drugs without violating the privacy protections within the Americans with Disabilities Act. A person need not disclose his or her medical conditions to an employer, so forcing the information to be disclosed in the drug testing is unlawful.

Negligently caused false positives will generally give rise to a cause of action against the employer and testing agency, particularly if that information is further communicated to supervisors or others in the organization or if it impacts the ability of a person to obtain future employment. Both to minimize the employer's liability and to comply with various employment laws, an employee generally has a right to retest lab results before any adverse employment action can be taken.

For employees in the public sector, the use of drug testing constitutes a search implicating the Fourth Amendment. There is no Fourth Amendment protection for employees of non-governmental employers. Even for public employees, the protection is limited. The Fourth Amendment merely requires some individualized suspicion of wrongdoing to be considered reasonable. Once this suspicion is present, a search of an employee may be conducted. No warrant or subpoena is required.

In addition, the Supreme Court has recognized that "safety-sensitive" positions meet the Fourth Amendment requirements even without the individualized suspicion. For example, the Supreme Court has held that the connection between impaired railroad employees and risk of train accidents was sufficient to find the "surpassing safety interests" justified a mandatory, suspicion-less testing program for railroad employees involved in train accidents. The Court held that railroad workers are positioned to "cause great human loss before any signs of impairment become noticeable to supervisors." Because of this, a general drug testing program was appropriate.

For some positions such as Justice Department attorneys, Customs Service staff, probation and parole officers, and similarly sensitive positions, pre-employment drug testing is permitted. Drug testing for these positions are just one of the many highly intrusive background checks required for such positions. Candidates for these jobs understand the level of intrusion that will be part of their employment and as a result, candidates for such positions are deemed to have a diminished expectation of privacy.

At the same time, however, a generalized governmental interest in efficiency or in the safe and effective delivery of public services are not sufficient to require universal drug testing of all job applicants. Instead, the government employer's concern must be very directly connected to the safety-sensitive concerns that make up the job duties or part of a position that establishes a diminished expectation of privacy in the public sector job.

4. Medical and Genetic Testing

Although it may seem like a futurist's claim, there is a concern that some employers use genetic and medical testing to screen applicants or to make retention decisions. The use of one's medical condition as the basis for future employment or job retention is a direct violation of the Americans with Disabilities Act. Unless directly related to the conditions of employment, genetic or medical testing is an intrusion into the privacy of the job candidates and likely to violate one or more antidiscrimination laws.

For example, in *Norman-Bloodsaw v. Lawrence Berkeley Lab.* (1998), the Ninth Circuit Court of Appeals found that plaintiffs had established a cause of action by alleging African American employees were being singled out and tested for sickle-cell anemia and women were being tested for pregnancy, both as conditions of employment. Such testing was a violation of the Americans with Disabilities Act of 1990 (ADA), conducted in a discriminatory manner in violation of Title VII of the Civil Rights Act of 1964, and the candidates' privacy rights. There are also examples of companies carrying out medical and genetic testing going back to the 1960s, including Dow Chemical Company and E.I. du Pont de Nemours & Company. These chemical companies screened out candidates who might be more medically susceptible to becoming sick from processing the chemicals sold by the company. Other companies used the medical condition screening to reduce the costs of health issues with their workforce.

In addition to the applicability of the ADA and other antidiscrimination laws, in 2008, Congress enacted the Genetic Information Nondiscrimination Act (GINA) to protect individuals from genetic discrimination. The law covers both employment and health insurance coverage discrimination. (It does not cover life insurance discrimination.) The genetic information protected by the law includes family health history, the results of genetic tests, the use of genetic counseling and other genetic services, and participation in genetic research.

GINA prohibits employers and insurance companies from basing decisions on hiring and promotion or on insurance coverage on genetic information they obtain. In most cases, the law also prohibits the employers or health insurance companies from requiring any genetic testing.

Both GINA and the Health Insurance Portability and Accountability Act (HIPAA) require the medical records of job candidates and employees be maintained as confidential records and limited to those who have a direct need for that information. Far fewer staff members at the company with need to access employee medical records than general personnel records. Therefore, the medical records should be kept separately and protected with a high degree of confidentiality and data security.

5. Third Party Investigations Under the Fair Credit Reporting Act

As employers narrow the field of potential employees, they often run background checks. These may include both criminal background screenings and credit reports. The Federal Credit Reporting Act (FCRA) defines third party consumer reports very broadly.

> The term "consumer report" means any written, oral, or other communication of any information by a consumer reporting agency bearing on a consumer's credit worthiness, credit standing, credit capacity, character, general reputation, personal characteristics, or mode of living. . . .

Although there are no privacy restrictions on unsealed criminal records, there are significant regulations regarding the use of consumer reports and credit reporting in the employment setting. If a third party collects the criminal history or other background information such as financial reports, employment history, driving records, or other reports that go to a person's mode of living, then those reports are subject to the notice and disclosure obligations of the FCRA.

Under the FCRA, a job applicant must be informed in writing that the potential employer is using a credit report as part of the background check. The notice cannot be part of a larger document, but must instead be a standalone notice and the employer must receive signed permission by the job applicant. If the person is not hired, then the employer will be considered to have taken an "adverse action" under the statute. This is true even if the job candidate was not hired for reasons unrelated to information provided in the report.

Once there is an adverse action, the employer must give notice of the adverse action. The Federal Trade Commission (FTC), which enforces the FCRA, summarizes the notice requirement, which must include:

- the name, address, and phone number of the consumer reporting company that supplied the report;
- a statement that the company that supplied the report did not make the decision to take the unfavorable action and can't give specific reasons for it; and
- a notice of the person's right to dispute the accuracy or completeness of any information the consumer reporting company furnished, and to get an additional free report from the company if the person asks for it within 60 days.

In addition, some employers use investigative reports that are based on "personal interviews concerning a person's character, general reputation, personal characteristics, and lifestyle." The

FCRA adds additional obligations under the FCRA. The employer must then inform the job candidate that he or she "has a right to request additional disclosures and a summary of the scope and substance of the report."

The reporting requirement under the FCRA is much broader than merely providing the job candidate a copy of his or her actual credit report. Most third-party reports collected as part of the hiring, promotion, or retention process are covered as a result of the broad definitions used in the FCRA.

6. Employee Polygraph Protection Act

There can be very few intrusions that invade privacy more deeply than a polygraph examination. Despite improvements in technology, the person under investigation is still subject to being taped with wires that check blood pressure, pulse, respiration, and skin conduction. The assumption underlying a polygraph is that a person with guilty knowledge about a question will have their biological indicators respond if he or she is hiding that information. Although the American Polygraph Association claims the accuracy can be as high as 90%, other critics peg the accuracy in the 65–70% range. The machines also have a tendency to report false positives, making investigators incorrectly believe in the guilt of suspects.

Polygraphs and other lie detector device results are not admissible in criminal court trials. As a general matter, state and federal law also prohibit them in the workplace, but there are exceptions. The Employee Polygraph Protection Act of 1988 governs the use of polygraph tests in the private sector. Similar laws govern public sector employees.

The Employee Polygraph Protection Act distinguishes between the use of polygraph tests for specific investigations into thefts, espionage, and other misconduct from the use in the pre-screening setting. In the pre-employment setting, the law allows for the use of polygraph tests only for "armored car, security alarm, and security guard employers," companies providing critical infrastructure such as dams, power supply, or currency production, and for "employers authorized to manufacture, distribute, or dispense a controlled substance."

The investigatory setting applies only to current employees. As summarized in the Code of Federal Regulations:

> [The law] provides a limited exemption from the general prohibition on lie detector use in private employment settings for employers conducting ongoing investigations of economic loss or injury to the employer's business. An employer may request an employee . . . to submit to a polygraph test, but no other type of lie detector test, only if—
>
> (1) The test is administered in connection with an ongoing investigation involving economic loss or injury to the employer's business, such as theft, embezzlement, misappropriation or an act of unlawful industrial espionage or sabotage;
>
> (2) The employee had access to the property that is the subject of the investigation;
>
> (3) The employer has a reasonable suspicion that the employee was involved in the incident or activity under investigation; [and]
>
> (4) The employer provides the examinee with a statement, in a language understood by the examinee, prior to the test which fully explains with particularity the specific incident or activity being investigated and the basis for testing particular employees . . . .

When polygraph testing is conducted in the workplace, the tests must be conducted by a licensed testing company. The information that results from the test should be considered highly confidential information. Any failure of a company to prevent the disclosure of the polygraph test could result in additional violations of the employee's privacy rights.

C. Workplace Monitoring

Since the beginning of the modern employment relationship, employers have regularly monitored the behavior and productivity of their employees. Employers monitor employee activities to promote efficiency of the employees; to encourage safety; to assure a workplace free from harassment and other inappropriate behaviors; to protect the trade secrets and confidential information owned by the company; to improve processes; and to document corporate compliance with various laws and regulations. These are all legitimate corporate interests, many of which benefit the workforce as well as the employer.

What has changed are merely the types of distractions from work and the means of surveillance. Since the introduction of Cyber Monday as a marketing strategy to promote online sales, surveys report that the majority of U.S. employees shop online while at work during the holiday season. Major sporting events sap companies of productivity as do the many other online distractions that enable workers to be on phones, social media, and other non-work activity.

For employees, the intrusion of the workplace into the rest of one's life has also been a growing concern. Writing a dissent in 1987, in *O'Connor v. Ortega*, Justice Blackman lamented the loss of privacy.

> [T]he reality of work in modern time, whether done by public or private employees, reveals why a public employee's expectation of privacy in the workplace should be carefully safeguarded and not lightly set aside.

> It is, unfortunately, all too true that the workplace has become another home for most working Americans. Many employees spend the better part of their days and much of their evenings at work.

Work had become a second home. Today, the home has become a second workplace. Online and Internet-connected technologies make it easier than ever for work to follow employees home, blurring the distinction between work hours and off-duty hours for exempt employees.

Employees do not automatically lose their privacy when at work; however, most waive away those rights as part of the contractual conditions of employment. The terms of the employment relationship are usually consolidated into an employee handbook. The employee handbook provides the key terms regarding an employee's expectation of privacy at his or her work. It describes the scope of the employer's right to monitor behavior and describes the obligations imposed on the employee to maintain the confidentiality, privacy, and data security of the company and its clients or customers.

1. Legal Authority to Monitor

The common law reasonable expectation of privacy does not extend to most areas of the workplace. Other than bathrooms, locker rooms, and nursing rooms, there is no common law right to seclusion. Instead, any privacy protections must derive from state or federal law.

For computers, phones, and other technologies, the laws which govern are the Wiretap Act and the Stored Communications Act of the Electronic Communications Privacy Act of 1986 (ECPA) as well as the Computer Fraud and Abuse Act (CFAA). The ECPA was introduced in Chapter 2. The ECPA includes both the Wiretap Act and the Stored Communications Act. As noted in that chapter, it is primarily designed to stop government intrusion into the private communications of citizens unless the government has a warrant or subpoena to obtain a person's private records.

The ECPA covers the electronic communications that take place in a private company. Rather than restricting a company from intercepting and recording communications, it has provisions that specifically authorize this conduct. The statute includes broad exemptions to the anti-interception law that enable an employer to monitor and control the communications that occur in the workplace. The most important exception to the application of the law is consent. Employment handbooks usually provide that the employer is entitled to monitor telephone calls and electronic communications for various corporate purposes, including quality control and employee training.

Under the ECPA, the consent is sufficient if either of the parties to the communication has agreed. Some state laws require both parties to consent. To meet this additional obligation, companies that record customer or other business calls add a disclosure at the beginning of each call to establish that all the parties to each call are aware—and therefore consent—to the recording.

In addition to the consent provisions of the ECPA, there is also another broad exception for monitoring electronic communications in the normal course of business operations. To the extent that the consent is somehow insufficient, the enterprise has the ability to intercept and record communications as part of its business operations when "incident to the rendition of his service or to the protection of the rights or property of the provider of that service." These interceptions of phone calls and electronic communications are fully exempted from liability as are the retrieval of communications stored on the employer's systems. These exceptions occur both for the communications covered by the

Wiretap Act and the Stored Communications Act, though the language of the statute varies slightly from section to section.

The other statute that directly authorizes the employer's monitoring of employees is the Computer Fraud and Abuse Act (CFAA). The CFAA has grown into a very expansive law, creating both civil and criminal liability for anyone who "intentionally accesses a computer without authorization or exceeds authorized access" on a computer and then obtains information or damages the computer, its software, or its data. The term "exceeds authorized access" means "to access a computer with authorization and to use such access to obtain or alter information in the computer that the accessor is not entitled so to obtain or alter."

In the employment context, it is the employer that owns the company computers and establishes the authorizations to use the computer systems. The federal government has empowered employers to set these parameters and then reinforces the employer's determination by providing both civil and criminal liability if an employee violates these parameters. In addition to creating criminal and civil liability for computer hacking, the law also covers situations where a former employee uses revoked credentials (or the credentials of a coworker) to steal corporate trade secrets or client information. The law makes very clear that employers have the authority to set policies on computer use and to manage the precise usage of those computers.

The laws create powerful authority for corporations to monitor the activities of their employees, but the actual authority to do so is also typically specified directly in the employee handbook. The ECPA consent provision is much broader than the business necessity exemption, and the CFAA creates authority to establish the authorization for computer access, but it does not specify the computer access. To implement the authority granted by the laws, an employer should specify its supervision policy in the employee handbook and obtain legally binding consent to the terms.

The terms for a typical employee handbook include the following:

- *Ownership of equipment and accounts*: The provisions will specify that all equipment provided by the employer remains the property of the employer and any accounts, including email accounts, social media accounts, cloud storage accounts, or other systems accessed by the employee are the property of the employer. The ownership of the accounts includes the corporate ownership of any usernames and passwords associated with those accounts. The provisions will also explain that the employer can access all information stored on its systems at all times, and warn the employees that they cannot store anything that they would wish to be treated as confidential.
- *Business use only for corporate accounts*: The provisions will specify that all accounts provided by the employer are for business purposes only; that the employee cannot use these accounts for any private purpose; and all content posted on these accounts becomes the exclusive property of the company.
- *Bring Your Own Device (BYOD) policies*: The provisions allows the employee to use one's own mobile device, portable storage, or other equipment, but gives the employer the right to monitor the use of that device, to track the whereabouts of that device, to install corporate security and monitoring software, and to authorize the remote deletion of all contents on the device. It

may also require the employee to consent to share information that might be personal to the employee with the employer if it is incidental to the information on the device. *Employees often give up significant additional privacy when they agree to let their employers have access to their personal devices, and they should be careful to limit this additional consent.*

- *Ownership of intellectual and intangible property provisions*: Employers generally own any copyrighted works made by employees within the scope of their employment and any patents invented if the employee was hired to invent the items. The provisions would contractually reinforce these legal norms. Except in creative and educational industries, content created by an employee is generally expected to be the property of the employer. Any content or files stored on the employer systems would generally be owned by the employer. This provision would extend to include any interest in trademarks, trade secrets, data, followers, or other intangible assets, so that anything created of value by an employee while employed would remain with the employer.
- *Internal confidentiality*: This provision requires that employees treat all internal company information as confidential and require that only official spokespersons for the company share any company information. For public companies, this provision is particularly important since any public disclosure can have the potential to affect market prices and implicate Securities and Exchange Act disclosures.

- *Obligations to respect privacy policies, anti-harassment policies, and computer use policies*: The provisions would establish expectations that the use of the corporate information systems could only be used for the benefit of the company, that the employee would not violate the rights of other employees, would not use harassing language targeted at other employees, would follow the terms of service on any accounts, would not install any unauthorized software, would not download or store any unauthorized content, and that the employee would follow all laws, regulations, and policies governing the use of computer and information systems.
- *System and workplace monitoring*: The provisions explain that the company maintains surveillance of the workplace to promote safety and efficiency as well as to improve business processes and meet regulatory obligations, so that the employee consents to the monitoring as a condition of employment. They provide a general summary of the monitoring of phone, wireless, and stored communications, video surveillance, and the use of tracking hardware and software in company-owned equipment.

Corporate handbooks tend to be drafted in very broad language, but this sometimes serves to undermine the goals of the policies. The employee handbook will often be very detailed regarding some of these provisions as needed for specific industries.

In practice, employers can log the activity of the computers with keystroke and screen capture software, review Internet traffic, check white-listed and black-listed Internet addresses, connect webcams, monitor the size of data flow into and out of an employee's account and take many additional steps to monitor the online behavior of each employee. The scope of the employer's surveillance efforts is generally tied to the sensitivity of the data available to the employee and the value of the nonpublic information.

2. Limitations on Ability to Monitor

For governmental employees, there are Fourth Amendment protections, though the reasonable expectation of privacy in the workplace is rather low. Some unions have been successful in negotiating less intrusive monitoring provisions through the collective bargaining process. More importantly, despite the broad scope of the ECPA and CFAA and attempts to draft very broad employee handbooks, there are limitations on the ability to monitor the electronic communications of an employee.

For example, an employer cannot monitor phone calls or electronic communications the employer knows are private communications since such communications are outside of the employee consent provisions and beyond the scope of the business operations exemptions. Employee phone calls with their union representatives or their legal counsel cannot be monitored. And once the employer realizes the nature of such a call, it has an obligation to stop any monitoring that may have started automatically.

Similarly, the use of a corporate computer to access a private, web-based email system or social media system does not transfer the rights to access that system to the employer, despite the statements to the contrary in the employment handbook. Even if employees are told not to access personal accounts during worktime or using work computers, the law does not strip employees of the right to retain their interests in their own accounts just because they violate these work rules. For example, where an employer accessed the email correspondence between an employee and her attorney on a website-based, personal email account, the employer was found to have exceeded its right to monitor the accounts and violated the rights of the employee. In contrast, when an employee used her work email account to correspond with an attorney, the company was not prohibited from reading the email. The difference between the two cases was that in the second example, the email account was also owned by the company.

There are also other forms of monitoring. The use of GPS monitoring is increasingly common. Most cell phones, for example, have "find my phone" technology which tracks the location of the device. Company-owned trucks and vehicles have location monitoring from a multitude of technologies. There is a valid business purpose to assure the proper use of the equipment and to protect the vehicles from theft and damage. Where the GPS is tracking an employee's private vehicle, there is no such business purpose. Instead, there may still be a strong expectation of privacy.

A relatively new concern involves more systemic monitoring of employees. Mobile apps installed on corporate cell phones, for example, can provide the employer with the tracking of those devices on a 24/7 basis. An employee, however, likely has an expectation of privacy that he or she not be tracked or monitored when away from work. The Supreme Court has found that such tracking violates the Fourth Amendment when conducted by the government without a warrant in a criminal setting. It follows then that there is also an employee's reasonable expectation of privacy to be free from pervasive tracking. To the extent the company is monitoring its vehicle, it is likely to be able to track the vehicle, but if the tracking is of the individual, this form of monitoring will likely violate the rights of the employee.

In addition, there seems to be very little business purpose for such tracking in most employment settings. An exception may exist where the employer has legitimate concerns for the physical safety of its employees due to stalking, paparazzi, civic unrest, or other external threats. In all but the most extraordinary situations, however, a company should not install or monitor tracking software for its employees. Where such technology is embedded in the cell phone or other hardware, the company should have a policy and practice to disable the technology and limit its use to those situations where the employee has requested the assistance and consented to its use.

3. Physical Surveillance Using Cameras, Recording Devices, and Biometrics

Video surveillance of workplaces is also quite common. Often the video surveillance is part of a broader physical security plan to reduce theft and to document that appropriate safety procedures are utilized. Audio surveillance, in contrast, is much less common. In part, this is because many states require that all parties to an audio recording have consented to the recording. In those states, it is not enough that the employer has agreed to the recording. Moreover, an audio surveillance system might inadvertently pick up conversations on speakerphone between parties that have not received any notice of the recording. The risk of inadvertent audio recording is too high for companies to implement blanket audio surveillance.

Even with video surveillance, there are limits. The expectations of privacy are somewhat higher in private offices than in public spaces within the work environment. Employees with private offices would not generally expect that those offices were subject to video surveillance. An employer could change that expectation by contract, but such surveillance would be surprising.

Areas where employees change clothing are subject to a much higher degree of privacy. Locker rooms, dressing rooms, bathrooms, nursing rooms and similar locations are expected to be used for their intended purpose. The personal nature of nudity raises the reasonable expectation of privacy and makes it inappropriate for video surveillance to be used. A company can monitor the entranceways into these locations if there are concerns about health, safety, or conduct issues, but they should never use photographic or video surveillance equipment where employees disrobe.

Many corporations use tracking-enabled devices such as ID badges with RFID or other monitoring equipment. Some use biometric data, including fingerprints, voice prints, facial recognition tools, or retinal scans. The use of these tracking devices throughout facilities and on printers, photocopiers and similar equipment can create a movement map for an employee. The collection of such behavioral data does not violate any general data collection laws. It should be limited, however, to information about activities while at work and while on the premises.

Given the concerns about employee tracking, a few states have already passed laws which prohibit employers from requiring employees to embed the tracking technology subcutaneously. In these states, it is illegal to "chip" employees. Fortunately, this form of physical marking of employees has not caught on as a necessary business practice.

4. *Related Issues for Labor Relations*

A related area to employee monitoring is the actions employers can take for perceived misconduct by employees on their personal social media accounts. For many, punishing an employee for his or her speech is a significant privacy intrusion. Nonetheless, many companies have policies that establish conduct and behavior expectations both at work and during one's off duty hours. In some cases, these provisions are written as a Code of Conduct rather than incorporated into the employee handbook. Examples include:

- Guidelines that require courtesy to company clients
- Expectations that employees are "brand ambassadors" at all times
- Requirements that employees treat each other with dignity and respect in all communications
- Obligations to treat all internal communications as confidential
- Policies that limit the use of the trademarks and service marks to work-related activities

Although policies such as these are positive values for an employer, they can raise concerns for the speech rights of the employees. For example, should a third party be able to complain to a person's employer regarding that person's conduct outside of work? There have been numerous examples of individuals being fired for their online posts that were unrelated to their work activities. In the private sector, there is no general right of free speech. Many employers are unwilling to retain employees who have posted inappropriate comments or publicized their inappropriate conduct.

Federal labor law does give employees limited speech protections under the National Labor Relations Act (NLRA) which is enforced through hearings held by the National Labor Relations Board (NLRB). Section 7 of the NLRA provides that "employees shall have the right to self-organization, to form, join, or assist labor organizations, to bargain collectively through representatives of their own choosing, *and to engage in other concerted activities for the purpose of collective bargaining or other mutual aid or protection . . . .*"

All employees are protected by the NLRA. The right to engage in concerted activities for mutual aid or protection is not limited to union employees. As a result, when employees discuss certain work related issues among themselves, they are protected by the NLRA from reprisals for their statements, even if made publicly online. For example, if employees use Facebook to organize a demonstration at their worksite regarding pay or working conditions, then the employee's right to concerted activities supersedes any code of conduct policies about posting about the company on social media.

The protection under Section 7 of the NLRA requires "mutual aid," meaning that it protects conversations among employees, but it can reach out to a single post, if the content is directed at fellow employees and covers collective bargaining or covered activities such as wages or working conditions.

While the NLRA protects some online discussions, it does not eliminate codes of conduct. Posts that are unrelated to mutual aid, including posted complaints about customers, personal attacks on supervisors, racist or discriminatory language, or other general rants are all outside the concerted activity umbrella, and the NLRB will uphold employee terminations for such conduct.

In addition to specific cases brought by employees seeking to have their jobs reinstated, the NLRB has also ruled on the enforceability of employment handbooks and codes of conduct.

In the *Boeing Company* decision of 2017, the National Labor Relations Board substantially revised the rules regarding the ability of employers to create enforceable codes of conduct. Prior to that decision, companies were finding it difficult to promulgate codes of conduct that were enforceable because their restrictions could easily interfere with the rights of the employees to bring concerted activity. The NLRB consistently found these codes of conduct to be overly broad because employees could reasonably construe the language to prohibit Section 7 activity.

In *Boeing*, the NLRB reversed the policy which prohibited all employment policies that "*employees would reasonably construe . . . to prohibit Section 7 activity.*" In place of that rule, the NLRB adopted a policy that "when evaluating a facially neutral policy, rule or handbook provision that, when reasonably interpreted, would potentially interfere with the exercise of NLRA rights, the Board will evaluate two things: (i) the nature and extent of the potential impact on NLRA rights, and (ii) legitimate justifications associated with the rule."

In the Board's shift in policy, it emphasized "the Board's duty to strike the proper balance between . . . asserted business justifications and the invasion of employee rights in light of the Act and its policy, focusing on the perspective of employees . . . ." This balance between the interests of the employer and the employees gives significantly more weight to the business purpose for the policy.

Any policy that explicitly restricts the rights under Section 7 remains unlawful. But if the policy is facially neutral, then the NLRB will now balance the potential negative impact on Section 7 rights with the employer's business justification for the rule. In *Boeing*, the rule in question was a no-camera policy which prohibited all cell phones, laptops, and other devices with cameras to protect the trade secrets and uphold the defense department requirements for the manufacture of its planes. The NLRB found that the need to protect the confidentiality outweighed the potential impact on the employee's ability to organize.

The NLRB also reversed the decisions of prior panels by finding that the entire category of conduct policies was now justified for the legitimate business purpose of the employers under the new approach. The policies previously invalidated that would now be approved included these:

- A rule requiring employees to "[k]eep customer and employee information secure"
- A policy requiring that "nurses and doctors should foster "harmonious interactions and relationships"
- A requirement to avoid conduct that "impedes harmonious interactions and relationships"
- The statement obligating employees to "[k]eep customer and employee information secure"
- A warning that social media use "may be violating the law and is subject to disciplinary action" if the employee engages in "inappropriate discussions about the company"

The *Boeing* decision makes it much easier for companies to promulgate employment handbooks and codes of conduct that will be upheld by the NLRB. Even if the policy is upheld, however, the provision will not be enforced if it impedes actual concerted activity for mutual aid or comfort or interferes with collective bargaining activity. Nonetheless, employees are much more likely to find their online presence subject to the review of their employers.

D. Workplace Health Data and Social Security Numbers

The scope of information collected by employers on their workforce is substantial. Because of compensation requirements and employee verification obligations, companies have the Social Security numbers for each employee. The employer will have all the information obtained from every background check. If employees seek ADA accommodations, medical leave, or family leave, then the employer will also have substantial healthcare data regarding the employee.

Many state and federal laws govern the use of Social Security numbers. While they vary widely, the general rules require that a Social Security number be kept confidential and not displayed on a record or file. While it had once been the practice for some public and private entities to use a person's Social Security number as their account number or identification number, these laws now bar such practice. If a company needs to display some portion of the Social Security number, one commonly permitted version is a truncated display of the last four digits of the number.

Employers have an obligation to keep employee Social Security numbers, health information, credit reports, and information collected through background checks secure from theft and treated confidentially. Only those individuals within the organization who have a legitimate business purpose for the knowledge can have access to these types of protected employee data. This requires that employers are diligent regarding the protections of the information.

The ADA, FCRA, and HIPAA each include statutory provisions obligating the recipient of an employee record or file to take reasonable and appropriate steps to secure the information so that it is not publicly available, to protect the information from theft, and to limit the access of the information to those with a legitimate business purpose for access to the information. The data security obligations of these laws are explored more fully in Chapter 6.

In addition to the federal laws, states including California and Massachusetts have been very active in creating additional state-based legal obligations to secure corporate data, including both customer data and employee data. The state laws vary considerably but generally require that the companies secure the data and minimize the access to the information both within and outside the business. In Pennsylvania, a state Supreme Court decision found that the employer's duty to protect the confidential records of its employees was part of the employer's "duty to others to exercise the care of a reasonable man to protect them against an unreasonable risk of harm arising out of the act." The Court explained further:

> [A]s a condition of employment, [The University of Pittsburgh Medical Center (UPMC)] required [employees] to provide certain personal and financial information, which UPMC collected and stored on its internet-accessible computer system without use of adequate security measures, including proper encryption, adequate firewalls, and an adequate authentication protocol. *These factual assertions plainly constitute affirmative conduct on the part of UPMC*. . . . [T]his affirmative conduct resulted in UPMC owing the employees a duty to exercise reasonable care to protect them against an unreasonable risk of harm arising out of that act.

As explained by the Pennsylvania Supreme Court, the employer had a common law duty in addition to any statutory obligations to maintain the confidentiality and security of the records it collected from its employees. These records included sensitive personal and financial information, such as names, birth dates, Social Security numbers, addresses, tax forms, and bank account information, which were collected as part of the condition of employment. Having created this relationship, the company had a duty to take reasonable steps to secure the information from risk of loss.

To meet the common law and statutory obligations to protect employee record confidentiality, there are common sense steps that every company should follow. The procedures begin with the ability to collect and store both physical records and electronic records in a secure, reliable manner. Chapter 5 provides the data security basics which must be followed to protect records from third party theft, and which help a company meet its common law duty to retain records in a reasonable manner. However, merely holding records in a secure computer system is not enough. There are additional steps that should be taken.

First, the company should develop clear policies that highlight the importance of privacy and confidentiality in the workplace. These policies should establish a priority of privacy and data security for customer information, employee information, and corporate information. The policies should make very clear that unauthorized access, disclosure, or use of confidential information is a violation of company policy and one's job duties.

Second, supervisor training should also reinforce this admonition, since supervisors often gain inadvertent access to information regarding those under supervision. There should be written policies regarding employee requests for health-related time off or accommodations since those requests can often entail medical information covered by the ADA or by HIPAA.

Third, documents provided to supervisors should be forwarded to centralized and secure storage. Supervisors and HR staff should not mix records covered by the FRCA, ADA, and HIPAA with general personnel records. Physical, printed copies of documents should be stored in a secure location using locked file cabinets and locked document rooms. Digital records should be stored using encryption and available only to the company's personnel who are directly responsible for matters covered by FCRA, ADA, or HIPAA. Neither senior management nor direct employee supervisors are generally entitled to such information.

Fourth, records under these federal laws and relevant state laws may need to be kept for a minimum number of years. Once the record retention limit is passed, a company should securely dispose of the information and carefully adhere to its record destruction policy. The record destruction policy should include both the secure shredding of physical documents and the secure deletion of digital files.

An employer that has implemented a sufficient data security system and created policies that meet the federal standards should be able to maintain the confidentiality of its employee records. These steps will not stop every inadvertent disclosure or sophisticated data theft, but they go a long way to assure the integrity of the information for a company's employees and reduce the risk of liability for the company.

Key Takeaways from This Chapter:

Workplace privacy is not protected directly by law. Instead, many of the interests of employees are protected by laws designed to protect the use of financial records, health care records, and consumer information. For those workers who are in unions, there are some privacy protections in the collective bargaining agreements, but for most employees, the rights are defined by the employment contracts. Most employment contracts, unsurprisingly, grant broad rights for the employers to monitor the conduct of employees in order to safeguard the workplace, protect intellectual property, and enforce customer privacy protections.

The laws that do protect employees also protect applicants for new jobs and protect employees who are seeking promotions or transfers. These laws include the FCRA when an employer is using credit reporting for purposes of employment screening or qualifications, HIPAA regarding certain health employment information, and various state laws.

States have protected employees from disclosure of their private social media accounts and passwords to their personal email. Some states have also added protections for use of biometric information without the employee's consent. Because state law is changing so quickly, it will likely be state laws that offer the greatest protections within the next few years.

Things to Know:

The National Labor Relations Act does not provide direct privacy protections, but it does protect certain communications among employees. Federal law also permits drug testing and the use of polygraph tests, but these intrusions are regulated and must be conducted within the constraints of the federal law. In contrast, genetic information cannot be used as part of the employment process.

Workplace monitoring is permitted under both state and federal law. The scope of the monitoring is typically mentioned in the employee handbook. The monitoring may include cameras throughout the workplace (other than bathrooms and locker rooms), access to all company-owned computer accounts, computer monitoring, phone call recording, and tracking of all data flowing through the company's computer systems. Except for activities protected by the NLRA, companies that follow their policies are free to monitor their operations in this manner.

The NLRA limits employee monitoring to the extent the employee was engaged in collective bargaining or involved in "concerted activities for the purpose of . . . mutual aid or protection." This requires companies to stop monitoring phone calls and other communications that are intended to address wages, working conditions, or similar issues of employment.

Things to Think About:

The employment relationship is very heavily regulated, so why has Congress chosen not to add employee privacy to the provisions of the NLRA or other federal laws?

If Congress were to add legislation, how might it change the conduct of employers and employees regarding privacy?

States have stepped in to pass laws barring employers and potential employers from using employees' social media passwords to screen their content. Were the federal computer security laws such as the CFAA insufficient? Why was additional legislation needed?

Employees are protected by some state laws regarding the privacy of personal information. To what extent do the general privacy laws influence employee privacy practices?

CHAPTER 5

Consumer Privacy

Throughout the twentieth century, the relationship between merchants and consumers rapidly changed. Retailers grew from small, local establishments to national chains. Customers began to rely on mail order companies and department stores rather than local shops for their trade. Advertising moved from newspapers to radio and television in an effort to reach national audiences. In 1890, when Warren and Brandeis penned “The Right to Privacy,” there were no concerns about commercial intrusion or consumer tracking. The local merchant was likely to know a lot about the customers because they were neighbors. The national chain, however, began to rely on demographic information to categorize and target groups of customers.

Radio and television introduced a new economic relationship. Broadcasters could not easily charge their customers for the over-the-air broadcasts, so instead the broadcaster sold advertising to the retailers. The consumers received free content in exchange for watching the ads. Advertisers worked hard to learn about consumer interest and trends, but the information rarely identified individual consumers.

Still, by 1973, artists Richard Serra and Carlota Fay Schoolman created an art installation which warned about the power of television and mass media. They wrote "[i]n commercial broadcasting the viewer pays for the privilege of having himself sold. It is the consumer who is consumed. You are the product of T.V." In 2010, Tim O'Reilly tweeted the updated version of this message. "If you're not paying for it, you're not the customer; you're the product being sold." In a similar vein, Sun Microsystems CEO Scott McNealy announced in 1999 that "you have zero privacy anyway. Get over it." At the time, he described consumer privacy concerns as a "red herring." Nonetheless, twenty years later, general consumer privacy continues to be a significant concern.

A. The Sectoral Approach to Privacy

What changed between 1973 and 2010 was the amount of information advertisers could obtain about their customers and the level of specificity the advertisers could obtain about individuals. Radio and television broadcasters could not know much about their customers without customer surveys. Instead, the Nielsen Company would hire families to enter their viewing habits into an electronic recording system. These families were intended to be demographically representative of the public. By tracking their viewing habits, they provided the advertisers and broadcasters with information about the popularity of the shows' broadcast.

The general assumption in the United States has been that there is no expectation of privacy in commercial transactions except by contract. If a contract between two parties specifies specific privacy protections, then the terms of that contract will be enforced. Otherwise, the expectation of privacy is limited to the protections afforded by the common law rights or traditional relationships. Attorneys, doctors, and clergy have been obligated to treat their interactions with clients, patients, and penitents as confidential by tradition. Other industries have business norms, but those are not the same as criminal or civil penalties for breaching confidentiality and privacy laws.

This general assumption, however, is rapidly changing as a result of expanded federal regulation under existing legal requirements for publicly traded companies, international regulations for companies that do business with non-U.S. customers, and expanded state laws in California, New York, and many other jurisdictions. Instead of no U.S. privacy protection, the law of the 2020s is becoming the law of competing privacy and data security regimes. Instead of companies being able to do anything with their customers' data, the rapid growth of regulation may now require that companies operate differently not just inside and outside the United States but also among states.

1. Federal Privacy Laws

In certain areas, the state and federal governments have taken specific action to increase privacy and limit the information that can be used about a person. Many states adopted laws to reflect the longstanding practices of attorney-client and doctor-patient relationships. Some states added laws to protect library records from being disclosed. State law will sometimes include privacy as part of broader industry regulation.

Because privacy laws focus primarily on certain sectors of the economy, the approach is known as sectoral privacy. These sectoral laws generally focus on health care information, financial information, governmental records, media transactions, or personal information regarding children under the age of thirteen. Most are described throughout the book. These are the key federal laws and their industry sectors:

- Health Care
    - Health Insurance Portability and Accountability Act of 1996 (HIPAA)
    - Genetic Information Nondiscrimination Act of 2008 (GINA)
- Banking and Finance
    - Fair Credit Reporting Act (1970) (FCRA)
    - Right to Financial Privacy Act (1978) (RFPA)
    - Gramm-Leach-Bliley Act (1999) (GLBA)
    - Fair and Accurate Credit Transactions Act (2003) (FACTA)
    - Securities Act of 1933 and Securities Exchange Act of 1934
    - Sarbanes-Oxley Act (2002) (SOX)
- Children's Privacy
    - Children's Online Privacy Protection Act of 1998 (COPPA)
- Education
    - Family Education Rights and Privacy Act (1974) (FERPA)
- Media and Speech
    - Cable Communications Policy Act of 1984
    - Video Privacy Protection Act of 1988 (VPPA)
    - Telephone Consumer Protection Act of 1991 (TCPA)
- Information Provided to the Federal Government
    - Administrative Procedure Act (APA)

  - Census Confidentiality Statute of 1954
  - Freedom of Information Act (1966) (FOIA)
  - Privacy Act of 1974
  - Taxpayer Browsing Protection Act (1997)
- General
  - Federal Trade Commission Act (1914) (FTCA)
  - Electronic Communications Privacy Act and Stored Wire Electronic Communications Act, together comprising the Electronic Communications Privacy Act of 1986 (ECPA)
  - Employee Polygraph Protection Act of 1988 (EPPA)
  - Driver's Privacy Protection Act of 1994 (DPPA)
  - CAN-SPAM Act (2003)

These categories are only general guides. As noted in Chapter 4, employee privacy includes the employee's health care, financial records and other information. Few of these laws were written exclusively to provide employee privacy, but provisions in many of them add to the rights of privacy enjoyed by employees. In that way, laws targeting one type of privacy often provide privacy rights in other areas. Federal and state laws often cover more than one narrow topic.

In addition to the federal laws, there are an increasing number of state laws that protect consumers and the general public. Some of these laws apply only to businesses organized in the particular states, but many apply to any customers residing in the state. As a result, companies that do business throughout the United States must take all state laws into account. There are also foreign laws that govern how multinational corporations must treat the information of customers outside the United States. In order to meet the obligations of these foreign jurisdictions, some U.S. companies are adding additional privacy protections for their U.S. customers as well.

2. Privacy Policies Vary in Goals and in Protection

Even where there is regulation, that does not mean that a company cannot use consumer data. Some of these laws merely require that a company notify its customers before using the data for marketing or other purposes. Some laws merely require that the consumer be informed how the information will be used while others bar the use of collected information other than for a narrow, specified purpose.

The GLBA, for example, requires that financial institutions provide customers with annual privacy notices and give customers the ability to opt out of the sale of the consumer's information to third parties. It does not stop the general sale of customer information or even require that the banks first get affirmative consent. As a result, laws like the GLBA have done little to slow the use of consumer information for sales and marketing. In contrast, HIPAA places rigorous obligations on companies to secure the data collected and clear restrictions on the sale and use of patient data for advertising and other non-health care related purposes.

The following provides a matrix for evaluating the strength of a privacy law:

- **Notice Only**—a requirement that the company collecting information provide some minimal notice that it has done so. An example would be a law requiring the posting of a privacy policy.

- **Opt-Out Notice**—a requirement that consumers receive notice that a company collects information or has access to components of a mobile device such as the camera or contacts app. Opt-out notice enables a consumer to refuse the service with a check-box or button. Despite the apparent control provided to the public through opt-out notice provisions, studies on consumer behavior consistently demonstrate that they make little difference. Most opt-out provisions go unread and unused by the public.
- **Opt-In Notice**—a requirement that consumers receive notice that a company collects information or has access to components of a mobile device and affirmatively consent through a check-box, button, or other form of consent. An example is the type of consent required from a parent to allow a child under the age of thirteen to allow a company to collect personally identifiable information about that minor.
- **Mandatory Usage Specification**—legal requirement that information collected by a company be used only for its specified purpose and not be allowed to be used for other purposes. An example would be videotape rental records that cannot be sold to third parties or used for marketing purposes.
- **Information Usage Prohibitions**—a legal requirement that information cannot be obtained and used in an unauthorized manner. Example of a usage prohibition are Title VII of the Civil Rights Act and GINA. GINA, for example, prohibits employers and insurance companies from using genomic data in

hiring and health care decisions. Title VII bars discrimination, which could occur when a company acquires information about the attributes or status of an employee and uses that information to discriminate. These companies may acquire the information through a variety of lawful activities. The law governs the use of the information rather than its collection or dissemination.

Laws vary on how they use these five categories of privacy management. Notice is always a component of any law requiring consumers opt-in or opt-out, but notice is usually not required when the law has a usage restriction. Over the past decade, the approach to privacy regulation has shifted from mandatory notice to some form of consumer control through opt-in or opt-out provisions.

3. *The Role of the FTC*

Given the wide range of federal laws governing U.S. privacy, there is no single agency that has overall jurisdiction to enforce privacy regulation. Privacy is a component of regulation in health, finance, education, transportation, and many other regulated industries. For the general public, however, the Federal Trade Commission (FTC) has grown into the role as the primary federal regulator for privacy.

The FTC's authority to regulate privacy violations began through its interpretation of its general mandate. Under Section 5 of the Federal Trade Commission Act, "unfair or deceptive acts or practices in or affecting commerce . . . are . . . declared unlawful." This is an extremely broad statement of authority. The FTC has explained these terms as follows:

> "Deceptive" practices are defined . . . as involving a material representation, omission or practice that is likely to mislead a consumer acting reasonably in the

circumstances. An act or practice is "unfair" if it causes or is likely to cause substantial injury to consumers which is not reasonably avoidable by consumers themselves and not outweighed by countervailing benefits to consumers or to competition. . . .

Certain elements undergird all deception cases. First, there must be a representation, omission, or practice that is likely to mislead the consumer. Practices that have been found misleading or deceptive in specific cases include false oral or written representations, misleading price claims, sales of hazardous or systematically defective products or services without adequate disclosures, failure to disclose information regarding pyramid sales, use of bait and switch techniques, failure to perform promised services, and failure to meet warranty obligations.

Second, we examine the practice from the perspective of a consumer acting reasonably in the circumstances. If the representation or practice affects or is directed primarily to a particular group, the Commission examines reasonableness from the perspective of that group.

Third, the representation, omission, or practice must be a "material" one. The basic question is whether the act or practice is likely to affect the consumer's conduct or decision with regard to a product or service. If so, the practice is material, and consumer injury is likely, because consumers are likely to have chosen differently but for the deception.

In addition to the general authority granted under Section 5, Congress has specifically tasked the FTC with primary jurisdiction in areas such as the Children's Online Privacy Protection Act. The FTC may bring criminal cases, but in the majority of actions, the FTC undertakes administrative hearings that can result in civil penalties. Violations of Section 5 do not create civil causes of action, but state laws sometimes provide the basis for a direct cause of action by victims of companies that are found to have used unfair or deceptive practices.

Among its wide range of duties, the FTC regularly brings administrative actions against companies that violate their published privacy policies, for those that ignore foreseeable data security threats, and those that use or allow their marketers to use deceptive practices in their advertising.

B. Published Privacy Policies

Federal law only requires privacy policies for those companies which operate in one of the federally regulated sectors. To supplement this, for the majority of businesses, the obligation to have a posted privacy policy comes from state law. The first of these laws was the 2004 California Online Privacy Protection Act (CalOPPA). States that added their own laws generally track the requirements of CalOPPA.

The statute provides that it applies to "[a]n operator of a commercial Web site or online service that collects personally identifiable information through the Internet about individual consumers residing in California who use or visit its commercial Web site or online service . . . ." California's Attorney General has interpreted "online service" to cover apps and other programs on mobile devices. Most commercial websites do not differentiate the location of their user for purposes of creating different disclosures, so CalOPPA applies to most commercial websites and app companies throughout the United States.

Since CalOPPA went into effect, two additional laws have been enacted which cover large businesses. The European Union's General Data Protection Regulation (GDPR) covers some businesses in the United States that do business in Europe. The California Consumer Privacy Act (CCPA) regulates California businesses that have annual gross revenue of more than $25,000,000 or meet other minimum requirements. Each of these two laws are discussed in their own sections of the book. For general business, the starting point is still CalOPPA.

1. Components of a Posted Privacy Policy

The purpose of the privacy policy is to explain what information is collected by a site and how that information is used. It is a notice provision. If a company collects no information, then it is not covered by the requirement. A privacy policy drafted to comply with CalOPPA will have sections explaining the types of personally identifiable information collected, sections detailing how the information is used and shared with other companies, and provisions on how information collected can be reviewed by the consumer and corrected.

CalOPPA requires the operator of a commercial website or online service to post a privacy policy on its website in a conspicuous manner. According to CalOPPA, conspicuously posting a privacy policy means:

- The privacy policy is shown on the website's homepage; or
- A link—via an icon that contains the word "privacy''—appears on the homepage and directly takes consumers to the privacy policy. In this instance, the icon must be in a color different from the homepage's background; or

- The privacy policy is linked to the homepage via a hypertext link that contains the word "privacy," is written in capital letters equal to or greater in size than the surrounding text; is displayed in a type, font or color that contrasts with the surrounding text of the same size; or is otherwise distinguishable from surrounding text on the homepage.

The content of the privacy policy must include the following information:

- The effective date of the privacy policy.
- The categories of personally identifiable information the operator collects.
- The categories of third parties with whom the operator may share the personally identifiable information.
- A description of the process (if any) by which the consumer can review and request changes to his or her personally identifiable information as collected by the operator.
- A description for how the operator notifies consumers of material changes to the operator's privacy policy.
- A description of any monitoring across multiple websites to build a profile of behavior and interests.

Personally identifiable information definitions vary considerably from one law to the next. Even the term varies. Laws differ on the term used to refer to protected data as personal information, including personally identifiable information (PII), personal information (PI), protected health information or personal health information (PHI), and electronic personal health information (ePHI), among the most common. CalOPPA uses a relatively short list of identifiable personal information, including any of the following:

- A first and last name.
- A home or other physical address, including street name and name of a city or town.
- An e-mail address.
- A telephone number.
- A Social Security number.
- Any other identifier that permits the physical or online contacting of a specific individual.
- Information concerning a user that the Web site or online service collects online from the user and maintains in personally identifiable form in combination with an identifier described in this subdivision.

Beginning in 2014, amendments to CalOPPA added provisions to promote do-not-track features, a technical solution to help consumers opt out of having their personal data collected across multiple websites. To meet this additional obligation, an operator must disclose how the site responds to Web browser do-not-track signals or mechanisms. If the do-not-track information is not a section of the privacy policy, then the operator must "provide a clear and conspicuous hyperlink in the operator's privacy policy to an online location containing a description, including the effects, of any program or protocol the operator follows that offers the consumer that choice."

Companies governed by additional laws and regulations will likely have to report a broader list of attributes that are recognized as personally identifiable information, and they will have additional disclosure obligations on the details of the privacy policy.

2. *Enforcement of a Posted Privacy Policy*

Once a company has made the decision to publish its privacy policy, both state and federal authorities can fine a company for failing to comply with its terms. Each of the fifty states has some form of Unfair and Deceptive Practices Act that operates in a manner similar to that of Section 5 of the FTCA. The FTC and many states have used those laws to take action against companies that fail to adhere to their posted privacy policies.

There have been many FTC actions regarding the failure of companies to meet their obligations under their posted privacy policies. In 2016, the FTC reported that it had brought actions in "over 130 spam and spyware cases and more than 40 general privacy lawsuits." Many are settled without any financial payment, but Facebook, which has been a repeat violator of its privacy policies, was fined a record $5 billion for ongoing privacy notice failures and failures to secure consumer information.

In the first few years following the passage of CalOPPA, FTC actions tended to focus on companies that failed to adhere to their privacy policies. As business practices have improved, companies now generally tend to follow their stated policies regarding the use of consumer data. These statements are often more forthcoming about the amount of information collected, the tracking tools permitted, and the sale of the information to third parties for advertising and consumer profiling purposes. Since the FTC and states can only act to enforce these policies, a candid privacy policy that explains the company exploits the information it collects will not trigger any liability.

The FTC also brings actions against companies that make untrue promises. In 2014, for example, it brought an action against

Snapchat for being unable to live up to its promise that a user's snaps would "disappear forever" after only a brief period, as specified by the sender. Instead, Snapchat knew of several simple ways that recipients could save snaps indefinitely.

An FTC action begins with an investigation. These are generally not public; however, the FTC will disclose the investigation if it determines the investigation is in the public interest. The FTC relies on public complaints, information from state authorities, and its own efforts to determine which cases to bring forward. Given the amount of press coverage regarding various privacy violations, there is often a great deal of public information available to the FTC before it takes action. The FTC is also quite modest in size and resources, so it only investigates a small percentage of cases involving potential violations of Section 5.

The FTC provides additional details about its process:

> Following an investigation, the Commission may initiate an enforcement action using either an administrative or judicial process if it has "reason to believe" that the law is being or has been violated. . . .
>
> *Administrative Enforcement*
>
> When the Commission has "reason to believe" that a law violation has occurred, the Commission may issue a complaint setting forth its charges. If the respondent elects to settle the charges, it may sign a consent agreement (without admitting liability), consent to entry of a final order, and waive all right to judicial review. If the Commission accepts the proposed consent agreement, it places the order on the record for thirty days of public comment (or for such other period as the Commission may specify) before determining whether to make the order final. . . .

If the respondent elects to contest the charges, the complaint is adjudicated before an administrative law judge ("ALJ") in a trial-type proceeding conducted under the Commission's Rules of Practice. The prosecution of a matter is conducted by FTC "complaint counsel," who are staff from the relevant bureau or a regional office. Upon conclusion of the hearing, the ALJ issues an "initial decision" setting forth his or her findings of fact and conclusions of law, and recommending either entry of an order to cease and desist or dismissal of the complaint. Either complaint counsel or respondent, or both, may appeal the initial decision to the full Commission. . . .

Upon appeal of an initial decision, the Commission receives briefs, holds oral argument, and thereafter issues its own final decision and order. The Commission's final decision is appealable by any respondent against which an order is issued. The respondent may file a petition for review with any United States court of appeals within whose jurisdiction the respondent resides or carries on business or where the challenged practice was used.

Judicial Enforcement

Even where the Commission determines through adjudication that a practice violates consumer protection or competition law, the Commission must still seek the aid of a court to obtain civil penalties or consumer redress for violations of its orders to cease and desist or trade regulation . . .

Section 13(b) of the FTC Act authorizes the Commission to seek preliminary and permanent injunctions to remedy "any provision of law enforced by the Federal Trade Commission." Whenever the

> Commission has "reason to believe" that any party "is violating, or is about to violate" a provision of law enforced by the Commission, the Commission may ask the district court to enjoin the allegedly unlawful conduct, pending completion of an FTC administrative proceeding to determine whether the conduct is unlawful. Further, "in proper cases," the Commission may seek, and the court may grant, a permanent injunction.
>
> The Commission . . . may seek not only permanent injunctions that bar unfair or deceptive practices, but also imposition of various kinds of monetary equitable relief (i.e., restitution and rescission of contracts) to remedy past violations. In some cases, the Commission may also seek to preserve the possibility of ultimate monetary equitable relief, by obtaining temporary restraining orders and preliminary injunctions that freeze assets and impose temporary receivers.

In recent years, the FTC actions have focused more actively on the duty of companies that collect personal information to properly secure that information. Companies including Twitter, Fandango, Credit Karma, VTech, and Wyndham Hotels were the subject of administrative actions or lawsuits for their failure to secure the consumer information they had collected. The FTC also focuses on other aspects of the online consumer experience, including the use of deceptive advertising, the role of social media influencers, and false claims made regarding privacy. One particular focus has been advertising targeted at consumers using online and mobile technologies.

C. California Consumer Privacy Act

Just as CalOPPA led the United States with its requirements for a privacy policy in 2004, California has again set a national standard with the California Consumer Privacy Act (CCPA), which went into effect on January 1, 2020. Although its reach is not as broad as CalOPPA, the impact it will have on commercial websites and mobile apps has the same potential to reshape accepted norms of privacy law. As the CCPA continues to develop, it has the potential to become the standard U.S. privacy policy.

The CCPA does not cover all businesses, but its reach is well beyond the sectoral privacy that existed prior to 2020. The law applies to any for-profit corporation or other business organization doing business in California that meet any one of these three criteria:

- Has gross annual revenues in excess of $25 million;
- Buys, receives, or sells the personal information of 50,000 or more consumers, households, or devices;
- Derives 50 percent or more of annual revenues from selling consumers' personal information.

The CCPA also covers any business that controls or is under the control of another company that meets any of these criteria. The CCPA does not apply to charitable organizations or to governmental entities, such as municipalities or state universities. Because of the contractual relationships among businesses, however, many companies that would not otherwise be obligated to comply with the CCPA may be required to adhere to its provisions. The same is true for GDPR (Europe's General Data Protection Regulation), but it is much easier for a company to demonstrate that it is not in a business covered by the GDPR than with the CCPA.

The CCPA grants residents of California new rights that had not previously been recognized under U.S. law. The California Attorney General's Office summarizes the rights as follows:

- The **right to know** what personal information is collected, used, shared or sold, both as to the categories and specific pieces of personal information;

- The **right to delete** personal information held by businesses and by extension, a business's service provider;
- The **right to opt-out** of sale of personal information. Consumers are able to direct a business that sells personal information to stop selling that information. Children under the age of 16 must provide **opt-in consent**, with a parent or guardian consenting for children under 13;
- The **right to non-discrimination** in terms of price or service when a consumer exercises a privacy right under CCPA.

Unlike CalOPPA, however, businesses implementing CCPA may make clear that the obligations in their policies extend only to California residents. Where the businesses do so, they will avoid having to be as responsive to non-California consumers. Nonetheless, the changes in business processes required by CCPA will likely benefit consumers nationwide.

1. The Right to Know About the Collection and Use of Personal Information

The definition for personal information is extremely inclusive, well beyond that in CalOPPA. This definition covers the rights to know, to delete, to opt-out, and to be protected from discrimination. A narrower definition is used for the provisions on data breach notification. For the consumer rights, the definition of personal information includes virtually all non-public information that can exist about a person, including the following:

(A) Identifiers such as a real name, alias, postal address, unique personal identifier, online identifier, internet protocol address, email address, account name, Social Security number, driver's license number, passport number, or other similar identifiers.

(B) Information that identifies, relates to, describes, or is capable of being associated with, a particular individual, including, but not limited to, his or her name, signature, Social Security number, physical characteristics or description, address, telephone number, passport number, driver's license or state identification card number, insurance policy number, education, employment, employment history, bank account number, credit card number, debit card number, or any other financial information, medical information, or health insurance information.

(C) Characteristics of legally protected classifications, *e.g.*, age, race, gender, religion, veteran status, disability status, marital status, sexual preference, and sexual identity.

(D) Commercial information, including records of personal property, products or services purchased, obtained, or considered, or other purchasing or consuming histories or tendencies.

(E) Biometric information.

(F) Internet or other electronic network activity information, including, but not limited to, browsing history, search history, and information regarding a consumer's interaction with an internet website, application, or advertisement.

(G) Geolocation data.

(H) Audio, electronic, visual, thermal, olfactory, or similar information.

(I) Professional or employment-related information.

(J) Nonpublic education records.

(K) Inferences drawn from any of the information identified in this subdivision to create a profile about a consumer reflecting the consumer's preferences, characteristics, psychological trends, predispositions, behavior, attitudes, intelligence, abilities, and aptitudes.

The only limitation on the broadly inclusive definition of personal information is that it excludes publicly available information. For purposes of this paragraph, "publicly available" means information that is lawfully made available from federal, state, or local government records. This is a much narrower definition than the public information gathered from sources other than the consumer.

The consumer has the right to know which pieces of information have been collected about that individual. This essentially requires the company be in a position to provide a report for each person in their database. The CCPA requires that such a report cover only the last twelve months of data collection. The report must be made available in a user-friendly format.

In addition to gaining the right to know what information has been collected, the California consumers get the right to know how that data are used, shared, and sold. This means that businesses must explain the business purposes for collecting the information and whether or not the company sells or shares the information with third parties. If there are third parties with access to the information, the companies must provide the categories of third parties that receive the information and what is done with the information. The information must be provided at or before the time of collection and included in the privacy policies for the company.

2. The Right to Control the Data Collected

The California consumer has new rights to control the collection and retention of their data. A business serving California consumers must provide a simple procedure to request that the consumer data collected be removed from the data stored by the company. The CCPA requires that the business provide a toll-free telephone number for consumers to make the request. If the business has a website, then the business must also provide an online process. Once the consumer requesting the removal is verified, the company must comply within 45 days. For many companies, this now means that the website needs to provide a "do not collect" button just like the do-not-track button required by CalOPPA.

While the CCPA requires the consumer have the right to receive the information removed, the law does not explicitly include any right to correct errors in the report. Of course, companies that rely on the data have their own incentive to keep the information correct. If a customer requests information be corrected and a company refuses, the customer can respond by demanding that all their information be removed. In addition, since many aspects of the information collected may be subjective, a separate right to correct information could create far more conflict than California regulators wanted to introduce.

The CCPA includes some limits on the right for a consumer to have one's personal information deleted. The most significant limitation is information collected for business purposes. As defined in the statute, "business purpose" means "the use of personal information for the business's or a service provider's operational purposes, or other notified purposes, provided that the use of personal information shall be reasonably necessary and proportionate to achieve the operational purpose for which the personal information was collected or processed or for another operational purpose that is compatible with the context in which the personal information was collected."

The business purposes must be listed in the notice and disclosure so that they can later be relied upon for data operations and data retention. The statute provides a list of acceptable business purposes, which can be summarized as follows:

- Auditing consumer transactions, including ad impressions and related measures.
- Protecting against security risks, including malicious, deceptive, fraudulent, or illegal activity.
- Debugging to identify and repair programming errors.
- Short-term, transient use, including the contextual advertising.
- Providing customer service, processing, order fulfillment, billing and payment, providing advertising or marketing services, providing analytic services, or providing similar services on behalf of the business or service provider.
- Undertaking internal research for technological development and demonstration.

- Managing or improving the quality or safety of a service or device that is owned, manufactured, manufactured for, or controlled by the business.

These activities constitute the core operations for the business. This is a significant limitation on the scope of the CCPA and will reduce the impact of requests to delete information made by a consumer.

In addition, the consumer can allow personal information to remain with a business while requiring that the business does not sell the information to third parties. The CCPA regulations provide that if a business sells personal information, then it must post a link titled "Do Not Sell My Personal Information" or "Do Not Sell My Info." Any app must have the link available as well. The web address must also be available in non-Internet publications. The Do Not Sell provisions do not include the same business exceptions, so these will be applied more broadly.

For information collected regarding minors, a company may not sell the personal information without express consent. The law requires affirmative, opt-in consent rather than relying on opt-out provisions. Unlike COPPA, the law covers minors under the age of 16. The law allows minors between the ages of 13–16 to opt-in for themselves. For younger children, the parent or guardian must provide consent. Because of the concerns that online social media companies and video-sharing services ignore the information they collect about the age of their clientele, the law also provides that "a business that willfully disregards the consumer's age shall be deemed to have had actual knowledge of the consumer's age."

3. The Right to Nondiscrimination

One of the most significant rights provided under the CCPA is the right to non-discrimination. This means that a business cannot condition its services on the customer agreeing not to opt-out of the data collection. A business can no longer require that cookies be used on a website or an email address be provided as a condition of seeing the content published on that site. Other forms of data discrimination are also prohibited, such as denying goods or services to the consumer, charging different prices for goods or services, using price discounts, imposing penalties, or providing a different level or quality of goods or services to the consumer.

In those situations where a business cannot legitimately provide its service to the consumer without the consumer information, the law gives the company authority to condition service on receiving the consumer information. For example, a company must collect shipping and billing addresses to ship its product and bill for its services.

The nondiscrimination requirement, however, is subject to a significant exception. "Nothing . . . prohibits a business from charging a consumer a different price or rate, or from providing a different level or quality of goods or services to the consumer, if that difference is reasonably related to the value provided to the business by the consumer's data." This allows for direct payment for consumer information or offer pricing incentives to opt into the data collection. It is somewhat contradictory to the provision that prohibits data discrimination.

Comparing the two different requirements, it seems that the law intends that any program of incentives must be clearly explained, be optional, require a clear opt-in model for consent, allow the consumer to opt back out at any time, and be fair. The fairness requirement comes from the last sentence of the law, which provides that a "business shall not use financial incentive practices that are unjust, unreasonable, coercive, or usurious in nature."

Taken together, the new rights provided by the CCPA will require that businesses servicing California consumers must institute very different procedures to collect their personal information, be able to report back to their consumers on what they collect, and disclose the nature of the collection at the time of collection. As additional regulations and clarifications come to the law, it will have a significant impact on how U.S. companies do business.

D. General Data Protection Regulation from the European Union

The European Union's General Data Protection Regulation (GDPR) went into effect in May 2018, almost two years prior to the CCPA. At the time, many analysts considered it to be the most significant potential change to U.S. privacy practice since CalOPPA. The EU positioned the law with this in mind, announcing that the GDPR "is the most important change in data privacy regulation in 20 years. The regulation will fundamentally reshape the way in which data are handled across every sector, from healthcare to banking and beyond." Despite the bold statements, however, the GDPR applies to far fewer companies than CalOPPA or CCPA and therefore has a more limited reach within the United States.

1. Limited Multinational Scope of the GDPR

Despite a great deal of fanfare in 2018 in the United States, the GDPR has had only a modest impact. To fall within the regulations of the GDPR, a business must have the personal information of an EU "data subject," meaning a person who is a citizen or resident of the EU or the European Economic Area. Multinational companies and organizations doing substantial business in Europe will certainly meet this requirement. For companies outside the EU, the GDPR applies to non-EU companies where they process personal information related to "the offering of goods or services, irrespective of whether a payment of the data subject is required" or "the monitoring of their behaviour as far as [the EU data subject's] behaviour takes place within the Union."

Additional guidance on the scope of the GDPR has also been provided by the European Data Protection Board (EDPB). The EDPB has made clear "that maintaining a website accessible in the Union is not on its own enough" to subject a company to GDPR jurisdiction. On the other hand, the GDPR does not include a size threshold requirement, so even a small online retailer will be subject to the law if it ships goods to European residents or collects and tracks the information of European residents.

Another important consideration is the reach of the EU regulators. The GDPR only provides a system to empower EU member states to fine companies for noncompliance. The consequences of noncompliance do not begin unless a European data protection regulatory office chooses to initiate an action against a company which has assets and operations subject to that state's legal system.

While the GDPR has extraterritorial scope, the regulatory agencies do not. For example, if a company sells a widget to a French citizen twice during the year from inside the United States but has no other contact in the EU, that company may well be governed by the GDPR. But the French regulator has little or no ability to investigate or fine the U.S. company. In addition, much like the FTC, the EU regulators are trying to undertake a regulatory review of every company doing business on the Internet. Unless a company is conducting significant business or the conduct is sufficiently outrageous, the company is unlikely to fall within the purview of any EU regulators.

The GDPR is far more than a paper tiger, but far less than an extraterritorial revision to domestic law. Companies that have significant international clientele should be careful to comply with the GDPR, but it should be understood to be another sectoral privacy law geared at international trade and multinational data management. Despite the marketing efforts of the EU, it is not a new global standard for consumer privacy. The CCPA is much closer to fulfilling that role in the United States.

2. Key Provisions of the GDPR

The GDPR uses a broad, general definition of personal information:

> 'Personal data' means any information relating to an identified or identifiable natural person ('data subject'); an identifiable natural person is one who can be identified, directly or indirectly, in particular by reference to an identifier such as a name, an identification number, location data, an online identifier or to one or more factors specific to the physical, physiological, genetic, mental, economic, cultural or social identity of that natural person. . . .

Online identifiers such as IP addresses, cookies, RFID tags, and other technologies are mentioned elsewhere in the regulation. Using information from multiple sources to identify a person, such as connecting the email from one interaction with a coupon used in another transaction, or the matching of email addresses with data acquired from a credit card company or data broker, would all qualify as targeting an identifiable data subject and fall within the scope of the regulation. Similarly, the process of "profiling a natural person, particularly in order to take decisions concerning her or him or for analysing or predicting her or his personal preferences, behaviours and attitudes," falls within the definition of personal data.

The GDPR is structured to make the processing of personal data unlawful unless that processing falls into one of six enumerated categories. In the United States, it is the right of speech that cannot be restricted, except in specific instances and for compelling reasons; under the EU directive it is privacy that holds this highest of regards.

> Processing shall be lawful only if and to the extent that at least one of the following applies:
>
> (a) the data subject has given consent to the processing of his or her personal data for one or more specific purposes;
>
> (b) processing is necessary for the performance of a contract to which the data subject is party or in order to take steps at the request of the data subject prior to entering into a contract;
>
> (c) processing is necessary for compliance with a legal obligation to which the controller is subject;
>
> (d) processing is necessary in order to protect the vital interests of the data subject or of another natural person;
>
> (e) processing is necessary for the performance of a task carried out in the public interest or in the exercise of official authority vested in the controller;
>
> (f) processing is necessary for the purposes of the legitimate interests pursued by the controller or by a third party, except where such interests are overridden by the interests or fundamental rights and freedoms of the data subject which require protection of personal data, in particular where the data subject is a child.

> Point (f) of the first subparagraph shall not apply to processing carried out by public authorities in the performance of their tasks.

Processing means "any operation or set of operations which is performed on personal data or on sets of personal data, whether or not by automated means, such as collection, recording, organisation, structuring, storage, adaptation or alteration, retrieval, consultation, use, disclosure by transmission, dissemination or otherwise making available, alignment or combination, restriction, erasure or destruction."

Despite the severity of the regulatory system, in practice, most EU companies have elected to rely on the controller's legitimate interest or contractual obligations regarding the processing. So long as there is a legitimate business purpose or a contractual duty for the processing of the personal data, the business does not need to obtain consent from the data subject.

Where companies do rely on consent for their right to collect subject data, the GDPR establishes significant limitations. The GDPR definition of "consent" is much more restrictive than in the United States. Under the GDPR, consent means "any freely given, specific, informed and unambiguous indication of the data subject's wishes by which he or she, by a statement or by a clear affirmative action, signifies agreement to the processing of personal data relating to him or her." Informed consent requires that the data subject be, at minimum, aware of the controller's identity and the intended purposes of processing the personal data. The GDPR Preamble states, "consent should not be regarded as freely given if the data subject has no genuine or free choice or is unable to refuse or withdraw consent without detriment." For companies that collect data for the company's own use, these purposes may suffice for most data collection.

Companies that resell data, however, will need to obtain meaningful consent. Consent must be asked for in plain language for specific purposes and be freely given without conditions. The data subject must also be able to withdraw consent as easily as the person was asked to provide it. Consent for minors under sixteen must come from parents or guardians and the source must be verified.

Where a company is relying on necessity for contracting or business operations, it should not first ask for consent. For example, map tracking software cannot provide the user his or her location on the map without the GPS turned on. Consenting to the use of GPS is a false choice for such a service. False choices violate the GDPR. If consent is requested, then the choice not to provide consent must be recognized and the service must not be diminished.

The consent provisions of the GDPR override the notion of contractual consent by altering the terms through which a contract can be formed. This operates in stark contrast to the multitude of "clickwrap" decisions in the United States, which has shifted the bargaining power between two contractual parties for specific types of goods and services.

The GDPR has also gained attention for the size of its regulatory fines. The maximum fine is the higher of 4% worldwide revenue or €20 million. For smaller infractions, a company is subject to administrative fines up to €10 million, or 2% of annual worldwide revenue, whichever is higher. One of the very first fines levied was against Google for €50 million.

Some analysts point to the $5 billion fine by the FTC against Facebook as evidence that the EU's influence has pushed the U.S. regulators to impose more meaningful consequences for lax privacy practices. The size of the fines provides an important reminder that those companies which operate under the auspices of the GDPR must take their obligations very seriously.

3. *Additional Rights Under the GDPR*

There are many aspects of data privacy policy that had not been required of U.S. companies before the adoption of the GDPR except in the area of health care. The CCPA has incorporated a few of those, such as the right for a customer to receive a report of the information collected and to request deletion of the information. This was introduced by the GDPR first, but is no longer unique to just that law. These additional obligations of the GDPR each have important implications for the design of a data policy and the process of compliance.

Clarity—The controller is expected to communicate in plain, simple language: "The controller shall take appropriate measures to provide . . . any communication . . . to the data subject in a concise, transparent, intelligible and easily accessible form, using clear and plain language, in particular for any information addressed specifically to a child." The controller is required to provide clear information about itself, the basis for collecting its data, the specific types of data collected, the uses intended for the data, and the amount of time it will be stored.

Rights of Access, revision, and erasure—This provision requires that the data subject be given the right to access the personal data collected and to be provided information regarding how that information is used. The data subject has the right to seek correction of the information collected by the company (known as the data controller) as well as to delete the data.

In addition, a person may request that information be "erased." The right of erasure is a more modest version of the earlier "right to be forgotten," which it replaces. Under the right of erasure, a person can make a request to have their information removed. A data subject may request the data removal when the person believes it is no longer needed by the controller, has withdrawn consent for its collection, believes it has been unlawfully processed or in similar circumstances. The controller must respond within thirty days, but there are grounds to refuse the request, including considerations of freedom of expression and information.

Where data has been corrected or erased, the controller will inform each recipient of the changes, unless it is impossible or disproportionately difficult to do so. If the data subject requests, the controller will inform the data subject of these communications.

Obligations of the controller—A controller subject to the GDPR that operates from outside the EU must designate a representative located in one of the EU member states. The representative provides the EU direct jurisdiction over a representative of the company.

The controller of the data collected for processing is required to institute sufficient technical and administrative procedures as required to keep the data secure from accidental disclosure or intentional piracy and theft. Like most data regulations, the law does not specify the particular steps necessary since the technological measures for encryption and data security are rapidly evolving. The nature of these cybersecurity obligations are discussed in the next chapter.

The GDPR does, however, identify data minimization and pseudonymization as data-protection principles that companies should employ, where appropriate, to reduce the risk of data loss and misuse.

The GDPR requires a stringent data breach notification provision that requires a company to notify the supervisory authority of any data breach, providing the nature of the breach, the scale, and the likely consequences of the breach. The notification should be completed "without undue delay and, where feasible, not later than 72 hours after having become aware of it." The company is also required to provide information regarding the remedial actions taken and those that will be forthcoming. Notification is not required where "the personal data breach is unlikely to result in a risk to the rights and freedoms of natural persons." This exclusion provides a powerful incentive to use strong encryptions, so that any theft of data or breach of control systems will not result in the exposure of customer or data subject records.

4. GDPR Challenges to U.S. Companies

The GDPR challenges for U.S. companies tend to fall into three broad categories: (1) disparity in data regulations among jurisdictions, (2) greater consequences of data breaches, and (3) conflict in U.S. and EU constitutional principles. As a result of these conflicts, some U.S. companies are striving to comply with the data management aspects of the GDPR while avoiding the duties that bring the U.S. company into direct contact with the GDPR regulators.

First, the usage of the data will be more restricted under EU regulation than its U.S. counterpart. Although the CCPA and GDPR are similar in their approach to business operations, the CCPA has not adopted the GDPR's restricted view of consent. Compliance with the CCPA can be accomplished through the use of opt-out notice provisions. Those do not meet the consent requirements of the GDPR. Within the EU, however, the importance of consent has been reduced as the essential requirements for business processing have allowed a greater range of activities to be conducted without consent. But the EU notices do not allow for opt-out consent, meaning the two systems remain somewhat incompatible.

Second, the challenges of data theft, ransomware, and disruption caused by external data breaches and internal employee misconduct may have a greater consequence for the corporate owners of the data and a higher cost for the response to each data breach when complying with the GDPR. The problem of lost and stolen data can trigger much more stringent reporting requirements from EU regulators. Both the GDPR and CCPA have introduced additional liability for data breaches under the two laws, but they are only similar in approach.

Third, and conceptually most challenging, is that GDPR restrictions may conflict with the U.S. fundamental right of free speech. The U.S. constitutional right in free speech grates against EU fundamental notions of privacy, like the right to erasure. Although this conflict may not be the most financially significant, it reflects the stark divide between EU and U.S. policies and political histories. Fortunately, the right to erasure has been made somewhat narrower than when first adopted, again allowing more harmony between the EU and the United States.

When first proposed, the GDPR was an extraordinary proposal requiring far more than most U.S. companies were prepared to address. As data protection policies and privacy notions have evolved, however, the requirements of other U.S. privacy laws and general expectations have moved steadily closer to the demands of the GDPR. Nonetheless, it still plays its primary role as a sectoral privacy law for multinational transactions.

5. Transactions Between U.S. and EU Companies

Even before the adoption of the GDPR, EU directives restricted the distribution of personal information from EU residents outside of the EU (and the European Economic Area (EEA)) without appropriate assurances that the information would only be used in a manner that provided at least adequate levels of data protection. Nonetheless, the economic ties between U.S. and EU based business makes the transfer of data a necessity for many commercial transactions.

In 2000, the U.S. and EU established "Safe Harbor Privacy Principles," a self-regulatory model operated under the FTC to allow U.S. companies to self-certify that they met the EU requirements for data privacy. In 2015, however, the agreement regarding the Safe Harbor Privacy Principles was declared invalid by the Court of Justice of the European Union. The self-regulation of the Safe Harbor Privacy Principles did not meet the "essentially equivalent" protections required to be adequate data protection under the EU Directives.

EU-U.S. Privacy Shield

The United States and EU recognized that there needs to be a mechanism to allow these data transactions for many business activities. In 2016, the parties agreed to a new system known as the "EU-U.S. Privacy Shield." The Privacy Shield was designed to address the limitations of the Safe Harbor Privacy Principles. Nonetheless, as of the time of the writing of this book, the Court of Justice continues to review the validity of the Privacy Shield. It is currently operating as an acceptable mechanism under which data transfers can take place, but a negative decision by the Court of Justice would require yet another agreement between the EU and United States regarding the protection of privacy in the United States for EU residents.

The Privacy Shield allows a consumer in the EU to conduct business with a U.S. company. The information needed to complete the transaction can be lawfully transferred to the United States provided that the U.S. company stores, processes, transfers, or otherwise uses the information in compliance with the rules established by the Privacy Shield. The obligations were once considered a significant burden on U.S. companies, but given the changes triggered by CCPA and the GDPR, the obligations under the Privacy Shield are now quite similar to the type of privacy being adopted under these other regulations. These include:

- Information regarding the types of personal data the company processes, and the purpose for using the data.
- Access to the personal information collected by the company.
- Information regarding any intended use to transfer the information to other companies and the right to opt-out to further transfers of the data collected.
- For sensitive information, such as race, gender, ethnicity, the right to transfer that data only with opt-in consent.

Companies that wish to engage in data transfers under the Privacy Shield protocol must apply and participate in what remains a self-certification process. In some instances, a company can certify through the Department of Transportation rather than the FTC. Companies subject exclusively to a different regulatory body such as financial institutions regulated by the Consumer Financial Protection Bureau are ineligible. The privacy notice used by the company must specifically reference the Privacy Shield and give the notice, opt-out, and opt-in rights described under the Privacy Shield understandings. Companies must also provide clear information for "recourse mechanisms" or complaint resolution, including the use of commercial mediation and arbitration, where appropriate. Additional rules apply to personnel and human resources data. The fee to apply for self-certification is based on the company's annual revenue.

The Privacy Shield also includes a complaint process and dispute mechanism that operates through the FTC in the United States. It establishes obligation on the FTC to provide this dispute mechanism for individuals and also to take affirmative steps to police against false claims that companies are in compliance with the Privacy Shield.

In its third year of operation, the Privacy Shield now has more than 5,000 participating companies, suggesting that it has become a very viable system for data transfers. In seven cases, the FTC brought enforcement actions against companies that falsely claimed they had been certified through the Privacy Shield process. Since the Privacy Shield is a self-certification process, no company is rejected if it correctly fills out the forms. The FTC has the ability to review the certified companies, but it generally provides only spot-checks of posted data at the rate of 30 companies each month. When compared to the number of self-certified participants, the FTC's role is quite modest.

The lack of aggressive oversight by the U.S. government continues to be one of the key concerns of the EU. At the same time, as companies agree to be regulated directly by the GDPR, the use of the Privacy Shield has the potential to become an ancillary part of that broader effort. The other concern with the Privacy Shield is that U.S. law enforcement and national security authorities have too great an ability to require the data stored in the United States. Since these are legal obligations for the companies operating in the United States, nothing particular companies wish to say about these concerns can be alleviated without changes to U.S. criminal law and national security law.

Binding Corporate Rules (BCRs) and Standard Contractual Clauses (SCCs)

The adoption of the GDPR included mechanisms that serve as alternatives to the Privacy Shield. The BCRs and SCCs cannot resolve the question of U.S. surveillance, but they provide a much stronger level of protection for EU companies than the oft distrusted self-regulation of the Privacy Shield. The Standard Contractual Clauses are a set of data contractual provisions published by the EU. There are three sets of the SCCs.

The SCCs are currently the most widely used mechanism under which data are allowed to transfer from the EU to third party countries. Although these are also under judicial scrutiny in the EU, these contractual agreements to meet the stringent GDPR standards are essential for companies that need to protect their data by using cloud and co-location systems that protect the data from natural disasters within the EU as well as for transactions that involve EU residents having business outside the Union.

Binding Corporate Rules are similar to SCCs in that they are agreements established at the entity level rather than by operative law. The BCRs are designed to create a legal regime within a conglomerate, primarily used within the operation of a business enterprise that might have separate divisions incorporated in different jurisdictions, such as a U.S. division and a German division. Since both of the corporations are under common ownership, a BCR can establish the rules by which privacy and security are protected for all the companies within the enterprise.

Both BCRs and SCC provisions have been expanded under the GDPR. Essentially, so long as every aspect of the enterprise or the contractual relationship complies with the GDPR requirements, then the BCRs and SCC provisions keep all of the EU resident data protected. These mechanisms do not stop the lawful review of the data by government agencies but in all other aspects, these provide a reasonable mechanism to address the data transfers.

E. Behavioral Advertising

The Internet changed advertising and consumer tracking. Instead of anonymous, generalized data, an advertiser can now collect specific information about the particular user. This information is used to decide which advertisement to show the consumer. As the advertising companies collect more personal information, the data are refined and profile improves, making the information about each consumer more valuable to the advertisers.

1. *Types of Advertising*

Broadly categorized, there are three types of advertisements. The first is generic advertising. A generic advertisement has no direct relationship to the content associated with the advertisement. For example, an ad for a car dealership that appears in the first section of the local newspaper will be purchased without the advertiser having any knowledge of the stories that will be printed on the page surrounding the ad. Journalistic codes of ethics kept advertising information and editorial information separate so that advertisers could not influence the coverage of the newspaper.

The advertiser in the newspaper might make certain assumptions about the readership. By assuming that men are more likely to read the business and sports sections, a car dealership might choose to purchase their ads in those sections. A department store might choose the local section or entertainment section, thinking that those sections will be more heavily read by women. But these gender-based assumptions are little more than stereotypes, with very low predictive value.

On a website, the advertisement shown to the person visiting can change for each viewer. The technology that allows the advertisement to be pulled from a separate database than the content on the site enables the advertising agency to provide much more personalized advertisements.

The first form of advertising personalization is contextual advertising. Contextual advertising uses the information about the content on the website to determine which ads to run. If the website has content about fashion, the ads will feature clothing and accessories. If, instead, the website has content about real estate, the ads might feature furniture, lawn care, or other products and services associated with real estate. These ads are more likely to be relevant to the consumer because they relate to the content the consumer sought out to read. Contextual advertising needs no particular information about the individual consumer to be effective.

The other form of advertising personalization is behavioral advertising. In behavioral advertising, the software that selects the ad chooses based on the information available about the recent activities of the individual consumer. At its simplest, if a consumer reads a story about real estate, for example, the software will feature ads about furniture and lawn care across multiple websites, until the consumer interacts with another category of advertisements that would be more profitable to promote. Behavioral advertising triangulates the information. If the consumer first visits a page about real estate and then a page about home financing, the ads might include moving companies, because the software is programmed to predict that a person financing a home is likely to be moving soon. At its best, behavioral advertising provides the consumer ads about the products and services the consumer is just about to need. After all, those ads are the ones most likely to attract the consumer's attention.

2. Types of Data Available for Tracking

Behavioral advertising works effectively by knowing as much about the individual consumer as possible. Using various tracking technologies, a website and its advertisers can now track the pages browsed on a website; the time spent on a site; the movement of the mouse interacting with the images and text; the clicks on links; the sites next visited after leaving a website; prior visits to that website and other websites; the geographic location of the device (including zip code—and hence demographic information); the time of day when the interaction occurred; and much more. If the device is a mobile phone instead of a computer, the website host and advertiser may be able to track the consumer's movements.

In addition, through services provided by data brokers, the unique information available for each website interaction can be combined with the geolocation information from one's cell phone and even the purchasing information from one's credit cards. Free email services will often scan the words used in email messages to connect the relevance of the advertising to the statements made in the private email communications.

Taken together, data brokers and advertisers can know precisely how and where each consumer spends money, times, and personal interests. There are few general laws that regulate the collection of this information. Certain industries have federal restrictions and increasingly state laws require certain amounts of disclosure regarding the collection of these data, but consumers in the United States are heavily monitored.

3. Regulations Regarding Behavioral Advertising

In 2009, after extensive review, the FTC promoted the development of a self-regulatory approach to the advertising. As a result, there is little or no federal regulation of the use of collected information for targeted advertising. One of the key aspects of the CCPA has been the introduction of do-not-track obligations to help thwart the use of technologies that monitor the activity of consumers as they navigate from one website to the next. Do-not-track operates as a setting in the consumer's computer and mobile browser that is designed to flag websites, ad networks, and analytics companies not to include the data from that consumer.

The CCPA was amended to require that businesses subject to CCPA make it simple to opt-in to the do-not-track service. This is required for both computer and mobile based websites and apps. As enforcement grows for the CCPA, the California Attorney General will provide additional regulations and guidance to implement this technology. Under the self-regulatory approach initially recommended by the FTC, the do-not-track technology has had no meaningful impact on reducing the tracking by online companies, data aggregators, ad networks and other information mining enterprises. The implementation of CCPA and similar laws in other states will likely shift this balance in years to come.

Key Takeaways from This Chapter:

Consumer privacy in the United States is still rather limited in scope. Through more recent laws in California and Europe, the number of companies subject to data privacy and data security laws are continuing to grow. Additional laws are under consideration across the country to continue to increase general consumer privacy.

Most U.S. privacy remains sectoral, focusing on health care records, financial information, information collected for employment, children under thirteen, and similar categories. Outside of these categories, the primary source of protection comes from the privacy policy posted by the company, as required by CalOPPA and enforced by the California Attorney General in California and by the FTC across the nation.

Outside one of the more heavily regulated areas, privacy policies merely require that the company explain how it collects and shares the personally identifiable information and how the company implements the do-not-track technologies. With the implementation of GDPR in 2018 and CCPA in 2020, many U.S. companies must now go much further and offer privacy policies that include some ability to opt-out of some data collection, to receive copies of the information gathered about them, to delete some of the information, and to be able to expect reasonable security of the data collected. Despite these improvements, most advertising continues to focus on behavioral tracking of consumers.

Things to Know:

Most U.S. privacy regulation still relies on voluntary guidelines. These do little to stop companies from collecting, aggregating, and sharing data about individuals.

The most important privacy rule is the policy posted to each website and app. Understanding what a company can do with the information remains the most important aspect of consumer privacy.

The GDPR and CCPA have limited scope. Companies often claim they are compliant, but they are meeting only a few of the requirements.

The meaning of personally identifiable information changes considerably from law to law, making it hard to predict what information is protected.

Things to Think About:

In the context of web browsing and shopping, advertisers suggest that privacy is not even needed. The information collected does not harm the consumer when used. To what extent is there a need for consumer privacy?

Should the U.S. law focus more on limits over the use of collected information rather than collection of information? Would this focus better protect the privacy interests of the public?

Privacy law continues to evolve. What are the consumer privacy laws likely to require ten years from now, and how does one plan for those changes?

CHAPTER 6

Data Security Basics for Business

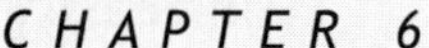

The modern economy runs on data. Nearly every company collects data as it advertises, markets its products or services, provides its goods or services to its customers, collects payment, and purchases goods or supplies from its vendors. The transactions are largely completed with electronic or credit card payments. The receipts are electronically stored. The customer information is maintained in a database. Social media and online tools are used to promote the brand and interact with customers.

These steps require that data are created, stored, sorted, and analyzed. The data collected on employees must meet state and federal requirements for the protection of the employee's confidential information. In certain industries, such as healthcare, finance, and videotape rental, and for products and services targeted to children under the age of thirteen, there are additional federal laws governing the collection of information. The FTC Act makes the failure to secure collected data an unfair trade practice. CCPA, GDPR and many additional state laws add requirements for data security for all but the smallest businesses.

To meet these requirements, the data collected by companies must be kept and used in a safe, reliable manner. This chapter will provide a basic overview of the security aspects of information privacy. It will outline the fundamentals every business must follow to keep the information it collects and utilizes secure and reliable.

A. What Data Wants—Accuracy, Validity, Reliability, Verifiability, and Security

To develop an appropriate understanding of information security, the corporation and its employees must first establish what makes for good data. Data, after all, are merely raw pieces of information. To be usable the data must be accurate, reliable and consistent. Different sources often use these terms interchangeably. The General Accounting Office explained a brief summary of these concepts:

- **Reliability** means that data are reasonably complete and accurate, meet your intended purposes, and are not subject to inappropriate alteration.
- **Completeness** refers to the extent that relevant records are present and the fields in each record are populated appropriately.
- **Accuracy** refers to the extent that recorded data reflect the actual underlying information.
- **Consistency**, a subcategory of accuracy, refers to the need to obtain and use data that are clear and well defined enough to yield similar results in similar analyses. For example, if data are entered at multiple sites, inconsistent interpretation of data entry rules can lead to data that, taken as a whole, are unreliable.

- **Validity** refers to whether the data actually represent what you think is being measured. For example, if we are interested in analyzing job performance and a field in the database is labeled "annual evaluation score," we need to know whether that field seems like a reasonable way to gain information on a person's job performance or whether it represents another kind of evaluation score.

These individual terms help understand the need for data a company can rely upon. First, reliable data are complete and accurate. Accuracy starts at collection. If a company collects incorrect or incomplete information regarding its customers, employees, operations, or vendors, it will not be able to utilize the information fully. Analysis of the information may result in faulty decision making. And the ability of the enterprise to check the reliability of the information will be compromised. Companies, for example, should be sure to confirm the information they collect with their customers, vendors, employees and others at the time it is entered into systems to assure it is accurate. If addresses are collected incorrectly, the efforts to ship goods will be frustrated, costing time, expense, and relationships. If geographical planning is based on collected area codes or zip codes, then inaccuracies or incomplete data will diminish the effectiveness of the planning.

Information also changes over time. Customers move, employees have children, vendors merge, and everyone ages. The data collected must be updated regularly and outdated information eliminated from all databases.

Second, the information must be valid. This means that the rules and definitions for structured data are followed carefully so that each piece of information represents what the company thinks it does. For example, a zip code, a Social Security number, and a bank routing number can each be comprised of nine digits. Collecting a nine-digit number from a customer only becomes useful when that number is properly labeled and stored. In this example, the customer providing a nine-digit number is correctly identified by the company to be a Social Security number and processed appropriately. Credit card payment systems, for example, often check the credit card number, customer zip code, and security code as a separate step before attempting to complete the payment processing.

Another aspect of data reliability is consistency, meaning that the same question will get the same answer each time (unless there has been a change of circumstance). If a person is asked how much an injury hurts on a five-point scale, the person will hopefully answer with the same response each time. If, instead, the person is asked for a score on a one hundred point scale, it is much more likely that a person's answer will vary for similar injuries. Similarly, while an objective math test will be accurate that a student achieved a particular score on a test, it will only be consistent if that test predicts how well the student will do on similar tests. If the test is not sufficiently representative of the knowledge being tested, it will not reliably predict the outcome on the next test.

Third, any data collected should be verifiable to the greatest extent possible. This means that information should be traceable, and a historical record should be created regarding the creation of transactions. In addition to collecting credit card information for a customer sale, for example, the credit card company collects location information and timestamps the transaction. The information is recorded both electronically and in print. Hospital records include signatures and acknowledgements by patients, nurses, and doctors to verify the patient data as it is being collected. While it may not be possible to independently verify each piece of data collected, the structure of the data collection process can help verify the context and increase confidence in the accuracy of the information.

Finally, the information and data collected and processed must be secure. Security means that the information and data collected cannot be used, deleted, manipulated, or copied without appropriate authorizations that the company has designed to maximize the use of the data and minimize the risk of harm or loss of the data. Without secure data, malicious third parties could change the data, rendering it unusable; they could publicly disclose the data to create embarrassment and civil liability; they could encrypt the data to render it unusable without the payment of a ransom; or they could copy the data for use in competition with the company. Security is essential to maintaining accurate, valid, verifiable, and reliable data.

The need for accurate, valid, reliable, and verifiable data is one of the key reasons that companies need secure data. If the data can be modified by accident or through the malicious conduct of hackers or thieves, then the company can never trust its data. Only by having secure data can a company ever achieve the other requirements essential for its data hygiene.

B. The Sources of Data Security Risks

Data security is essential to reliability because any information that can be altered while in storage cannot be trustworthy. Financial institutions must constantly fight attempts by thieves to create false transactions and falsify banking data. School districts and universities are constantly thwarting attempts to break into computer systems to change student grades or add credentials. Every industry has some degree of fraud or theft. In the absence of good security, these efforts would financially ruin companies.

Lapses in security can come from hackers, software malfunctions that inaccurately index data, human error, human misconduct, or other external forces that alter, destroy, corrupt, or improperly disclose the data. The various risks are sometimes called "attack vectors." This merely means that threats to data security can come from both outside and inside a company.

External attacks have many motives. They may be launched by thrill-seekers, social or political activists, individual criminals, organized criminal enterprises, or nations under the guise of cyber espionage, cyber terrorism, or cyber warfare. Even if a company is an unlikely target for organized crime or cyber espionage, its computer system could be used by such third party attackers to build opportunities to infiltrate companies that do business with the small business or to exploit the computing power of thousands of similar small businesses. Since every company is networked to every other company through the Internet, attackers are always seeking to find vulnerable links to infiltrate the network.

Security lapses, however, are just as likely to come from within an enterprise as outside it. Internal threats come from mistakes made by employees, ill-advised shortcuts, and from intentional misconduct. Loss or theft of laptops or cell phones with unencrypted customer, patient, or employee data will give rise to state and federal liability. Misuse of corporate data by current employees can create significant legal problems. Misuse of corporate data by leaving or former employees is often a source of data insecurity and theft of confidential information. Even when information is being managed by employees authorized to do so, the failure of the organization to have complete data policies and effective training can result in data loss, corruption, or misuse.

In addition to the risks posed by attacks from outside attackers, mistakes from loyal employees, and misconduct by disgruntled employees, there are also more abstract threats. Companies can face the loss or corruption of their data due to the failure of the business resources such as the equipment, vendors, supply chains, or other operational disruptions. In addition, companies increasingly face risk from environmental factors such as fire, flood, storm, power outages, riots, and other natural or man-made disasters.

Each of these risks can be predicted, so companies can take steps to mitigate the harm and improve their resilience to the threats. The best model for data security is based on the regulations required for health care data under HIPAA. These regulations require that there are physical safeguards, technical safeguards, and administrative safeguards to protect the health care records. For non-health care data, the steps may not be as rigorous, but the general approach should be the same.

Software, hardware, and other countermeasures should be deployed to protect the integrity of information and data from outside threats. Encryption should be used for any sensitive data. Well-designed data systems should store copies of nearly up-to-date data in a system that cannot be encrypted by the same attack that crippled the primary site. There are a multitude of resources to help a company reduce the risks of an outside attack and to respond efficiently when that breach inevitably occurs.

C. Data Security Basics

Planning cybersecurity falls into three broad categories: technical, administrative, and physical safeguards. This approach is based on the "Security Rule" developed by the U.S. Department of Health & Human Services, but the general approach provides an excellent framework for data security at any institution. The goals of the Security Rule model are to assure that all businesses—

- Ensure the confidentiality, integrity, and availability of all [protected information] they create, receive, maintain or transmit;
- Identify and protect against reasonably anticipated threats to the security or integrity of the information;
- Protect against reasonably anticipated, impermissible uses or disclosures; and
- Ensure compliance by their workforce.

Broad-based data security laws were initiated with the development of the HIPAA Security rule, but changes to state laws and federal regulations beginning in 2018 mandated this approach much more broadly. The Gramm-Leach-Bliley (GLBA) Safeguards Rule provides a very similar requirement for all financial institutions. (These are explained in Chapter 10.) The New York SHIELD Act, the California Privacy Protection Act, and similar laws in Massachusetts, Rhode Island, and other states all have similar data security requirements. While they vary considerably in how they are described, each of the laws provides a framework for businesses to establish reasonable security measures, based on the potential risks that the company will face, the size of the business, and the sensitivity of the data that could be stolen, altered, or destroyed.

Even for the smallest business, these steps are essential to protect it from data security threats and data privacy breaches. For companies subject to HIPAA or GLBA requirements, the specific obligations are much greater than described in this introduction. In general, the protection philosophy requires that companies strive for the greatest protection and lowest amount of access that is reasonable, given the nature of the business and the sensitivity of the information.

In addition, the safeguards plan must include the vendors and contractors that do business with the company. If a vendor gets access to any computer systems or any data, then the vendor must be included in the safeguard procedures to assure that physical assets are secure, encryption and data minimization is in place, and the vendor has the lowest possible access. Many data breaches have occurred because vendors' systems were corrupted by third parties and the vendors were not sufficiently diligent to stop the intrusions from spreading. Hackers know that service and repair companies connect with thousands of other companies, so they are a common target for malicious software and other attacks.

1. Physical Safeguards

Physical safeguards range from the physical plant where the company operates to the tracking of each mobile device. All doors, computers, cell phones, and data storage devices need physical security. Companies should start with their location. Doors should be locked, or they should be staffed. A retailer, for example, keeps its customer doors open throughout the day, but it has employees on staff to see all patrons enter and exit. Office areas that are not staffed should be locked.

Computer rooms, whether large server rooms or small closets, should have door locks that allow only authorized personnel into the area. For small companies, a simple key might suffice. For companies storing more sensitive or heavily regulated data, the door locks should include tracking information so that the company has logs of which employees entered and exited the computer server areas in case of any data breach.

Both physical keys and access cards must also be logged and carefully monitored so that they are not duplicated and shared without authorization. When an employee changes positions within a business or leaves, the keys must be collected. Since it is very easy to duplicate physical keys, most companies invest in electronic locking systems that can be updated quickly as employees are hired, change roles, or leave.

Each computer, mobile device, or other networked machine must also have physical safeguards. This generally means that the device is password protected with secure passwords not written down next to the machine and multi-factor personal authentication procedures. This also requires that physical and technical policies reduce the ability to copy and remove protected information using email, cloud storage, USB drives, and other media.

Good physical security also includes the use of an inventory system so that each device is assigned to a custodian/user and the custodian is responsible to keep track of the device. One of the technical safeguards should be strong encryption so that if a device is lost or stolen, it has both password protection and encryption to thwart access by thieves or other unauthorized users. Similarly, all laptops and mobile devices should be equipped with remove data erasure technologies so that the information can be eliminated from any lost or stolen device. This remote erasure is also appropriate for secure corporate information if it is allowed on personal devices.

2. *Technical Safeguards*

The public generally thinks about cybersecurity through its technical safeguards. These are the steps necessary to fight fire with fire: hacking with firewalls. These steps are certainly among the most important, but technical safeguards only work with the appropriate physical and administrative safeguards also in place.

At the broadest level, technical safeguards are designed to protect access into accounts, to restrict data transfers out, to audit the use of all systems and equipment, and to provide integrity checks so the company has confidence the data has not been altered or destroyed. In addition, there must be technical safeguards to assure that data are not intercepted while in use or in transit and there are appropriate back-up and retrieval strategies in place in case anything goes wrong.

Access controls start with system basics. Every company network should utilize firewall protections, antivirus software, and regular updates for all software. When installed, every system should be checked to make sure that default passwords are replaced with unique and secure pass phrases. Companies also get in trouble by using outdated software operating with known vulnerabilities. This is a very common cause of data breaches and can easily be avoided through simple procedures to keep all software up to date. While cost is certainly a factor in business decisions to continue using outdated software, the cost of a data breach or ransomware attack is much greater than the maintenance costs of any software service. If software cannot be updated, then it should be removed from the systems.

Where companies allow remote access, they should provide virtual private networks (VPNs) to minimize the ability of third parties to monitor and access the information transmitted. There is always a risk that log in credentials are exposed when using a public network. A VPN allows remote access in a much more secure environment.

Access controls also include segmentation of systems. For many businesses, the majority of employees have no need to be on the system that stores customer, patient, employee, or client information. By operating two systems, the employees who do not need access to the more secure data cannot ever have access to that network and therefore no third-party intrusion or employee misconduct from one system can penetrate into the other system. Guest networks also keep the customers and public off the network and away from sensitive information in the same manner.

For employees with access to the primary system, access controls should include strong authentication protections and data minimization. This means that each person who can log into the system must use multi-factor authentication to gain access. The system itself should be designed to give each person access to the minimum amount of data and management control needed for that person to complete his or her duties.

The auditing aspects of technical safeguards should allow the company to know which employees are on the system, what systems are being used, patterns of data flows, and network activities. This will enable a company to track attempts to log into the network from unauthorized locations, attempts to send or exfiltrate data to unapproved devices, to track whether employees or others are attempting to access information for which they do not have permission, and other examples of attempts at system breaches. Managing the system to create alerts for unusual activity will often allow the companies to catch attempted intrusions well before they occur. The audit systems should also track changes to software so that attempts to install viruses and malware are stopped and the attempts are tracked.

The integrity controls are designed to assure that the data maintained by the company are accurate and untampered. This is required for health data and is very important for other critical data such as financial data and educational records. These are sophisticated procedures designed to authenticate where and how changes to patient and customer records occur so that only authorized changes are allowed. These also assist the company in being sure that data do not become corrupted through errors that occur as a result of storage and transfer.

3. *Administrative Safeguards*

Companies tend to underplay the administrative safeguards, but these aspects of data security are as important as the physical and technical safeguards. Administrative safeguards are the policies, procedures, training exercises, and institutional culture, and ongoing evaluation that drives data protection.

Data security begins with the corporate culture of the institution. If the leadership of the organization does not take data security seriously, then the employees will ignore the mandates and underplay privacy risks. If instead, the leadership advocates and invests in data security, then it will be able to promulgate a culture of security and hold the workforce responsible to meet the challenge. It takes both financing and attention for leadership to shape this culture. Speeches by the CEO will do little if there is no funding for adequate security measures. And a well-funded IT department will not gain any institutional respect if the senior leadership ignore its recommendations.

When there is a partnership among senior leadership and security personnel, then the culture of data privacy and security will flourish. Senior leadership must be subject to each aspect of the data privacy and security system, including the data minimization, the training, and the accountability. Even the CEO should not be permitted to see patient or customer files unless that CEO has a true business purpose for the information. The CEO and other senior leadership must participate in appropriate training on the security requirements, and they must be held accountable if they intentionally breach the policies of the organization.

Second, administrative safeguards require comprehensive, well-written policies and procedures that are shared with all employees. These include sections in the Employee Handbook, training manuals, and regularly updated user information.

Employees cannot be expected to meet expectations unless they are clearly written and widely available.

Third, the administrative safeguards require that all employees are trained on the various technologies and systems used in the business and taught how to avoid the common risks of data intrusion and theft. Employees must be trained to use the company systems and to respect privacy policies. Employees must also be trained on the best ways to avoid efforts by hackers, and they must be educated regarding the consequences of any intentional misconduct on their part.

The employee training should not be limited to hourly employees. Senior executives must also be trained that they should not use their leadership in ways that could put the physical or technical safeguards at risk. CEOs should never ask that a firewall be dropped or that they be allowed to log in from an unsecure hotel or coffee shop server rather than through the corporate VPN. The inconvenience to a senior business executive is still far less damaging than the possibility that the corporate data become vulnerable. These protections are part of the corporate culture of security and they also reflect common attack vectors for hackers and other third parties.

Proper administrative safeguards include consequences for failing to adhere to the privacy and security policies and procedures of the business. These consequences should also apply across all levels of the organization so that new employees, senior leadership, and everyone in between remain part of the training process and accountability process of the company.

Finally, administrative safeguards are not static. Evaluation and response become an essential part of a healthy data security process. The laws regulating data privacy and security are continuing to evolve, the risks associated with data attacks continue to grow more sophisticated, and the personnel working at a business often change. For these reasons, it is important to continually refresh the policies, procedures, and training to keep the administrative safeguards current and dynamic. A culture of compliance requires a very active engagement with all aspects of the physical, technical, and administrative safeguards.

To keep the development active, companies must consistently evaluate their systems to assure that the efforts they are undertaking are working, to learn about where the company's systems can improve, and to gain lessons from the changes in the industry. The evaluation then helps the company update its efforts and reinforce its culture of privacy and security.

4. *System Backups and Managing Catastrophic Risk*

One of the important obligations for any data security system is to keep the data secure from destruction as well as from theft. In recent years, the threat of ransomware has increased. Ransomware is a form of data intrusion in which all of a company's information is encrypted without authorization. The hacker then ransoms the decryption code back to the company in exchange for a payment. Another threat for destruction of data comes from natural causes, including fire, flood, hurricane, blizzard, earthquake, or other catastrophic failure. Similar risks can occur from equipment and software failures, particularly for smaller businesses that rely on a single work computer.

Data suggest that companies often fail to recover from catastrophic data loss, even if the loss is not accompanied by physical destruction. The cost to business operations, revenues, and relationships can often be fatal for small businesses.

To manage the risk of both manmade and natural disasters, a company must have an established and tested data backup and recovery plan in place. At a minimum, this means having a very recent set of duplicate copies of all data stored at a location other than the company's place of business. This can be done through the use of backup media such as storage tapes. In the age of cloud computing, it is no longer difficult to find services that will store backup files off site and in multiple locations.

A system that includes true backups of data is essential to protect a business. Because of the threat of ransomware attacks, it is best to have one or more backups that are not merely synced copies of the active data. Synced copies of data are protected from hardware crashes and natural disasters, but software errors, intentional deletions, and unauthorized encryptions can travel across the synced formats and wipe out the secondary copies. Syncing is a partial solution, but it should not be the entire solution.

In addition, it is essential to test the backup systems before there is a catastrophic situation requiring data recovery. Backup systems have many settings, so a company needs to test the system when it is first configured to be sure it is collecting the correct data and that the restoration functions work properly. Moreover, because systems change, the steps to assure that the backup is working properly should be conducted on a regular basis. Depending on the amount of data and sophistication of the system, the process should be evaluated on anywhere from a monthly to an annual basis.

There are also smaller steps companies can take to avoid the necessity for disaster recovery. Installing uninterruptible power supply systems and backup generators can keep machines operable to provide additional time to plan for shutdowns. Cloud services that guarantee distributed service from multiple locations also help considerably.

Finally, despite the promise of a paperless office, keeping paper backups of critical documents and files remains a useful strategy to assure the integrity of data and provide a comparison to the information stored on the computer system. In the case of a ransomware attack, the paper files will remain unaffected as well.

D. Special Considerations for Credit, Debit, and Payment Cards

Credit card systems have been transferring financial information for decades before the Internet and World Wide Web were made commercially available. The largest companies involved in these financial transactions have always undertaken steps to assure that their systems were protected from fraud and theft, both to reduce the cost of operating and to address the obligations imposed by regulation on the banks for losses associated with the use of credit cards, debit cards, and other card payment systems.

In 2006, American Express, Discover, JCB International, MasterCard and Visa Inc. joined together to form the Payment Card Industry Council and publish the Data Security Standard (PCI DSS). The PCI DSS serves as the trade association's regulations for every merchant that uses a point of purchase device to collect credit card information or otherwise contracts with a bank to accept payments through credit, debit, or payment cards.

The PCI Council stresses the importance of continuous updates to merchant security to guarantee protection from theft and fraud. In many ways, the PCI system is very similar to the HIPAA system, but focused narrowly on the devices and operations related to merchant payment systems. Each of the member banks works directly with the merchants to provide the merchant the point of purchase equipment and to assure the vendor's compliance with the data security obligations.

The PCI Council describes the compliance process as a three-step, continuous process:

- *Assess.* Identifying cardholder data, taking an inventory of IT assets and business processes for payment card processing, and analyzing them for vulnerabilities.
- *Remediate.* Fixing vulnerabilities and eliminating the storage of cardholder data unless absolutely necessary.
- *Report.* Compiling and submitting required reports to the appropriate acquiring bank and card brands.

The PCI process involves twelve steps that are required for any merchant that wishes to accept the cards issued by member banks.

- Build and Maintain a Secure Network
    1. Install and maintain a firewall configuration to protect cardholder data
    2. Do not use vendor-supplied defaults for system passwords and other security parameters
- Protect Cardholder Data
    3. Protect stored cardholder data
    4. Encrypt transmission of cardholder data across open, public networks
- Maintain a Vulnerability Management Program
    5. Use and regularly update anti-virus software or programs
    6. Develop and maintain secure systems and applications
- Implement Strong Access Control Measures
    7. Restrict access to cardholder data by business need-to-know

8. Assign a unique ID to each person with computer access
9. Restrict physical access to cardholder data

- Regularly Monitor and Test Networks

10. Track and monitor all access to network resources and cardholder data
11. Regularly test security systems and processes

- Maintain an Information Security Policy

12. Maintain a policy that addresses information security for employees and contractors

The most significant aspect of the PCI DSS is the role that the member banks play in supervising their merchants. The obligations to have firewalls, updated password systems, data encryption, antivirus software, access controls, and physical access controls are all fundamental steps for good data hygiene. It also reminds merchants that the merchant should never collect and store the cardholder data. Merchants are no longer allowed to retain the payment information.

The PCI DSS also requires that the equipment used by vendors has been approved and to regularly check the equipment to assure that no one has installed malware or skimming devices to steal with credit card information.

Even with these efforts, however, the risks to credit card collection continue to grow. In early 2020, the FBI issued a warning regarding the expanded use of credit card skimmers to the online environment. Described as e-skimming or "Magecart attacks," thieves have developed techniques for installing software on the virtual shopping cart of major retailers.

The FBI identified some of the victimized websites, including Macy's, Puma, Ticketmaster-United Kingdom, and British Airways.

These companies represent just a few of the many companies where this unauthorized, criminal software is likely to be installed. As the consumers enter their credit and debit card information, the thieves collect that information to resell. Buyers then use the credit and debit cards to shop online or to print working, falsified cards.

The PCI Council stresses that the greatest risk for credit card data theft comes from the failure to adequately maintain each of the PCI DSS obligations. It notes that new vulnerabilities are always being discovered and out-of-date systems can lead to easy access by criminals. E-skimming likely exploits just this form of vulnerability. The PCI DSS provides a very reasonable solution that is based on the core fundamentals of proper data security. By keeping software and hardware up to date, by using strong pass phrases, and by monitoring a company's system carefully for intrusions, a company can greatly reduce the risk of data breaches.

E. What to Watch for—Common Vectors of Security Intrusions

The security protocols required are designed to respond to particular types of threats. The following summarizes the most common threats a company can face regarding its information and data. All businesses face both internal and external data security risks. The frequency of the risk will depend on the nature of the business.

1. *The Malicious Actors*

Data security risks generally come from a well-known group of threatening sources, the actors who hack into computer systems. In the early days of the Internet, most of these threats came from young computer enthusiasts who cracked systems just to prove they had the skills to do so. The hacker culture still exists, but it represents just a small fraction of the data breaches and malicious online conduct. Today, the risks are much more intentional.

The following provides a brief introduction to the individuals and groups creating data security threats:

- **Committed Employees**—The greatest risk most companies face is from their employees, both current and former. The best employees strive to work as efficiently as possible. Security systems often slow down operations and make it difficult to get work done. Employees write down passwords because companies implement systems that change the passwords too often or make the passwords too difficult to memorize. Employees create backdoor access so they can work at home to meet challenging deadlines. Employees move sensitive data to unsecured equipment because they prefer their home machines. Employees let colleagues log into systems without authorization because clients and customers need problems resolved in a timely manner. Each of these steps is taken by an employee trying to do the job better, faster, and more conveniently. Unfortunately, each of these steps undermines data security and reliability.
- **Disgruntled Employees**—The leaving employee is a less common but greater threat than the employee that makes innocent but harmful mistakes. Leaving employees often wish to take proprietary information, trade secrets, and business knowhow with them to their next employment. Some leaving employees believe that since they created the materials for their former employer, they are entitled to copies of their work notwithstanding the

law and the company policies. Other leaving employees want payback or revenge for perceived mistreatment and wish to harm their former employer. Former employees have been responsible for malicious software that destroys hard drives, for reformatting company servers to destroy the information held by the company, for creating vulnerabilities for third party attacks, and for the theft of company information.

- **Teen Hackers**—Every year, another group of children turns thirteen. For some teens, there is an allure to challenging security systems and thumbing their noses to the institutions of society. The goal is the ability to beat systems rather than to do damage or make money. These hackers generally do not intend significant harm, though the consequences of their data intrusions sometimes create substantial harm. A few of these hackers continue through into their twenties but most either transfer their youthful indiscretions into backgrounds in professional cybersecurity or move onto other activities.

- **Hacktivists**—The cyberspace community has always had a fondness for its counter-culture ethos, even though it has evolved to become the largest segment of the global economy. At the heart of this digital counterculture has been the notion that civil unrest is an essential component of political change. Laws of segregation could not have been struck down without courageous individuals willing to be jailed for challenging those laws. Hacktivists intentionally break laws and attack institutions to further what they believe to be important social agendas. Like civil rights protests, hacktivism ebbs and flows with the prevailing social and political environment.

- **Individual Criminals**—Willie Sutton was famously quoted for answering the question why he robbed banks with the answer "because that's where the money is." Sutton denied the accuracy of the quote, but he acknowledged that criminals seek the easiest money. Today, money exists in digital wallets, electronic accounts, and in the value of data. Criminals are drawn to the wealth that exists online. In addition, online criminal conduct is much safer than street crimes, drug cartels, or sophisticated commercial heists. The criminal plans are much easier to conduct, the likelihood of prosecution is much lower, and generally the criminal sentence for those convicted are much lower.
- **Criminal Syndicates**—Because online crime is much more efficient than the drug cartels and large-scale corruption of prior generations, large criminal syndicates have moved online, either as an extension of their gambling, racketeering, prostitution, drug sales, and money laundering operations or as a replacement. The online environment does not have the geographic restrictions of cities and towns, so the turf warfare that pitted one criminal syndicate against another is much less of a threat to the organized crime enterprises. Individual criminals may find themselves the targets of larger organizations, but there have not been any reports of gang battles starting from online conflicts among the syndicates.

- **State Funded Hackers**—More than any time in the modern era, war is waged between nation states and non-state actors such as terrorist organizations and state-funded militias. The same is true in cyberspace. Government-funded organizations operate to commit industrial espionage, interfere with military operations, and threaten the critical infrastructure of foreign enemies while offering their state sponsors the ability to deny direct governmental involvement. Such attacks have been responsible for attacks on dam management and powerplant software in the United States, hospitals in Ukraine, and airport operations in many countries.
- **Military and Governmental Intelligence Agencies**—The Cold War, the War of Southeast Asia, and the Mideast Conflict have moved to cyberspace. All major military powers and national intelligence agencies have a presence online. Every major conflict of the twentieth century that followed World War II continues through online surrogates. In 2013, Cambridge University Press published the "Tallinn Manual on the International Law Applicable to Cyber Warfare" (the Tallinn Manual), written through a multinational global consultative process that involved many of the NATO members and UN Security Council countries regarding armed conflict. The authors then published Tallinn 2.0 in 2017 in an effort to extend the international principles to other state acts of aggression. The U.S., Russia, and other participants, however, have been unwilling to recognize the proposed norms of Tallinn 2.0. The expanded manual would limit a nation-state's ability to operate offensively in cyberspace. The reluctance

of the UN Security Council member states to be bound by international agreements regarding their online offensive activities helps illustrate the ongoing and fluid nature of military and national security activities that continue to involve both governmental and private institutions.

2. *The Common Attacks*

There are a wide range of possible cyberattacks which occur from internal and external threats. The following provides a brief summary of the most common threats.

- **Social Engineering**—is a category of attacks in which the perpetrator pretends to be another person to gain access or influence. Social engineering occurs both in cyberspace and in the real world. For example, the theft or use of counterfeit identification is a form of social engineering. Calling a customer service line to convince the company to change access information is another form of social engineering. Social engineering would also include the pressure one employee puts on another employee to allow unauthorized access into the computer system.
  - **Phishing**—This attack is a form of social engineering conducted through email or social media. The attacker may send an email requesting that an account be updated. Instead of coming from the victim's bank, the falsified request directs the customer to a web page doctored to look like the victim's bank. When the person enters the login information, the attacker can use those captured login

credentials to open the victim's actual bank account and transfer out all the funds.

- **Vishing** is a variation of the conduct that occurs over the phone.
- **Spear phishing** reflects an attack that is highly focused and targeted. A spear phishing attack may develop over time to gain the trust of the victim, usually someone with significant authority at the target organization. Senior executives and IT personnel, with their higher level of institutional access, are typically the targets of such directed attacks.

- **Credential Harvesting**—Cyberattacks do not occur in isolation. Modern attacks build on the information collected in prior attacks. Billions of individuals have been the victims of credential theft worldwide. As a result, most people have had their username and password stolen. If a user continues to use a username and password combination that has been stolen and sold on the attacked site or other sites, then an attacker can use that published access to gain control of the victim's account. This is why it is so important that users do not reuse username and password combinations from one location to the next.
  - **Brute Force Attack**—A variation of credential harvesting is to run software that tries to open the victim's account by running a list of common passwords. The FBI refers to this technique as a "password spraying attack." If a victim uses 123456789, 2001, or "password" as the password, the account will open quickly.

Common pet names and other popular terms fill the database for brute force attacks. The phrase should be long, use more than all lower-case letters, not be too obvious, and be reasonably easy for the user to remember. While "tosleepperchancetodream" is much better than "password," it is sufficiently popular to make it into brute force attack databases. Replacing each 'e' with a '3' will make it less likely to be guessed.

- **Computer Viruses**—are forms of malicious software that can be introduced into the victim's computer system. A computer network without firewalls and password protections, for example, can be recoded by anyone. Systems without these fundamental protections are highly susceptible to computer viruses. If there are firewalls and password protections on the ability to update the software, then the computer virus must also be able to overcome these protections. Computer viruses are often self-executing, meaning that when the conditions occur for them to infect the software, they will begin to run.
  - **Malware**—describes the broad category of computer viruses.
  - **Ransomware**—is a form of computer virus designed to reside in the system until triggered. The malware encrypts all the data stored on the system and sometimes on the backups and synced copies of the network. This process will usually occur late at night so it cannot be stopped by shutting off the system. The

malware will then send a ransom note to the user demanding a payment in hard-to-trace cryptocurrency to be exchanged for the encryption key. Some ransomware attackers honor their promise to restore the data; others do not. Another variation of the ransomware is that the threat is to publish the data rather than to destroy it.

- **Spyware or Trojan Horse Attacks**—another form of malware, this is software introduced into a victim's computer system that monitors the activities on the system and shares the information with the attacker. Spyware can include keyboard loggers so that passwords can be harvested and financial account information collected. Spyware is often integrated into freeware products and free apps so that victims intentionally download and install the software.

- **Attacks on Outdated Systems**—Hackers and security analysts are constantly trying to find vulnerabilities in computer networks and the software and apps that run on those systems. The security analysts generally try to identify and patch those vulnerabilities before the public is aware of the problem so that attackers cannot exploit the vulnerability. Once a vulnerability becomes public, however, it is a race between the security services and the attackers to protect or exploit the vulnerability. Companies that do not use security services, such as firewalls and antivirus software services, will become victims of various forms of attacks.

- **Drive-by-Downloads**—If a system has a known vulnerability due to lack of updated security, then any attacker can update and rewrite that system to take control of the operations.

- **Zero-Day Exploits**—The term refers to the amount of time a company has to patch its software before the vulnerability becomes public. It is not a technical term nor a particular piece of software. Instead, the term refers to any vulnerability that is about to go public. These are particularly problematic if a software user discovers a vulnerability and discloses it as a warning to the public rather than privately to the company. When this happens, the company and the antivirus companies do not have any lead time to create solutions to fix the vulnerability.

- **SQL Injection Attack**—SQL is a Microsoft programming language specially created to handle large amounts of data in a relational database management system. The Structured Query Language injection attack takes advantage of a vulnerability in the SQL server to expose the data in the database, particularly if the software allows queries from sources that are not validated or do not limit the nature of the queries permitted. It can also allow the attacker to modify or destroy the data and to run administrative commands to do additional harm.

- **Distributed Denial of Service (DDoS) Attack**—This attack is designed to interrupt a website or network from operating. In a DDoS attack, the targeted site is bombarded with requests and inputs that overwhelm its ability to respond in time. By flooding the victim's system with requests and activity, it either crashes the system or makes it inaccessible to the legitimate users of the system. The DDoS attack does not generally result in data theft, but the denial of service can be a significant business disruption. As networks become larger, DDoS attacks take substantial computing power. Attackers sometimes hack the public's computers and poorly secured IoT devices (smart plugs, doorbells, printers, and toasters, etc.) to greatly magnify the scale and disguise the source of the attack.

- **Man in the Middle (MITM) Attack**—An attacker takes over a communications node such as a WiFi device or cell tower to become the intermediary in information and communications traffic. Neither party in the interactions is aware that an attacker is listening into the communications or that the attacker could be altering the information flowing from one party to the other. For example, a Man in the Middle attack could be used to change the banking routing and account information flowing in and out of a financial institution to steal all the money being wired for the duration of the attack. The attack can also operate surreptitiously, with the parties never being aware of the eavesdropping.

Cyberattacks often involve a combination of the strategies listed above. Phishing to gain a person's access privileges is often essential to deliver the malware needed to infiltrate a system. Cyber attackers are often quite sophisticated, and they build their efforts to attack an organization with patience and through a wide range of tools and techniques.

3. The Goals of Malicious Behavior

The purposes of online malicious behavior are generally consistent with the nature of the actor creating the online attack, though the goals are often entwined. Criminals and criminal syndicates, for example, are focused on earning money from their cyberattacks. They can make money by gaining access to financial accounts and transferring the funds from those accounts into their own accounts through untraceable transactions. Criminals can use ransomware to extort payment from victims in exchange for unencrypting their files. They can also collect personal information to use in blackmailing the victims of cyberthefts.

A description of famous attacks helps illustrate the range of cyberattacks and their aftermath. The Sony attack was described in Chapter 1. The Stuxnet virus attack against Iran demonstrates the power of cyberwarfare, particularly during the inexorable lead-up to armed conflict. The Yahoo and Target attacks illustrates the industrial consequences of a successful attack while the Ashley Madison attack shows how an attack can transform from one purpose to another.

Stuxnet.

The Stuxnet virus is often described as the world's first cyberweapon. The malware was commissioned by the governments of five Western nations, the United States, Israel, the Netherlands, Germany, and a fifth country generally reported to be either the United Kingdom or France. Iran remains at war with Israel dating back to Israel's founding and is subject to sanctions from the United States dating back to the hostage taking of U.S. embassy employees in 1979. The target for the Stuxnet virus was the uranium enrichment centrifuges built based on designs stolen from the Netherlands. The Western governments asserted that Iran was using the equipment to create weapon's grade uranium to let the country become a militarized nuclear power, although Iran claims it was only seeking to enhance its domestic nuclear energy program.

The virus was inserted through a USB by a Dutch agent into the software at Natanz, one of the companies developing and servicing the centrifuges. None of the Iranian equipment was ever connected to the Internet or exposed to a network attack. Through the introduction in a single USB, the software spread to other machines at the vendor's company and to other Iranian vendors servicing the centrifuges. To antivirus software, the Stuxnet software looked like part of the Microsoft operating system. It replicated itself only in machines that had specific software essential for the centrifuge management. When operating, it both altered the operations of the centrifuges and it created false reports to show the operators that the equipment was operating correctly. As a result of the Stuxnet software, Iran's centrifuges operated at dangerously high speeds and essentially tore themselves apart, ending Iran's effort to create weapons-grade uranium. The disclosures of the strategies used to create, introduce, and execute the cyberattack on Iran have become increasingly detailed in the past three years.

While it was likely not the first government-backed piece of malware used to physically destroy an enemy nation's infrastructure, it is the first to be acknowledged and hailed as a success. The Iranian enrichment program was stopped without the use of a bombing raid, and it led directly to the short-lived Iranian nuclear accord of 2017. It demonstrated how malware could be introduced to a computer system protected by the greatest possible security measures, how to use software to get a widespread network to target very specific devices, and how to hide the operations of the attack until it was far too late to stop its effect. Although the Stuxnet virus attack was an unqualified success from a military standpoint, it also introduced the world to a new level of cyberwarfare and aggression.

Yahoo and Target.

In 2013, both Target and Yahoo were the victims of widescale cyber-attacks. Yahoo's systems were breached by a Russian organization led by two men who served in Russia's Federal Security Service (FSB), the Russian military agency responsible for helping foreign intelligence agencies track cybercriminals. Verizon was acquiring Yahoo at the time of the sale for $4.8 billion and downplayed the scope of the data expropriation. It was not until 2017 that Yahoo admitted that all three billion users had their information stolen, making it the largest data breach in history. Verizon renegotiated its merger price, reducing the acquisition by $400 million. Analysts were never sure whether the attack was authorized by Russia or carried out illegally by the agents who were later indicted for their own illegal purposes. The names, email addresses, passwords, security words and other information all appeared for sale in the years following the attack.

Target was also compromised the same year. A company providing heating and air conditioning services to the Target stores was hacked and the attackers used this point of entry to infect the point-of-sale credit card machines at Target. Over 110 million credit card users shopping at Target had their information stolen. The attack resulted in more than a $160 million loss for Target during the 2013 holiday shopping season and a drop in its share price of more than ten percent. Because the attack was focused on credit cards, it was particularly disruptive for Target's shoppers. From a technological standpoint, the attack highlighted the threat posed by authorized vendors creating risks and insecurities to corporate systems as well as the ability of malware to spread from one system to an unrelated system. The point of sale machines were operated in a manner wholly separate from the heating and air conditioning systems, but the common access by members of Target's personnel and the shared infrastructure was enough to create an opportunity for the malware to spread and do its work.

Ashley Madison.

The 2015 attack on Ashley Madison remains one of the most controversial hacks in the Internet age. Ashley Madison was operated as a dating site targeting men seeking affairs. It used the tag line "Life is short. Have an affair." The company was considered a moral affront to many, including many feminist groups. It was also regularly accused of fraud. There were claims that as many as ninety percent of the female accounts on the sites were actually software bots designed to keep men online and paying fees. It did not verify the user emails and addresses, so public figures were often added to the company membership without the knowledge or participation of these spoofing victims.

When Ashley Madison's system was breached in 2015, the attackers announced that they would be disclosing the names and emails of thirty million users. Ultimately the entire database of Ashley Madison subscribers became public and hundreds of credit card accounts were also released.

Immediately on the heels of the Ashley Madison data breach, another group of criminals jumped on the opportunity. They began to spam people across North America, threatening to reveal their participation on the Ashley Madison platform to the people in the victim's contact book if blackmail was not paid. In most cases, the spammers did not have any additional information and they had not breached the contact information of the target. Millions of threatening emails were sent and the fractional percentage of victims who responded still paid enough to reward the attackers handsomely.

A second fraud emerged. Attackers spammed men and women promising to remove their names from the publicly released Ashley Madison data dump. Again, these promises were fraudulent. The spammers took the money of those fearful of exposure, victimizing them a second time.

Even more seriously, at least three suicides were tied to the release of the spousal cheating information, including two in Toronto and one by a pastor in New Orleans. The database release was reported to be a useful source of information in many divorce proceedings as well. Despite the social damage caused by the breach and the financial settlement for $11 million, the company continued to operate despite the attack.

These four attacks reflect the financial, political, social, and military justifications for cyberattacks. Most, of course, are motivated by greed. But many others are driven by personal motives and efforts to send a political message or forward an agenda for a political purpose. Moreover, the costs of cyberattacks go well beyond the costs of fixing the computer vulnerabilities. The costs include the loss of customers, litigation over the harm done to clients, and damage done to public trust, and the distractions to respond to the crisis caused by the data breach. These costs quickly magnify, making data breaches an area of great concern for most businesses.

Key Takeaways from This Chapter:

Companies required to provide patient, customer, or client privacy must also protect the collected data from theft, destruction, or corruption. To maintain a valid data system, the data must be collected in a manner that assures it is accurate, reliable, and secure. Once collected the systems employed by a company must maintain the accuracy, reliability, and security of the information collected.

To keep data secure, every company collecting and processing data must institute a series of physical, technical, and administrative steps to assure that the information is protected. These may be very simple steps of keeping doors locked, using firewalls, updating passwords, maintaining antivirus software, and training staff on the steps needed to keep the data protected. For larger enterprises, the steps may involve much more complex network system management, usage logs, VPNs and other advanced tools, but the categories and strategies remain the same. Merchants accepting credit cards have additional duties and commitments to the card-issuing banks.

Risks of data vulnerabilities come from both inside a business and from the outside. Well-meaning employees may accidentally or intentionally circumvent data security efforts as part of their work to get their jobs completed. Disgruntled employees and leaving employees are sometimes motivated to take the confidential information of their former employer or to do damage to an employer they believe was responsible for their mistreatment. Hackers, activists, criminals, syndicates, and governments all have interests that may result in efforts at data breach information theft. All these threats must be taken seriously by companies, since every company has a duty to maintain its data in a secure and reliable manner.

Things to Know:

Data must be managed to be accurate, reliable, verifiable, and secure beginning with the collection of the information and at every stage in its processing and use. If the information becomes inaccurate at any stage in the process, it undermines the value and reliability of the data.

Threats to data come from both inside and outside an organization. Companies must assure that their systems take both categories of threats seriously. Threats also come from natural disasters and catastrophic events that can compromise the systems used for collecting data.

The physical, technical, and administrative steps needed to keep data secure can be scaled to the size of the company. But all three aspects of data security must be part of every plan to keep information secure. Every aspect of the data security program must be updated regularly, including the updates to antivirus software and the need to keep operating programs up to date.

Things to Think About:

Companies that do not have effective data security can never meet their obligations for data privacy, since unauthorized access can open the information to criminals or to the general public. Security comes before privacy.

Data breaches are often caused by the failure of companies to follow their own rules. How does a company enforce its policies so that the protections are not ignored by senior leadership, vendors, or hourly employees?

Is there a better system of data security than the one currently being used? What approaches would make data security simpler, cheaper and more efficient for most companies?

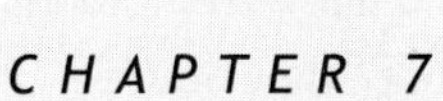

Data Breach Notification Laws

A. Introduction

Despite the many steps described in the prior chapter designed to protect private data from theft and disclosure, data breaches are common occurrences. The 2013 Yahoo data breach resulted in three billion users having their online information stolen and eventually sold. In 2019, despite the tremendous emphasis on data security, First American Financial Corp. implemented a weak data protection system that exposed 885 million accounts to hackers. Marriott International had multiple incidents in 2018 through 2020 because a subsidiary did not maintain adequate security.

Given the number of accounts exposed in some of the largest data breaches, it is likely that all people who maintain online accounts have had their accounts exposed at some time or another. It is also likely that there are many more thefts and intrusions than the ones that are reported each year.

California was the first state to require that data breaches suffered by companies be disclosed publicly with a law that went into effect in 2003. Today, there are laws in all 50 states as well as the District of Columbia, Puerto Rico, Guam, and the U.S. Virgin Islands that require notification to that jurisdiction's residents of a data breach. Alabama was last, enacting its law in 2018. There are also additional federal regulations that cover some enterprises, and the provisions of the GDPR apply to those companies subject to the EU's international jurisdiction. These laws are similar to each other, but they differ on certain requirements, making the actual compliance with the obligations to disclose a data breach very costly and time consuming. This summary does not attempt to list the rules of the 54 jurisdictions. Instead it highlights the common elements in all the data breach notification rules and illustrates the range of policies adopted on some of these key features.

While some state laws focus on regulations for for-profit companies or more generally for any holder of public information, other states focus on the obligations of governmental agencies to report on any data breaches. These may include school systems, departments of motor vehicles, or tax and revenue departments. Each state approaches these issues uniquely, so there is no universal approach to the disclosure laws.

Increasingly, states want data breaches publicly disclosed. As noted below, states have increased the types of personal information that triggers a data notification obligation, reduced the minimum number of residents affected to trigger a notification requirement, and eliminated the requirement that the breach cause substantial harm.

A data breach triggering the notification will typically be defined as an "unauthorized acquisition of computerized data that compromises the security, confidentiality, or integrity of personal information" stored by the company. Theft of the data or proof of data tampering is not necessary to establish a data breach. Once a company learns that a third party had the ability to access its customer or client data, it has an obligation to notify those customers or clients under the statute.

Statutes generally exclude the unauthorized access by employees from the definition of a data breach unless the unauthorized access by employees results in an additional disclosure to third parties. This distinction is a practical one. There are often situations where employees sometimes gain inadvertent access to customer information that they do not generally need. This can occur during IT maintenance, staff training exercises, job realignments, personnel investigations, and many other times. There is very little likelihood of harm to the customer or any evidence the unauthorized disclosure occurs. The employee who gains the additional access to the information still has a duty not to disclose that information. So, the likelihood of real harm is very low. States do not want to confuse these situations with real theft of data, so they exclude these internal incidents from the definition of a data breach for purposes of the notification laws.

The purpose, presumably, of increased data breach notification obligations is to encourage greater data security systems and use the costs and public pressure of the breach notification as motivation to get companies to install better data protection systems and take more aggressive steps to train their employees. Data security is costly. But if the cost of a data breach remediation is even more expensive, the thinking goes, then companies will be willing to pay the costs to avoid the breach rather than taking chances with their customer information.

Slightly more than one third of the jurisdictions also provide a private cause of action under the data breach notification statute. This means that a person harmed as a result of the data breach may bring a lawsuit. Most of these, however, require that the person bringing the lawsuit to have suffered actual financial damage as a result of the data breach. Although there are a great many data breach violations, only a small percentage of these result in direct financial harm to the consumers. Where these harms occur, however, the law will generally hold the companies that stored the data responsible for the losses that do occur. Since the companies are aware of this obligation, they generally respond quickly to minimize the financial damage and avoid expensive litigation.

B. Structure of a State Data Breach Disclosure Law

Each of the data breach disclosure laws provides that if the personal information of a specified number of customers, clients, or patients is accessed without authorization or is disclosed to third parties, then the enterprise must provide notice of the data breach. In some instances, the notification must go to the state's attorney general. In most instances, the notification must be made using specific language provided by the state law to the victims of the data breach.

Each law will also provide for the time guidelines for the breach. The typical requirement in the United States is within 30 days of learning about the breach, though this varies considerably from state to state. The shortest time period for required reporting has dropped to three days, which is also the time period allowed under the GDPR. The timelines for public notification may be delayed if the victim of the breach is working with state or federal law enforcement and the enforcement agency requires confidentiality to pursue its investigation.

The law will also establish the penalties that may result for failing to comply with the data breach notification requirements and the rights of the state's citizens regarding the breach. Each of these standard elements may vary considerably from jurisdiction to jurisdiction.

1. Personal Information

The definition for personal information has expanded considerably since data breach notification laws first went into effect in 2003. They have expanded well beyond the name of the person, the account number, and the password. Jurisdictions are regularly updating their laws to expand the list of potential identifiers used by companies to target individuals.

The California law, for example, has been expanded to include the following items as relevant to trigger the obligation to notify the attorney general and the victims. This definition is narrower than the general CCPA definition of personal information, but it is still a very inclusive list:

1. A username or email address, in combination with a password or security question and answer that would permit access to an online account.

2. The user's first name, or initial and last name, along with a second element:

- Social Security number.
- Driver's license number, California identification card number, tax identification number, passport number, military identification number, or other unique identification number issued on a government document commonly used to verify the identity of a specific individual.
- Account number or credit or debit card number, in combination with any required security code, access code, or password that would permit access to an individual's financial account.
- Medical information. "Medical information" means any information regarding an individual's medical

history, mental or physical condition, or medical treatment or diagnosis by a health care professional.

- Health insurance information. "Health insurance information" means an individual's health insurance policy number or subscriber identification number, any unique identifier used by a health insurer to identify the individual, or any information in an individual's application and claims history, including any appeals records.
- Unique biometric data generated from measurements or technical analysis of human body characteristics, such as a fingerprint, retina, or iris image, used to authenticate a specific individual. Unique biometric data does not include a physical or digital photograph, unless used or stored for facial recognition purposes.
- Information or data collected through the use or operation of an automated license plate recognition system. . .

The California statute excludes personal information that is public, but only if it is "lawfully made available to the general public from federal, state, or local government records." Other states treat public information as an exclusion from the obligations to report a data theft and some jurisdictions include all public information rather than just public information published by the government itself.

Like California, many states have increasingly added biometric information to their notification laws, though this change has not been adopted universally. Arkansas, for example added a requirement to report the theft of biometric data, defined broadly as:

data generated by automatic measurements of an individual's biological characteristics, including without limitation: (a) Fingerprints; (b) Faceprint; (c) A retinal or iris scan; (d) Hand geometry; (e) Voiceprint analysis; (f) Deoxyribonucleic acid (DNA); or (g) Any other unique biological characteristics of an individual if the characteristics are used by the owner or licensee to uniquely authenticate the individual's identity when the individual accesses a system or account.

Generally speaking, the personal information does not include the unique IP address of the computer or the digital profile of a device. Advertisers and data aggregators can profile and identify a computer or mobile device from a combination of the device's IP address or configuration of installed hardware and software without ever identifying the person who owns the device. For many advertising purposes, that form of near-anonymous data tracking can prove useful. The unidentified owner of a particular cell phone can be tracked web browsing and shopping at certain locations, making the behavioral data sufficiently accurate to track the device without ever knowing the name, gender, race, or economic status of the consumer. In many jurisdictions, the lack of the name or username and other personal traits would be sufficient to exclude any obligation to disclose a data breach.

2. *Materiality, Encryption and Other Safe Harbors*

In the early years of data breaches, the obligations to inform the public and the state were typically triggered if the result of the breach could cause material harm for those consumers. Unless a breach involved credit card information or information that could be used to access bank accounts or otherwise commit fraud or identity theft, regulators had a difficult time demonstrating that material harm was likely in most data breaches. Unlike the situation of Ashley Madison, merely being publicly known to be a customer was usually unlikely to trigger the material harm requirement. In at least ten jurisdictions, however, the requirement for materiality was not made a component of the law or it has been eliminated from the law by amendment.

Arizona provides an example of a state taking a middle approach. The lack of material harm will eliminate the need to send out consumer notices, but the determination of the harm must be made by a third party rather than by the company. To rely on this exemption, the company must permit either the law enforcement agency or a forensic auditor to conduct an investigation. If the investigation establishes that the breach is not likely to result in economic loss to the victims, then no breach notification is required. In some jurisdictions, the state allows the company to make this determination, while other states do not limit breach notification to those situations where there is a risk of harm.

In contrast to Arizona, Alaska provides that a company can undertake its own investigation. But if a company determines that a breach *does not* create a reasonable likelihood of harm to the consumers, it must document this determination and provide notice of the determination to the Attorney General. In this way, Alaska is putting the obligation on the company to prove the lack of harm.

In most states, there is a safe harbor if the data stolen were protected by encryption. If the information was stolen in an encrypted form, then the data breach notification obligations are not triggered. Of course, if the encryption keys were also stolen then this safe harbor is not available. Nonetheless, this is an important exception to the data breach notification obligations and an important additional motivation for companies to institute encryption systems.

Other states extend this safe harbor to information that is redacted in a manner that the information cannot be re-identified to particular individuals or rendered unreadable in some other manner. Encryption, redaction, and alteration all serve to make the information unusable to data thieves, so if the efforts are effective, the data loss will not have negative consequences for those who have had their information stolen.

In a typical situation, a corporate laptop might be stolen from an employee or vendor. The thief stealing the laptop has no particular interest in the laptop's data. Instead, the thief plans to wipe the laptop and sell it as a piece of used equipment on eBay or Craigslist. If the laptop contains an unencrypted copy of a customer database, that theft will trigger the data breach notification obligations whether or not the thief was intending to take advantage of the information.

If, instead, the laptop has password protection and encryption, then the thief is unlikely to be able to access the information. The encryption greatly reduces the risk the information on the device will be copied and sold online. An untold number of data breaches are caused by lost or stolen equipment. The thieves and finders of the equipment are not mining the data inside these devices. Nonetheless, without encryption, the companies must treat these events as security breaches triggering notification requirements. While it is best not to store customer databases on portable equipment, it is also essential to encrypt those databases wherever they are located.

Ohio has enacted a safe harbor into its law to promote good data security practices. Among the ways to be protected by the Ohio safe harbor, a company must "create, maintain, and comply with a written cybersecurity program that contains administrative, technical, and physical safeguards for the protection of personal information and that reasonably conforms to an industry recognized cybersecurity framework. . . ." The statute also provides details on what such a cybersecurity program would look like.

Other states exclude data protected by federal law under HIPAA or GLBA. In these situations, the company suffering the data breach must inform federal officials but then they are not obligated to follow the regulations of the states where the patients or customers reside as an additional obligation. As noted in Chapter 8, the department of Health and Human Services (HHS) has a much stronger set of regulations, including substantial fines for data breaches. Allowing HHS to be the agency responsible for health data breaches still assures that the data breach will be addressed without using up state resources.

3. Engagement with Data Breach Victims

Data breach notification laws require that every person who has been victim of a data breach be informed about the breach. The numerical threshold is used to trigger the reporting to the state attorney general's office, office of consumer protection, or another designated agency. In providing information to the victims of the data breach, the company should be considering the potential damage that can be caused because of the sensitivity of the information and the likelihood of the information's misuse.

The company should also consider the nature of the attack and the ability to misuse the public information. The disclosure of a dataset of IP addresses likely has little risk of real harm to the public. In contrast, a sophisticated and targeted attack to collect the Social Security numbers and home addresses of a patient list is likely to be used for sophisticated identify theft. The more targeted the attack, the more proactive the company must be in informing its customers.

In addition, some states require that companies inform the credit reporting agencies (such as Equifax, Experian and TransUnion) if more than the threshold of customers are impacted. Most states set the threshold at 1,000, though Texas has established this requirement only for breaches that exceed 10,000 residents. In practice, companies should provide this notice when sensitive information like Social Security numbers, driver's license numbers, or credit card numbers are stolen, without regard to the size of the data breach. The FTC advises that it is the nature of the harm as much as the size of the breach that matters.

Most companies today provide the victims of data breach a year of free credit monitoring. This may be required by some states, particularly for larger breaches. In California, for example, credit monitoring is required if the company was the cause of the data breach but not if the data breach was caused by a third party. In addition, offering credit monitoring also helps reduce the risk of true economic harm that could arise from the breach and may serve to reduce the liability for the company that suffered the data breach.

Most state laws specify the information that must be provided to the victim of a data breach. The California law provides a useful example. It includes both mandatory disclosures and voluntary disclosures:

- The name and contact information of the reporting person or business.
- A list of the types of personal information that were or are reasonably believed to have been the subject of a breach.
- The date of the notice.
- The date of the breach or an estimated date or date range.
- Whether notification was delayed as a result of a law enforcement investigation, if that information is possible to determine at the time the notice is provided.

- A general description of the breach incident, if that information is possible to determine at the time the notice is provided.
- The toll-free telephone numbers and addresses of the major credit reporting agencies if the breach exposed a Social Security number or a driver's license or California identification card number.
- If the person or business providing the notification was the source of the breach, an offer to provide appropriate identity theft prevention and mitigation services, if any, shall be provided at no cost to the affected person for not less than 12 months along with all information necessary to take advantage of the offer to any person whose information was or may have been breached if the breach exposed or may have exposed personal information defined in subparagraphs (A) and (B) of paragraph (1) of subdivision (h).

At the discretion of the person or business, the security breach notification may also include any of the following:

- Information about what the person or business has done to protect individuals whose information has been breached.
- Advice on steps that people whose information has been breached may take to protect themselves.
- In breaches involving biometric data, instructions on how to notify other entities that used the same type of biometric data as an authenticator to no longer rely on data for authentication purposes.

4. Notification of Government Officials

The obligation to notify victims of a data breach and to notify the appropriate state agency varies significantly from as little as three days to as long as 45 days following the date that the organization learns of the data breach. Idaho does not enforce any time limit. Companies suffering significant data intrusions should always involve law enforcement in the situation. In many cases, the law enforcement agencies will begin an investigation that can trigger the need for confidentiality while the investigation attempts to track the data theft. This is particularly important for thefts committed by online organizations and for thefts committed by employees and insiders.

Notification obligations will be tolled during the criminal investigations. This time can be very useful for companies to get ahead of their reporting and remediation obligations.

Data breach notification laws were initially targeted at serious breaches, so the laws required a substantial number of records being compromised before the notification obligations were triggered. States often set this number at 1000. As more states enacted laws and the laws became more demanding, the record minimum dropped to 500 in some states and 250 in others.

Most states have requirements that describe what must be provided to the state attorney general or state regulator. For example, most states will require that a sample of the notice being provided to victims of the data breach is provided to the attorney general as well. The attorney general's office may request additional information regarding the nature of the company's security efforts and the efforts the company is undertaking to respond to the data breach.

Nebraska's online notification form for the attorney general has a checkbox system that allows the company to identify the form of the breach by selecting among a group of categories:

- Theft of computer, device, or media
- Insider wrongdoing
- Phishing
- Inadvertent disclosure
- Loss of computer, device, or media
- External systems breach (i.e. hacking)
- Other (specify)

The form also requires the company identify the manner in which it provided its customer notice of the data breach notification (written, electronic/email, telephone, or substitute), to describe the circumstances surrounding the breach, to list the types of personal information acquired, and to upload a copy of the notice being sent to affected customers. In many ways, the form both simplifies and focuses the information being sent to the attorney general.

The primary role for the attorney general is to be sure that the notification meets the obligations under the jurisdiction's statutes. Every state also has its own version of the Unfair and Deceptive Trade Practices Act, the state version of the FTC Act, however, so the information in the disclosure can trigger additional responses from the attorneys general who receive the notification. If an attorney general believes that the failure to protect the customer information was the result of unfair or deceptive trade practices stemming from bad data security practices or repeated failures by a company to secure its data, then the attorney general can take additional steps to require remediation or to fine the company.

Typically, the attorney general's office will start with a demand for additional information. If incidents continue, however, the attorney general's office can establish either informal obligations or a formal consent agreement with the company. In extreme situations, the attorney general can file a lawsuit and seek substantial penalties. This will typically happen only if there are repeated instances of data security mismanagement.

5. *Notification of Public and Other Third Parties*

Although there is no affirmative duty to notify the press and public, many companies end up sharing their data breach information publicly. For publicly traded companies, there may be a duty to disclose the data breach as part of the company's SEC securities filings. The disclosures to the customers and clients are not confidential, so the receipt of a data breach notification can easily trigger an investigation by journalists. In larger data breaches, it is statistically likely that the customers affected will include members of the press or public officials.

In addition to the information being shared with the news media as part of the reporting process, companies may actually choose to use the media as part of their notification strategy. For large breaches, companies struggle to reach all of their customers. Having to send the data notification through first class mail becomes very expensive. The information collected by companies may not include mailing addresses. And the accuracy of customer mailing addresses declines over time as customers move, marry, and die.

Statutes in states such as California and Massachusetts provide for a substitute notification in three situations. The substitute notification can be used when the company does not have the contact information to inform the residents of the data breach. The substitute notification can sometimes be used if the company can establish that the cost of informing the residents exceeds a financial threshold of $250,000. And the substitute notification can be used if the data breach impacts more than 500,000 residents. Each state looks at these thresholds for its own residents, not the size of the total breach.

Where substitute notice is appropriate, the company must place information about the data breach on the home page of the company website and the company must alert major statewide media. This is typically done in the form of a national press release that covers the same types of information that would otherwise have been put into the individual notification letter.

The real benefit to national breach disclosure through the media is the cost mitigation it allows. The additional scrutiny that press media brings to a data breach increases the likelihood of a lawsuit arising from the breach, of additional third-party data attacks from hackers, and negative stories harming the share price of a company's stock if it is publicly traded. In the example of the Target breach, the news coverage fueled a decline in shopping and a considerable loss of sales revenue.

Negative press is generally harmful. Nonetheless, public disclosure is a core element of data breach notification. Failing to be forthright regarding a data breach will likely cause even more negative consequences in the long run.

There also may be an obligation to notify third parties. The FTC notes that a company may have access information to an account but not the information in the account. Merchants, for example, generally should not retain customer's credit card information on file. But the merchant may have access information in its data. In such a case, the merchant should inform each of the financial institutions to which it has access. Similarly, if Social Security numbers have been stolen, the company should report this to each of the three major credit bureaus.

C. New York Shield Act and WISP Requirements

New York's "Stop Hacks and Improve Electronic Data Security Act" (SHIELD Act) provides a useful model for state data privacy regulation. New York is one of a handful of states including Massachusetts, California and Rhode Island that requires a "written information security program" (WISP). The law is very broad in scope, applying to all persons that collect private information on New York residents.

Since the law focuses on the obligation to provide reasonable security pursuant to a written security policy, it is a general law rather than being focused on any particular industry sector. Each of these laws applies to its own residents, but the SHIELD Act, for example, does so in a manner that makes companies doing business in New York adhere to its standards for all consumers.

Although WISP laws could be categorized as a data breach notification law because it includes those provisions, it stands out as an example of a state data security law because it creates an obligation to provide reasonable administrative, physical, and technical measures to protect the information collected by the entity.

The SHIELD Act uses both personal information and private information as two separate categories of protected data. Personal information is "any information concerning a natural person which, because of name, number, personal mark, or other identifier, can be used to identify such natural person." Private information, in contrast, is the personal information plus identification numbers such as state IDs, Social Security numbers, credit and debit account numbers (even without the PINs or access codes to those accounts), or other account numbers. Private information also includes a broad biometric category, not limited to fingerprint, voice print, retina, facial, and other unique physical representation or digital representation of biometric data. Finally, the private information category also includes "a user name or e-mail address in combination with a password or security question and answer that would permit access to an online account."

The SHIELD Act is both a data safeguards law like that of HIPAA regulations and a data breach notification law. The Safeguards provisions require reasonable physical, administrative, and technical safeguards of data regarding New York residents provided in a written plan that is audited and assessed on a regular basis. The SHIELD Act treats companies compliant with similar regimes as compliant with the law, so companies regulated under HIPAA or GLBA do not need to provide a second data security regime. There is some limited flexibility for small businesses, defined as those that have fewer than 50 employees; less than $3 million in gross annual revenue; or less than $5 million in year-end total assets.

The HIPAA discussion in Chapter 9 provides a more detailed description of the physical, administrative, and technical safeguards. The SHIELD Act and similar WISP laws follow the general model of the HIPAA Security Rule with less detailed versions of those obligations.

Physical Safeguards.

Companies must plan their operations to assure that the physical storage of personal and private information is secure from theft, misuse, loss, and manipulation. These obligations include

- The physical facilities in which the data are stored.
- The manner of securing the data.
- The ability to limit who within the organization has access to the data.
- The process of destroying and disposing of data that should no longer be retained.

- A system for auditing or assuring that these physical systems have not been breached.

Administrative Safeguards.

The administrative safeguards are the most critical and most overlooked aspect of information security. The WISP laws, like the HIPAA Security Rule, typically start by requiring that a senior level security officer be identified as the person responsible for implementation of all data security efforts. If the company is small, the identified security officer can also fulfill other roles at the company, but every company must have a designated individual.

The person designated as the lead for data security will generally be one member of a team of employees focused on data security. Because the SHIELD Act and other WISP laws now focus on access to information in addition to theft or destruction of information, training of employees becomes increasingly important. Unauthorized access of information can be the basis for a security incident, and this will often occur by an existing employee with access to the system. A reasonable data security program will address both internal and external risks.

Training, auditing, updating, and recognizing the types of issues that the company can face are all part of the administrative safeguard obligations. Reasonable administrative safeguards also include an assessment of the manner used to select service providers that may be storing data, providing software, or otherwise accessing computer networks of the business.

Technical Safeguards.

The technical safeguards are the computer systems, data minimization steps, audit controls, segregation of networks, firewalls, antivirus protection, installation of software patches, and similar steps that a company must take to stay abreast of its data security obligations. The technical safeguards must focus on data at each of the storage, transmission, and processing steps. Encryption is essential in every stage where it is a feasible alternative.

Technical and physical safeguards together provide some strategies for data stored on mobile devices that are at greater risk of loss or theft. Encryption is a first step. In addition, companies should have systems to track the devices, to remotely remove the data, and to audit the disclosure of that data during the process.

The Safeguards obligations under the SHIELD Act are comparable to those of HIPAA or GLBA, but scaled appropriately to the nature of the data and the size of the organization. The data breach notification obligations under the SHIELD Act are typical of the examples provided earlier in the chapter.

The SHIELD Act has some interesting new features. For example, the law makes clear that email notification of a data breach cannot be used if it is a breach related to an email account. New York does not want the breach notification to go to the compromised account. The law also requires a company which is a covered entity under HIPAA to notify the New York Attorney General within five business days of notifying HHS of any security incident. While the SHIELD Act exempts covered entities under HIPAA from following the New York safeguard's rule, the state still wants to be involved in notices and potentially in the civil penalty process.

In addition, the New York Attorney General has enforcement rights but much more modest fines than under HIPAA. Civil penalties can be as high as $5,000 for each violation with a cap of $250,000. There is no private right of action under the law, but the failure to meet reasonable security standards may trigger a common law negligence action.

D. Response Procedures for a Data Breach Incident

A data breach should be avoided, if at all possible. Companies should take preventative measures seriously and invest accordingly to avoid the costs and disruption of a serious data breach. Most of the steps necessary to recover from a data breach should have been taken before there was an incident. The FTC provides this advice: "The only thing worse than a data breach is multiple data breaches. Take steps so it doesn't happen again." If a company wants to stay in operations following a data breach, it must take its obligations to respond to the breach very seriously.

Very soon after a data breach has been discovered, the company will need to work with its management to keep senior leadership informed, forensic experts from outside the organization to assess the scope of the breach and assist with remediation, law enforcement, lawyers to assist with the notifications and communications with regulators, the company's human resources department to assist with training and to address any theft of employee information, and other departments or outside consultants.

1. *Anticipate the Potential Costs*

When a company suffers a data breach, there are a number of financial consequences to the company. Depending on the type of company and the size of the breach, some breaches may be handled without much business disruption while others have the potential to bankrupt the company and close the business. These are the primary costs associated with a breach:

- *Investigatory costs*. The victim of a data breach must identify the source of the breach and correct any security issues. Forensic experts and data breach specialists are typically hired to help assess the failures of the current security system. It is generally a good idea to utilize a company that was not part of establishing the system that was successfully breached.

- *Notification costs.* Since each of the 54 U.S. jurisdictions has its own law, and non-U.S. customers may also need to be notified, the cost to manage the complex notification obligations is very high. This is usually done through a contract with a law firm and communications firm that work together to meet the legal obligations in each jurisdiction.
- *Business disruption.* Depending on the nature of the security incident, a breach can significantly interfere with the operations of the company. A ransomware attack, for example, that destroys the customer, client, or patient data of a company can shut down the company for days, weeks or longer. There have been hospitals and other businesses that have never reopened because the loss of data made it impossible for the company to operate and the cost to recover the data was too high to be absorbed.
- *Loss of customers.* For some retailers, the impact of a significant data breach can result in customers refusing to do business with the company. Large retail enterprises are most at risk of losing market share because of a major security incident. Generally, this only lasts a few months, but the loss of revenue can be very significant.
- *Increased security.* Outside hackers and criminal organizations often test companies that have had security incidents. The news of the data breach may

become public before the company has fully implemented its corrective measures, providing a roadmap to conduct a second breach. Even if that vulnerability is corrected, the breach flags that the company has been at risk and creates an environment that encourages attacks. Companies that suffer data breaches generally have to invest to upgrade much of their security operations, not merely the one area that suffered the breach.

- *Impact on share prices*. For a publicly traded company, the negative news surrounding a major data breach can cause investors to sell the share of the stock. Investors worry about the potential flight of customers, fines, and the distraction caused by the company's leadership needing to focus on the security incidents.
- *Credit monitoring*. It has become customary for the company that suffered a data breach to provide credit monitoring for the victims of the data breach. This is a much less expensive strategy than fighting in court with the victims of the data breach over the potential damage caused by the breach.
- *Direct litigation and liability for actual harm*. A company that had a data breach resulting in actual harm through identity theft will likely be sued by the victims of the breach to recover the cost of the harm. Those lawsuits will claim negligence, breach of contract, a failure to comply with the state law, or other similar claims. If there is actual harm, the company suffering the breach will likely choose to settle the lawsuit. If the lawsuit goes to court, plaintiffs who can establish actual injury are in a

strong position to win their cases. Even if the company wins the lawsuit, there will still be considerable attorneys' fees and expert witness costs.

- *Regulatory fines.* The FTC, HHS, CFPB or other federal regulator has the power to assert fines for security breaches, and these fines are increasing substantially. In addition, many of the larger cases involved a partnership between the federal regulator and one or more state attorneys general, who also have the authority to levy fines.

- *Class action lawsuits by victims.* Many of the larger data breaches trigger class action lawsuits. A single law firm will lead a class of most victims of the data breach. Class action lawsuits are very expensive to defend. The lawyers can seek injunctions and other forms of relief that will still enable them to win the lawsuit and seek to recover the attorneys' fees.

- *Shareholder derivative lawsuits.* Companies traded on public stock exchanges are required to provide material information about the stock to their shareholders and the public, including information regarding the data privacy and data security for the company. A data breach suggests that the company was not accurate regarding its security and that means it is possible that the information it provided in the securities filings was materially misleading as well. Like class action lawsuits, these actions are very expensive to litigate and defend, even if the company ultimately wins its case.

Not every company will encounter each of these costs. Different incidents have different consequences. The loss of customer data on a laptop will trigger a different response from evidence that the corporate network has been compromised or a ransomware attack has begun. Each type of security incident needs an appropriate response. The scope of damage caused by an incident will determine whether the company can continue to operate while the investigation proceeds or whether the company will be forced to shut down temporarily while the investigation takes place.

As companies take the steps necessary to respond to a data breach, the senior management must take into account how the breach will impact the company. Investing in credit monitoring and enhanced security early may help to avoid the litigation costs and loss of customers. The goal of a security incident response is to manage each of these potential costs and mitigate the damage caused by the breach, not merely to send a simple notice to the affected customers.

2. Secure the Data and the Evidence

The discovery of many data breaches starts with a small piece of information that discloses a much larger problem. An IT staff member notices a problem with a piece of software or an unexplained log entry. From there, an investigation reveals other problems until the internal team begins to understand that there has been a sufficient problem to suggest a breach.

As soon as this process starts, it is essential to secure the evidence of the breach from tampering or removal and to secure other aspects of the system. Using the physical, technical, and administrative framework as a guide, the company must make sure its physical security is in place and updated if the situation requires it. The company may need to make an additional set of backups to retain forensic evidence and it may need to retain a set of older backups that would normally be copied over.

In some situations, the company may need to request that its employees update their passwords or temporarily reduce system access. As the outside forensics team begins to consult with the internal staff, it can help provide a roadmap to security for both the evidence needed to track down the breach and to maintain the current systems. This may require the replacement of all user credentials and the use of new equipment to avoid allowing the intruder to reestablish its presence.

3. Contact Legal Experts and Law Enforcement

The legal teams that specialize in data breach notification have developed highly specialized practices that enable them to address the many variations in the laws of the 54 jurisdictions. A company victimized by a data breach is generally better off working with a team that is experienced in data breaches than relying on its corporate counsel.

An experienced legal team will help the company identify and consult with the appropriate law enforcement agency. Depending on the nature of the incident, the lawyers may reach out to the FBI or they may consult with state law enforcement officials. Local police departments are not prepared for addressing most data breach incidents, but states and larger cities have created special units trained to work on these situations. Involving the correct law enforcement agency is essential to make progress addressing the data beach incident. In some situations, the U.S. Secret Service and the U.S. Postal Inspection Service might also be involved.

If the data involved health information, there will be additional obligations under the HIPAA Data Breach Notification Rule, which requires the company to notify the Department of Health and Human Services.

4. *Execute a Communications Plan*

In addition to the assistance of legal experts, the company may wish to retain a media and communications consultant that specializes in disaster recovery. At a minimum, the communications must include each individual who is entitled to a data breach notification and to any regulator covered by statute or regulation. This means that the company and the legal team must assess the scope of the breach to determine who has had their information disclosed or potentially disclosed for each of the 54 jurisdictions in the United States as well as international customers.

The legal team will prepare the communication for the individual customers and the regulators, but for larger breaches, the information will also become public information. The media consultants will help manage the press relations and public disclosures through the media. For publicly traded companies, there may also need to be communications to the securities regulators and to the shareholders.

For larger or more wide-ranging breaches, the communications plan must include internal communication to the company's employees. Employee information is often captured in large data breaches, so employees will want to know whether or not this occurred and what steps the employer is taking to protect the employees from financial or other harm. For companies that use large independent contractor workforces, the communications must also include these part-time and semi-autonomous employees as well.

Depending on the nature and size of the breach, the company may also need to reach out to its vendors and suppliers. This is particularly true if the breach involved a vulnerability caused by a vendor or consultant. The forensics experts may recommend temporary or permanent changes in the operations between the company and its vendors as a result of the incident. The vendors will need to be made aware of these changes as early as possible to minimize disruption of the company's operations.

In all the communications, it is important that the information be factually correct and not misleading. If the investigation has only just begun, the company should avoid making blanket promises that try to minimize the harm. The FTC also notes that a company should not "withhold key details that might help consumers protect themselves and their information." At the same time, the FTC notes that a company responding to an incident should not "publicly share information that might put consumers at further risk." In other words, the public statements should not highlight specific vectors of attack that copy-cat attackers can exploit.

Communications plans involve two-way communications. The plan should anticipate that the customers, employees, regulators, vendors, and the general public will all have questions. Companies should anticipate the questions to the extent possible and be sure to provide contact information for each of these categories of stakeholders so that there is enough information to address the situation. Early communication is also very helpful, and it is reasonable to explain that the information will be updated as more is learned.

While the communications plan should be candid, it must also be respectful of the needs of law enforcement. The communications consultants and the company should work closely with law enforcement to assure that the information provided to the public is made available on a schedule that furthers the law enforcement efforts and that does not disclose information which will harm the police investigation.

The communications plan should explain the next steps the company plans to take in order to minimize the risk of additional victimization of the consumers harmed by the data breach. For example, the company likely has no plans to call victims on the telephone. The letter to the victims and the public disclosures should explain that all communications will be done through mail so that scammers cannot use the data breach as the basis for a telephone scam. The communications should also remind the public that the company will never ask for Social Security numbers or credit card information.

The communications plan may also consider providing information to the public from the FTC and other government agencies. The FTC maintains identitytheft.gov as an excellent resource for members of the public who have been the victims of a data breach. It provides a series of steps on how to report identity theft, how to work with local police, how to remove unauthorized charges from credit cards, and even how to address debt collection issues.

5. Establish Heightened Data Security Procedures

As noted by the FTC, the worst thing a company can do regarding a security incident is let it happen again. Once a vulnerability becomes public knowledge, other attackers will attempt the same exploit. Companies that have been the subject of data theft incidents are more likely to be targeted by hackers simply because the media attention has increased the awareness by criminals. Other hackers may want to teach companies that have insecure data practices a lesson. And hackers know that many companies are not good at learning from their mistakes.

Companies that suffer a data breach must secure their systems from that vector of attack before disclosing the breach. This is one of the key reasons that companies are provided some time to act before making public disclosures. In addition, the company must introduce sufficient short-term fixes to protect the system from the original attacker and from copycats.

As the forensic investigation assesses the system, it should be answering two different questions. The investigation must first answer questions about who attacked the company and how did it accomplish that attack. Secondly, the forensic investigation should provide a roadmap to harden the company from future attacks. The forensic experts should help the company identify vulnerabilities in its physical, technical, and administrative safeguards that can be improved to reduce the risk of a follow-on attack.

Companies that have a publicly disclosed data breach are much more likely to be targeted more aggressively in the future. Those companies, therefore, need to plan to invest more heavily than companies with similar operations and size which have not been victims of a publicly disclosed data breach. What may have been a reasonable data security plan for a company without any incidents will likely be insufficient for a company that has suffered such a breach.

E. SEC Disclosure Requirements

As the concerns about cybersecurity have increased, the SEC has also become increasingly active in addressing cybersecurity concerns among financial institutions and for the "issuers," public companies that issued securities on a public market and have their stocks traded on national security exchanges. Noting the significance of data security risks, the SEC published guidance stating "that it is critical that public companies take all required actions to inform investors about material cybersecurity risks and incidents in a timely fashion, including those companies that are subject to material cybersecurity risks but may not yet have been the target of a cyber-attack."

Under the SEC regulations, companies must adopt appropriate security procedures, publish adequate privacy policies, and inform the public of material risks to their cybersecurity. Although

Congress did not adopt a new law directly related to cybersecurity for a publicly traded company, the SEC required that such a company "consider the adequacy of their cybersecurity-related disclosure" when meeting their disclosure requirements under the Securities Act and Securities and Exchange Act.

The SEC also warned that a trading risk exists for corporate insiders who are aware of material cybersecurity incidents or risks and who trade their securities while in possession of this material nonpublic information. A corporate executive who is aware that the company is cooperating with law enforcement regarding a recently discovered, but nonpublic, cybersecurity incident cannot trade privately owned stock without risking violations of insider trading laws.

> The materiality of cybersecurity risks or incidents depends upon their nature, extent, and potential magnitude, particularly as they relate to any compromised information or the business and scope of company operations. The materiality of cybersecurity risks and incidents also depends on the range of harm that such incidents could cause. This includes harm to a company's reputation, financial performance, and customer and vendor relationships, as well as the possibility of litigation or regulatory investigations or actions, including regulatory actions by state and federal governmental authorities and non-U.S. authorities. . . .
>
> We expect companies to disclose cybersecurity risks and incidents that are material to investors, including the concomitant financial, legal, or reputational consequences. Where a company has become aware of a cybersecurity incident or risk that would be material to its investors, we would expect it to make appropriate disclosure timely and sufficiently prior to the offer and

sale of securities and to take steps to prevent directors and officers (and other corporate insiders who were aware of these matters) from trading its securities until investors have been appropriately informed about the incident or risk.

In addition to the duty to disclose material risks, the publicly traded companies also have a duty to correct disclosed information so that they are accurate. If earlier disclosures are later found to be inaccurate then there is a duty to update the disclosure. For example, if a publicly traded company incorrectly states the scale of a data breach, then the SEC disclosure obligations mandate that the company update and correct the information it had previously published.

The SEC provides the following list of considerations for public companies to use in considering the appropriate scope and timing of their cybersecurity disclosures. It also reminds companies that to provide context for these risk factors, companies may be required to describe prior incidents to put these risks into context for potential investors. Considerations include:

- the occurrence of prior cybersecurity incidents, including their severity and frequency;
- the probability of the occurrence and potential magnitude of cybersecurity incidents;
- the adequacy of preventative actions taken to reduce cybersecurity risks and the associated costs, including, if appropriate, discussing the limits of the company's ability to prevent or mitigate certain cybersecurity risks;
- the aspects of the company's business and operations that give rise to material cybersecurity risks and the potential costs and consequences of

such risks, including industry-specific risks and third party supplier and service provider risks;

- the costs associated with maintaining cybersecurity protections, including, if applicable, insurance coverage relating to cybersecurity incidents or payments to service providers;
- the potential for reputational harm;
- existing or pending laws and regulations that may affect the requirements to which companies are subject relating to cybersecurity and the associated costs to companies; and
- litigation, regulatory investigation, and remediation costs associated with cybersecurity incidents.

The risk factors identified by the SEC are broader but more general than the types of disclosure needed for victims of a security incident. The concerns for the SEC go beyond the information in a particular breach and instead cover the more general threat to the stability and longevity of a publicly traded company that can be put at risk because of a poor cybersecurity plan.

Like the state disclosure laws, the underlying goal for the SEC is most likely to push companies to invest in cybersecurity before incidents occur and remind the corporate executives that the consequences for cybersecurity breaches may include insider trading review and other serious consequences to the organization. The SEC focus on cybersecurity should help motivate corporate executives to invest in the physical and technological safeguards essential to good cybersecurity hygiene and to invest their time and effort in the administrative safeguards so that cybersecurity is a priority in every publicly traded company.

Although the SEC does not use the term administrative safeguards, it emphasizes its importance. The SEC emphasizes that "a company must include a description of how the board administers its risk oversight function." It then incorporates cybersecurity oversight into this standard. "To the extent cybersecurity risks are material to a company's business, we believe this discussion should include the nature of the board's role in overseeing the management of that risk." The SEC specifically notes the importance to include disclosures regarding a company's cybersecurity risk management program, noting that "how the board of directors engages with management on cybersecurity issues allow investors to assess how a board of directors is discharging its risk oversight responsibility in this increasingly important area."

The ongoing disclosure requirements for cybersecurity hygiene obligate public companies to engage a combination of legal counsel, forensic experts, and communications counsel for its ongoing corporate compliance as a nonpublic company would do in the case of a material breach. For publicly traded companies, their cybersecurity reporting obligations have become quarterly events, even when no specific incident has occurred.

Key Takeaways from This Chapter:

The data breach notification laws adopted in every state have a number of common components, but each has its own obligations for compliance. There is no one-size-fits-all response because each state requires its own forms and specialized language.

All states require companies to have robust cybersecurity protections and to be able to explain the nature of any cybersecurity incident. Depending on the size of the data breach, a company suffering an incident needs to quickly be able to consult with law enforcement, forensic experts, communications specialists, and legal counsel to meet the statutory obligations regarding the company's response.

States do not require a data breach notification if the information lost or stolen is in an encrypted form. Some states treat unreadable and unusable data in the same manner as encrypted data. Many states do not require notifications unless there is a likelihood of harm resulting from the data breach, but at least ten states do not have a material harm threshold. And once the information about a data breach is made public to some of the consumers, the general public will learn of the incident.

If the breach involves sensitive information such as Social Security numbers, then many states will require the company to provide credit monitoring as a response to the incident. Companies often extend this service even in states that do not require it to reduce the risks that real economic harm will result in expensive lawsuits by the consumers who have had their data exposed.

Things to Know:

Every company should have a cybersecurity data breach plan in place before there is an incident. The company should identify its teams of lawyers, forensic experts, and communications consultants before the crisis occurs.

The information required in a data breach disclosure provides a useful reminder of the cybersecurity obligations that every company must address. Most data breach notification laws are designed to encourage companies to be more proactive in their cybersecurity efforts in order to block data breaches rather than to document the incidents once they occur.

The more a company does to reduce the risk of breach and to lessen the impact of any incident, the easier it will be to report and the lower the costs of remediation.

Things to Think About:

There is no universal data protection requirement or privacy requirement in the U.S., yet every jurisdiction has been able to enact a data breach notification law. What is it about the notification law that has made it easier to enact than actual privacy or cybersecurity legislation?

Would data breach notification laws be as important if there were stronger privacy and cybersecurity laws instead?

Would a single, national data breach notification law be preferable to the patchwork of 54 national laws? How would a national data breach notification law differ from the various state laws?

CHAPTER 8

Sectoral Privacy: Children's Online Privacy

The United States does not have a single privacy or cybersecurity policy that covers all businesses. Even the state laws that have the largest reach often distinguish between for-profit business organizations and nonprofit corporations and government agencies. Many of the strongest data privacy and data security laws in the United States are federal laws and regulations that focus on particular industry sectors or populations. There are laws focused on student records, driver's licenses, and other narrow uses of information, but these regulations do not have significant scope.

The area where there has been the greatest bipartisan political support for privacy and cybersecurity regulation has been in the field of child privacy. The Children's Online Privacy Protection Act (COPPA) has been passed by Congress and updated through the collaboration of Congress and the FTC. This chapter summarizes and explores COPPA and its role in providing privacy protection to children and other consumers.

A. Introduction and Origins

In the late 1990s, the recently commercialized Internet was growing faster than almost anyone had predicted. There were few regulations, and the Internet was often described as "the Wild West" or a space without laws. In 1998, an FTC survey found that 85% of all websites were collecting the personal information of their visitors and most of these sites had inadequate privacy policies. The FTC raised concerns about online privacy and the use of personal information for fraud and misuse of the information being collected. The FTC Commissioners noted that "the Commission has been committed consistently to the proposition that industry self-regulation . . . is preferable to a detailed legislative mandate. However, [the] self-regulation, so long promised, was quite disappointing."

Despite the change in position by the FTC, there was little bipartisan appetite for general data privacy and data security regulation. There was, however, broader agreement with regard to privacy concerns and unauthorized marketing targeting children age 12 and under. In particular, the FTC noted that very few of the sites addressed privacy practices targeted at children, even among those sites that provided children's content, goods, and services. Shortly after the FTC hearings, the White House adopted a similar mandate, calling for stricter regulations for health care information and to protect children's privacy online.

Congress responded to the concerns by passing the Children's Online Privacy Protection Act of 1998 (COPPA). The legislative history of COPPA provides an outline of its central goals:

(1) to enhance parental involvement in children's online activities in order to protect children's privacy;

(2) to protect children's safety when they visit and post information on public chat rooms and message boards;

(3) to maintain the security of children's personal information collected online; and

(4) to limit the collection of personal information from children without parental consent.

Congress recognized that the operational aspects of online privacy were rapidly evolving. Rather than pass a law with stringent requirements that would quickly fall out of date, Congress assigned the duty to create and maintain regulations to the FTC. This was also the first explicit act of Congress recognizing that the FTC had become the de facto privacy regulatory body in the United States, and its passage helped to provide the FTC the de jure authority the agency needed to enforce privacy rights more generally.

COPPA extended the FTC's broad authority to prohibit unfair and deceptive acts or practices through the use of fines and civil penalties. By using the unfair and deceptive trade practices framework, Congress was also able to extend authority to state attorneys general to enforce COPPA. An attorney general choosing to bring an enforcement action merely needs to provide the FTC written notice and the COPPA Rule provide authority to move forward under the law. Attorneys general can also rely on their state unfair and deceptive trade practices law to bring state actions.

Congress did provide specific requirements giving parents or guardians the right to control their children's personal information on the Internet. It included a general requirement that websites and online services directed to children obtain verifiable parental consent prior to collecting, using, or disclosing children's personal information.

The COPPA Rule was promulgated by the FTC the following year, becoming effective on April 21, 2000. With the growth of social media, the Internet of Things (IoT), and mobile devices, the FTC found that certain aspects of COPPA had grown out of date, and the Commission updated the COPPA Rule in 2013. In the 2013 expansion of the COPPA Rule, the FTC expanded the definition of children's personal information to add online cookies, geolocation tags, and information contained in audiovisual content including videos and shared photos.

Although the stated goal of COPPA is to give parents more control over the information collected from children under the age of 13, the structure of the COPPA Rule is designed to discourage the collection of personal information from those children. Reducing the amount of information collected by children was one of the four goals expressed by Congress in the legislative history. A second goal of COPPA is to require improved privacy notices for companies that collected children's information, including a large number of general purpose websites where the operators knew that they were collecting children's information in addition to the adolescents and adults visiting the sites.

B. COPPA Requirements

COPPA sets out obligations for operators or online websites collecting the personal information of children. Each of these terms has a particular meaning under the COPPA Rule that together define the scope of COPPA regulation.

1. Scope of COPPA Coverage—Operators Collecting Children's Personal Information

Operators. The COPPA Rule applies to operators of commercial websites, mobile apps and devices, Internet-connected toys, and online services directed to children under 13 that collect, use, or disclose personal information from children. It also applies to websites, apps, and devices that target general audiences, if the operators of those sites do so with actual knowledge that they are collecting, using, or disclosing personal information from children under 13. Companies that run ad networks or plug-ins are also covered by the rule if the operators have actual knowledge that the site or service collects personal information and which targets users under 13.

In addition to actions against website operators offering content directed at children, the FTC had brought actions against more general website operators including Google and YouTube for advertising and media channels targeting children under 13, and toy manufacturer VTech Electronics for collecting children's data through its Internet connected line of toys. VTech's data collection practices were made public after a cybersecurity breach exposed the trove of personal information VTech had been collecting on its customers.

The COPPA Rule is designed to capture the connected devices and platforms without regard to particular technologies. Although originally focused on online commercial websites, the COPPA Rule now covers websites, mobile devices such as cell phones and tablets along with the various software, apps, and widgets that operate on them, networked toys and other devices connected through the Internet as Internet of Things protocols, voice-over internet protocol services, and any other toy, tool, or technology that allows a machine or device to collect personal information and share it with an operator or company that collects, sells, or processes that information. It does not, however, extend to pencil and paper.

Collecting. The COPPA Rule also uses a broad definition of "collect" regarding the information. Unlike policies where the consumer, client, or patient can choose to disclose their personal information, COPPA is written on the assumption that the consumer is a child under 13 and it is the child's parent who must consent to the collection of information. As a result, sites that collect information "voluntarily" from the site users are not meeting their obligation to obtain parental consent. The COPPA Rule addresses this concern with the following definitions for collects:

> *Collects* or *collection* means the gathering of any personal information from a child by any means, including but not limited to: (1) Requesting, prompting, or encouraging a child to submit personal information online; (2) Enabling a child to make personal information publicly available in identifiable form. An operator shall not be considered to have collected personal information under this paragraph if it takes reasonable measures to delete all or virtually all personal information from a child's postings before they are made public and also to delete such information from its records; or (3) Passive tracking of a child online.

Under this definition, a prompt to collect information would trigger the rule even if the requested information was entirely voluntary and the service operated in a nondiscriminatory manner, meaning that the service worked with or without the information provided by the child.

Under the second clause in the definition of collect, a social media site would be responsible to have software or staff to delete any personal information that a child posted on the child's social media account. Some children's software solved this challenge by allowing social media software to select from menus of prewritten words and sentences rather than allowing children to post their own text and images.

Personal information. With the 2013 expansion of the COPPA Rule, the regulation now uses a very broad definition of personal information:

> (1) A first and last name;

(2) A home or other physical address including street name and name of a city or town;

(3) Online contact information, meaning an email address or any other substantially similar identifier that permits direct contact with a person online, including but not limited to, an instant messaging user identifier, a voice over internet protocol (VOIP) identifier, or a video chat user identifier;

(4) A screen or user name where it functions in the same manner as online contact information, as defined in this section;

(5) A telephone number;

(6) A Social Security number;

(7) A persistent identifier that can be used to recognize a user over time and across different Web sites or online services. Such persistent identifier includes, but is not limited to, a customer number held in a cookie, an Internet Protocol (IP) address, a processor or device serial number, or unique device identifier;

(8) A photograph, video, or audio file where such file contains a child's image or voice;

(9) Geolocation information sufficient to identify street name and name of a city or town; or

(10) Information concerning the child or the parents of that child that the operator collects online from the child and combines with an identifier described in this definition.

The language of the personal information definition was intended to be both broad and forward-looking, so the definition could not be circumvented by new technologies.

2. *COPPA Rule Obligations*

The COPPA Rule has specific obligations for the commercial operators of websites and online services. The failure to meet any of these obligations is unlawful and the operator is subject to fines or civil penalties for failure to meet these obligations. Some of these obligations, such as the duty to employ appropriate security measures have a very broad application, while obligations regarding parental approvals are quite specific to the children protected by COPPA.

The FTC has summarized the statutes with this outline of duties. Under the COPPA Rule, an operator must:

- Post a clear and comprehensive online privacy policy describing their information practices for personal information collected online from children;
- Provide direct notice to parents and obtain verifiable parental consent, with limited exceptions, before collecting personal information online from children;
- Give parents the choice of consenting to the operator's collection and internal use of a child's information, but prohibiting the operator from disclosing that information to third parties (unless disclosure is integral to the site or service, in which case, this must be made clear to parents);
- Provide parents access to their child's personal information to review and/or have the information deleted;
- Give parents the opportunity to prevent further use or online collection of a child's personal information;
- Maintain the confidentiality, security, and integrity of information they collect from children, including

by taking reasonable steps to release such information only to parties capable of maintaining its confidentiality and security; and

- Retain personal information collected online from a child for only as long as is necessary to fulfill the purpose for which it was collected and delete the information using reasonable measures to protect against its unauthorized access or use.

Many of these obligations are similar to policies present in other data privacy regulations. These include the duty to provide an accurate notice regarding the type of personal information collected and an accurate description of how the personal information is used; the ability to review the information collected; and the ability to delete the information that is inaccurate. These practices have become part of the CCPA and GDPR laws as well. The duty to maintain the confidentiality, security, and integrity of the information collected is part of many privacy laws, and treated as an implicit part of the duty imposed on any business that collects personal information under the state and federal unfair and deceptive trade practices laws.

The unique aspects of COPPA are the obligations to provide direct notice to parents and obtain verifiable parental consent before collecting personal information online from children. The additional rights of parents to review, stop further collection, and delete the information collected are not unique to COPPA, but COPPA still represents the broadest obligation to require such data management.

3. *Verifiable Parental Consent*

The obligation to ensure that the parent of a child under 13 receives the notice of the sites' privacy policies and that it is the parent who consents to the access by the child is one of the key elements of the COPPA Rule and one of the larger challenges to its implementation. The COPPA Rule requires an opt-in assent by parents to the collection of personal information regarding the minors. Despite using an opt-in consent model, the COPPA Rule is drafted with some flexibility, requiring only that operators "make reasonable efforts, . . . taking into account available technology" to meet the operator's obligation.

To make parental consent even more difficult, the COPPA Rule requires that consent must be obtained before any information is collected for the child. There are limited exceptions to the obligation to collect the information before collecting information from the child, generally focusing on collecting sufficient information from the child to be able to reach the parent and request consent.

The challenges to the verifiable parental consent made these provisions largely aspirational when the law was first passed. In the 2013 revisions to the COPPA Rule, these provisions were significantly updated to make them more practical and enforceable.

The FTC lists a number of acceptable parental verification methods:

- Providing a consent form to be signed by the parent and returned via U.S. mail, fax, or electronic scan (the "print-and-send" method);
- Requiring the parent, in connection with a monetary transaction, to use a credit card, debit card, or other online payment system that provides notification of each discrete transaction to the primary account holder;
- Having the parent call a toll-free telephone number staffed by trained personnel, or have the parent

connect to trained personnel via video-conference; or

- Verifying a parent's identity by checking a form of government-issued identification against databases of such information, provided that you promptly delete the parent's identification after completing the verification.

As originally conceived, the credit card requirement was generally considered to be the most practical and reliable. Minors under thirteen, it was assumed, would not have their own credit cards. By charging a credit card, went the thinking, an adult was sure to be part of the transaction. This form of verification has some obvious limitations. First, it was never clear that the holder of the credit card was a parent rather than an older sibling or other person. Second, there were many instances of children using their parent's credit cards without their parent's consent. And third, many of the vendors using this method wanted to avoid having an actual financial transaction or quickly reversed the transaction, lowering the likelihood that the adult would object to unauthorized financial transactions. Nonetheless, the credit card provides a useful barrier to children under thirteen signing up for websites, so it continues to be used as a reasonable, if flawed, method of verification.

One high-tech approach was approved by the FTC in 2015, based on an application by Riyo Verified Ltd. The company developed what it calls "face match to verified photo identification" (FMVPI) to verify that the person providing consent for a child to use an online service is in fact the child's parent. The FTC explained that FMVPI is a two-step process. In the first step, a parent uploads a photo ID, such as a passport or driver's license. The company verifies the photo ID using external tools. The parent then uploads a picture taken through a web cam. The web cam is sufficiently live to establish that the second photo was not a picture taken of a preexisting photograph. The company then uses facial recognition software to confirm the web cam image is a match to the verified photo ID. This process requires a very substantial level of parental identification, but it significantly reduces the ability to falsify the parental consent. The FTC approved this as an acceptable approach for parental verification.

These approaches are all rather extensive, requiring significant and active participation from the parent. The FTC recognizes that for companies that collect but do not disclose any information, these efforts might be unduly burdensome. For companies that do not share the information with third parties or allow the information to be posted online by the minors, the risks are lower, and a less rigorous form of consent is acceptable. For such use, the FTC allows companies to use the "email plus" method of consent. A parent is sent an email requesting consent that includes all the information in the privacy notice and includes a second—or plus—step of additional verification. The second step can be as little as a second email reconfirming consent by the parent or a request in the first email for the parent to confirm by providing a telephone number.

4. *Safe Harbor Provisions*

To help industries be assured that they are not the targets of FTC action and to help the FTC extend a culture of compliance, the COPPA Rule includes the ability for the FTC to approve safe harbor policies or enforcement systems that companies can use to assure that they are in compliance and to assure that the FTC will not take adverse actions.

The safe harbor provisions are generally used by trade associations and industry groups that impose their own management. For example, the Entertainment Software Rating Board (ESRB) is an organization owned and managed by the major videogame companies. It is responsible for publishing age guidelines for video games. The ESRB is a very aggressive regulator of its members, empowered to bring substantial fines against companies that do not abide by the age guidance obligations published by the association. It first joined the safe harbor program in 2001 and has received approvals from the FTC to update its policies every few years thereafter.

For a company or trade association to meet the safe harbor requirements, it must apply to the FTC and provide the text of its proposed guidelines, an analysis showing that the proposed guidelines meet all the FTC requirements, and statements that describe how it plans to enforce its policies within its membership and how its enforcement system operates in other contexts. In the case of the ESRB, for example, it has an extensive handbook for member conduct, a staff that regularly audits the age-based reporting obligations, secret-shoppers who test that the age verification requirements are used by retailers, and a mechanism for levying and collecting fines. With that kind of extensive system of enforcement, the FTC has been quick to approve letting the ESRB receive a safe harbor and serve as the enforcement body for COPPA in the video game industry.

Given the significant obligations to serve as an enforcement agent under the safe harbor, there are only seven organizations that have been extended safe harbors. They are:

- Aristotle International Inc.
- Children's Advertising Review Unit (CARU)
- Entertainment Software Rating Board (ESRB)
- iKeepSafe
- kidSAFE
- Privacy Vaults Online, Inc. (d/b/a PRIVO)
- TrustArc/TRUSTe

TrustArc, originally operating under the name TRUSTe, was the first organization to receive certification as a safe harbor under the FTC program. It also served to provide other privacy protection certifications. TRUSTe did not have a particularly good reputation for enforcing privacy obligations, and it came under continuous scrutiny for what appeared to be a permissive model towards privacy violations. Finally, in 2014, the FTC finally responded to years of mounting complaints. Although complaints against TRUSTe began as early as 2002, the FTC complaint stated that "from 2006 until January 2013, TRUSTe failed to conduct annual recertifications of companies holding TRUSTe privacy seals in over 1,000 incidences, despite providing information on its website that companies holding TRUSTe Certified Privacy Seals receive recertification every year." The FTC also accused TRUSTe of misusing its nonprofit status. Nonetheless, although the FTC levied a $200,000 fine, it did not revoke the safe harbor for the company.

Another one of the companies holding a safe harbor verification is Aristotle. It operates the Integrity Privacy Compliance Program and sells age verification service for COPPA compliance as well as alcohol, tobacco, and adult websites. It offers thirteen different technologies for age verification for COPPA. Companies that may struggle to implement their own COPPA systems can purchase these services from Aristotle and become members of its safe harbor program.

Both CARU and ESRB are trade associations that have incorporated the COPPA safe harbor provisions into their broader membership obligations. These efforts work, but only to the extent that the trade associations take seriously their obligations to police the conduct of their members.

C. The COPPA Experiment

COPPA was the largest effort made by the FTC to create a new, mandatory culture for online privacy. The success of the program remains unclear. Like other laws that declare conduct unlawful, the laws themselves often do little to eliminate the unwanted behavior. The history with serial violators like TRUSTe suggests that the good intentions of the FTC are not necessarily lived out through actual enforcement.

COPPA has had both successes and failures. For companies and industries that want to meet the goals of COPPA, the guidance provided by the FTC and the best practices established by COPPA have created models to improve consumer privacy. Certain trade organizations, such as the ESRB, have instituted very comprehensive regulations within their own voluntary bodies. The ESRB, which also provides age-ratings for videogames, has a substantial operation to assure that its members meet all the organization's standards. The ESRB is much better positioned than the FTC to take action if its members fail to adhere to the policy required under the ESRB's safe harbor approval.

At the same time, the number of actual cases against companies failing to adhere to COPPA are tiny in comparison to the number of websites that target content to minors or operate knowing minors under thirteen take advantage of the platforms. Social media and communication platforms like Facebook, MySpace, TikTok, WhatsApp, and others all have substantial popularity among children of all ages. Many such companies assert compliance with COPPA by asking the user to provide an age or date of birth. If the age is under 13, the service is denied to the child. But there is no age verification, so the same child can increase the reported age and get access to the service. One service, for example, asked high school and college age users for the name of their school. If the subscriber listed an elementary school or middle school, the program would deny them service. But the person could simply create a new account listing a high school or college to gain access to the service.

Despite the criticisms that COPPA is too easy to evade, there are also critics raising concerns that the minors disenfranchised from social media platforms actually have free speech rights independent of their parents, and these children are entitled to use these services without interference by federal government regulation. Speech concerns have not been addressed, likely because the minors can so easily find ways to overcome the restrictions that COPPA imposes.

The greatest success COPPA has had is to establish a national framework for increased privacy and security. It represents a small first step at a national approach to data security and privacy. Many of its features have been incorporated into subsequent legislation. But the difficulties in implementation have also served as a reminder to privacy advocates and governmental regulators that the enforcement of privacy and securities laws is difficult and expensive. Like any first effort, it has provided useful guidance on how to continue building toward the future.

Key Takeaways from This Chapter:

With its adoption in 1998, COPPA became the first comprehensive consumer privacy law. Although it was targeted at companies collecting information on minors under the age of 13, the requirements for a privacy notice and data security helped improve these standards for all online businesses. With the amendments to the COPPA Rule in 2013, the scope of personal information is among the broadest in data regulation.

COPPA provides the parents and guardians of children under 13 the right to control consent to collect the personal information collected about the minors. It is an opt-in privacy system that also gives parents and guardians the right to see what information has been collected, the right to request deletion of information collected, and the right to stop the further collection of information. Many of the consumer protections later enacted in the GDPR and CCPA were first introduced as law in COPPA.

Things to Know:

COPPA remains limited in scope. Although the CCPA increases the age protections to 16, COPPA remains at 13. The FTC regularly brings enforcement actions, but the number of enforcement actions cannot begin to truly police the collection of minor's personal information, particularly at websites and services that are available to the general public and used actively by children under 13.

COPPA remains a powerful regulation, and the vast majority of businesses that collect personal information try to adhere to the COPPA Rule. Many companies use one of the seven companies that have received a safe harbor to verify their compliance with COPPA.

Things to Think About:

When Congress enacted COPPA, the legislative history restated the preference for self-regulation instead of governmental regulation. As a result, there is no generalized data privacy protection. Instead, there are complex state-by-state data breach notification laws and conflicting consumer privacy laws for companies subject to either GDPR or CCPA. To what extent would online businesses have benefitted from a single federal regulation?

Is the current system of sectoral privacy laws and competing state laws too well established to replace with a single federal law?

Does the opt-in nature of COPPA work better than the opt-out systems provided in other data regulations regimes?

CHAPTER 9

Sectoral Privacy: Health Care Privacy

A patient's health information has been protected by confidentiality and privacy from the time of Roman law to the present. As the technology of medicine has changed and the rights of patients have increased, the nature of the regulations have evolved. Health care organizations are a popular target for ransomware attacks because these companies are so reliant on their electronic records. At least two health care organizations have been driven out of business in 2019 and others have been forced into bankruptcy as a result of malware attacks and the inability to continue operations as a result of the data breach.

In modern U.S. legislation, the Health Insurance Portability and Accountability Act represents the single most comprehensive set of privacy and data security regulations enacted in the U.S. While not nearly as comprehensive, the Genetic Information Nondiscrimination Act provides legal protections from particular forms of misuse of private information. This law is particularly important since it represents a different approach to privacy, focusing on regulating the harm that may be caused by using the information rather than regulating the disclosure of the information.

This chapter summarizes and explores the role of privacy and the obligations of data security in the health care fields.

A. Doctor-Patient Confidentiality

Congress did not have difficulty requiring comprehensive privacy and data security in the health care sector because the doctor-patient relationship has always included strong confidentiality. The confidentiality of the relationship is included in the Hippocratic Oath promulgated in Greece in the fourth or fifth century B.C.E. The doctor taking the oath vowed that "whatsoever I shall see or hear in the course of my profession, as well as outside my profession in my intercourse with men, if it be what should not be published abroad, I will never divulge, holding such things to be holy secrets."

1. In General

The obligation of confidentiality continued in Roman and English law. The purpose for the confidentiality is to encourage patients to trust their physicians and be willing to seek treatment. The confidentiality also promotes honest and frank discussions between the patient and the doctor.

The confidence is controlled by the patient, meaning that the patient is not bound by confidentiality and can share the information provided by the doctor for any reason, including such purposes as getting second opinions or bringing claims of medical malpractice by the doctor. Doctors do have limited abilities and obligations to breach their confidentiality. For example, certain forms of children's abuse or spousal abuse evidence must be reported by a treating physician and cannot be protected by confidentiality. Doctors can also share necessary medical treatment information when defending claims of medical malpractice by the patient who holds the privilege.

To establish the confidential relationship, the doctor must be serving to treat or at least consult with the patient. If no doctor-patient relationship has been established, then there will be no duty. This means that advice at social gatherings or through online websites may not rise to the level of a doctor-patient relationship, but each situation must be analyzed on its own facts. In addition, the information disclosed to the doctor must be relevant to the medical treatment. If a patient mentions the person's criminal misconduct, those criminal activities are not part of the treatment and can be disclosed. So, for example, if a patient mentions to a treating physician that he received a concussion when he was clubbed by a police officer while robbing a liquor store, then information about being at the liquor store can be reported to police.

Contrary to presentations on popular detective shows, doctor-patient confidentiality survives the death of the patient. The doctor cannot share the confidential information of the patient merely because the patient died.

At the same time, doctor-patient confidentiality is not the same thing as a doctor-patient privilege. A privilege is a legal doctrine that prohibits a judge from ordering testimony in a criminal or civil matter, either in court or through the use of a warrant or subpoena. The confidentiality will keep a doctor from disclosing the confidential information to the press, family members, or from gossiping, but only the legal privilege will stop the doctor from being compelled to disclose the information in a court proceeding.

Federal law does not specifically recognize the doctor-patient privilege, so in federal criminal and civil cases, the court is more likely to order the information be disclosed. But even though there is no affirmative federal privilege, the Federal Rules of Evidence that generally disfavor testimonial privilege also recognize the common law tradition that recognized the doctor-patient relationship. As a result, the application of the rule in federal courts is very inconsistent and highly fact specific.

Most states have addressed the privilege by statute. State laws generally recognize the privilege, but they vary considerably in the extent to which they can be overcome if the party needing to establish the testimony of the physician can establish the need before the court. States, for example, may provide for the doctor-patient privilege in civil cases but not in criminal matters. Other states will extend the privilege in all cases but give judges some discretion to establish that the privilege needs to be waived because of the factual situation.

2. An Exception to Confidentiality—the Duty to Warn

There are exceptions to doctor-patient confidentiality for highly communicable diseases and epidemic outbreaks. In these situations, there may be state or federal mandatory reporting requirements so that the public health risk can be reduced and greater outbreaks averted. The obligation to report must be established by law or regulation, and in the absence of a legal obligation, the doctor must respect the confidentiality of the patient.

In *Tarasoff v. Regents of University of California* (1976), the California Supreme Court held that a psychologist who was treating a dangerous patient had a duty to warn the intended target of the victim's violence. The court explained that the patient's right of confidentiality was secondary to the risk of harm. The court stated that once a "patient presents a serious danger of violence to another, [the physician] incurs an obligation to use reasonable care to protect the intended victim against such danger." This California decision significantly changed the attitudes towards physician-patient confidentiality and has been followed in many states.

As genetic testing and medical treatments continue to improve, states and medical organizations are struggling to establish rules regarding the obligation to inform family members of patients who test positive for genetically transferred medical conditions. In some legal decisions, courts have held that the doctor's obligation is satisfied by informing the patient of the results of the test and also explaining the likelihood that other family members will have the same genetic disorder. In other states, however, the courts have required that a doctor who learns of a genetic disease inform the family members who are likely to carry the same disease.

Genetic test warnings are similar in structure to laws adopted by some states or cities that have adopted HIV partner-testing laws. In these jurisdictions, a person who is HIV positive has a legal duty to inform sexual partners of the risk of transmission. Some of these jurisdictions also place an obligation on the physicians to provide this information to the partners. The Ryan White HIV/AIDS Program, a federally funded grant program which provides primary medical care for low-income individuals, includes a mandatory disclosure component for notification to the married partners of HIV/AIDS patients.

In areas such as sexually transmitted diseases, genetically transmitted diseases, and epidemics, the public policy of confidentiality typically gives way to the need for public disclosure and protection of those who may be impacted by the spread of a disease.

B. Health Insurance Portability and Accountability Act of 1996 (HIPAA)

In 1996, as part of a national effort to reform health care practices and reduce the rapidly rising cost of U.S. health care, Congress adopted the Health Insurance Portability and Accountability Act (HIPAA). The long title of the act provides an introduction to its goals:

> An Act To amend the Internal Revenue Code of 1986 to improve portability and continuity of health insurance coverage in the group and individual markets, to combat waste, fraud, and abuse in health insurance and health care delivery, to promote the use of medical savings accounts, to improve access to long-term care services and coverage, to simplify the administration of health insurance, and for other purposes.

More than two decades later, the aspect of HIPAA that has the most continued impact are the law's protection of portability from insurer to insurer. Not listed in the title was an outcome of even greater impact—the aggressive development of privacy and information security standards incorporated into the administrative simplification regulations.

1. *Introduction to HIPAA and the HITECH Act*

The law included five separate sections or titles, the first of which was designed to protect the right of an employee to retain health coverage when switching employers. The second section, named the Administrative Simplification, was designed to establish standards for electronic health records. The third section revised the rules for pre-tax medical spending accounts, the fourth section focused on updates to group health plans, and the last section updated the regulation of company-owned life insurance policies.

Title II of HIPAA focused on efforts to control fraud and abuse, to authorize the Administrative Simplification rules, and to mandate the Department of Health and Human Services (HHS) to create the standards under the Administrative Simplification mandate.

To implement the Administrative Simplification, HHS developed rules in five focus areas. Two of these rules, the Transactions and Code Sets Rule and the Unique Identifiers Rule, focus on the payment and billing process for health care providers, insurance companies, and related vendors and business entities. The remaining three rules are the Privacy Rule, the Security Rule, and the Enforcement Rule. Together, these three rules transformed healthcare privacy and data security, setting a new, national standard for governmental regulation of data. The HHS Office for Civil Rights administers and enforces the Privacy and Security Rules.

Although intended to create a more streamlined health care system, HIPAA met with considerable industry opposition, and federal regulators struggled to implement HIPAA in the manner they intended. In particular, the electronic health care record mandate of HIPAA was largely undermined by hospitals and insurance companies. They provided electronic records as graphic images (jpg and non-scannable PDFs) rather than machine-readable data sets, making the electronic record even less useful than paper copies. As part of the economic stimulus laws in 2009, Congress enacted the Health Information Technology for Economic and Clinical Health Act (HITECH Act) to force better compliance and stop the behaviors interfering with HIPAA.

The HITECH Act extended HIPAA and focused on the need to transition to usable electronic health records and their electronic personal health information (ePHI) that would be shared among doctors, hospitals, insurance companies, pharmacies, and other entities. With the expansion of electronic health records, Congress recognized that the need for regulation of data privacy and data security needed significant enforcement as well. The HITECH Act expanded data breach notification obligations and increased the level of fines that are levied for failure to protect the personal health information in these records.

HIPAA is implemented and enforced through the rules established by HHS. Various changes to the Privacy Rule and Security Rule made during the rulemaking process and through amendments in recent years have tried to balance very stringent privacy protections with practical implementations that protect patients without frustrating the medical industry and patients alike.

With the authority of HIPAA and the HITECH Act, HIPAA regulations provide the strongest data privacy and data security regulations in the United States, establishing the highest requirements for security efforts in any legal regime. Companies that need stringent data protection seek out HIPAA certified providers because this certification represents the most exacting set of physical, administrative and technical standards for data protection.

The failure to meet the obligations under HIPAA trigger significant fines and can lead to criminal convictions. The HHS Office for Civil Rights manages the investigations into security incidents and compliance, collaborates with entities to assure they meet the standards, and levies the fines for noncompliance. The Office for Civil Rights can also refer cases to the Department of Justice for criminal prosecution. The fines range from $100 per violation or record to $50,000 per violation with an annual cap of $1.5 million. The enforcement actions are detailed in the Enforcement Rule.

2. What HIPAA Means to Patients

HIPAA was initially enacted to assure insured employees that they would be able to continue their health coverage when moving to new employment. For employees with serious medical issues, the risk of losing insurance because of preexisting conditions meant that a change of job could have disastrous financial consequences.

The provisions of Administrative Simplification and electronic record protocols were enacted at the start of the online business expansion. Neither the government nor the public wanted the health industry to be governed like the wild west of the Internet. In response, HHS became the leading government agency in promoting patient rights for the protection and ownership of their personal information.

Under the Privacy Rule, patients are entitled to receive specific information from each covered entity in the form of a privacy notice:

(1) a description of patients' rights under the rule and how to exercise those rights;

(2) the legal duties of the covered entity;

(3) a description of the required and permissible uses and disclosures of PHI;

(4) how an individual can file a complaint with the covered entity or the HHS Secretary;

(5) how the covered entity will provide a revised notice if it needs changing; and

(6) a contact person for additional information.

HIPAA created a culture of confidentiality that transformed the nature of the doctor's office. Although doctor-patient confidentiality has existed throughout all of modern medicine, it was sometimes treated rather cavalierly. With the enactment of HIPAA, doctors' offices and health providers were forced to take a much harder look at their regular practices. Offices that asked patients to sign in by writing down their medical issue on a page open to every other patient in the clinic found they needed to create more respectful procedures to sign in patients. Similarly, pharmacies stopped giving medical advice at the checkout counter and instead offered patients the ability to consult with the pharmacist away from the listening ears of the other customers in line.

At first, doctors and pharmacists were concerned that HIPAA privacy would require the installation of soundproof consultation rooms and expensive changes to their facilities, but much more modest adjustments have been permitted that serve to separate a person seeking medical consultation from the observation of others waiting nearby for service. Many offices updated the manner in which they stored files, so that the print copies were not easily accessible; enhanced the training of their personnel to prioritize privacy; and paid more attention to the environment in which medical information was shared. Most offices required only modest improvements to meet the Privacy Rule requirements, although it served as a wake-up call for others.

HIPAA also empowered patients. HIPAA includes rights for patients to obtain copies of their medical records. For the first time, patients were able to demand their medical records, making it much easier for patients to control and direct their own medical treatment. Through the HITECH Amendments to HIPAA, individuals have a right to receive the ePHI as an electronic record. They can request that the record is delivered electronically and directly to another provider and to receive an accounting of the disclosures that have been made. In addition, the covered entity is required to follow a patient's request not to disclose to information about a specific health care item or service paid for out-of-pocket. This is an important addition, because it allows an individual to share some of the person's health care record without automatically revealing medical treatment that the person feels is more intimate or personal.

As with other privacy laws, it is the patient who controls the privacy. A patient is free to invite a family member or friend into the doctor's office, particularly when the patient needs assistance understanding or addressing the medical advice being given by the doctor. The Privacy Rule permits a doctor or other health care provider to "disclose to a family member, other relative, or a close personal friend of the individual" medical information that pertains to the patient's care. Consent to share the information with a friend or family member can be obtained by verbal consent or through consent by conduct. In other words, if a patient invites an adult son or daughter to attend a doctor's visit and consult with the doctor, the act of bringing the offspring to the appointment provides the consent needed. The doctor's office does not need to have the patient sign a release or consent. If the doctor's office insists on the patient signing a release, which some do, it should not claim that the HIPAA Privacy Rule requires it.

3. *Privacy Rule*

While the Privacy Rule prohibits companies covered by the regulation from disclosing the protected health information to unauthorized third parties, it enables the patient or person with protected health information to obtain a copy of the record, request corrections to those records, and gives the patient the authority to refuse to consent to the transfer of protected health information when it is used for purposes other than treatment, payment, or health care operations. Although simple in practice, the HIPAA regulations are highly complex and detailed.

In the 2000 publication of the Privacy Rule, HHS summarized the Congressional goal for Administrative Simplification and the importance of privacy to that goal:

> Congress called for steps to improve "the efficiency and effectiveness of the health care system by encouraging the development of a health information system through the establishment of standards and requirements for the electronic transmission of certain health information." . . . Congress recognized the fact that administrative simplification cannot succeed if we do not also protect the privacy and confidentiality of personal health information. . . .

The regulation's preamble noted that there were many state laws governing privacy but the patchwork of state laws and regulations did not cover all aspects of patient privacy, and they failed "to provide such basic protections as ensuring a patient's legal right to see a copy of his or her medical record." The Privacy Rule preempted existing state laws in most regards and established a single, national standard for the privacy and security of patient health information.

Health care privacy always covered doctors, but as the Privacy Rule evolved, it expanded to include a much broader set of companies. HIPAA uses the term "covered entity" to identify any business that is subject to the law. The law categorizes the covered entities into three groups: Health Care Providers, Health Plans, and Health Care Clearinghouses. In addition, there is a fourth category, the business associate, that is covered because of its contractual relationships with one of the three categories of covered entities.

Health Care Providers. A health care provider is an individual or company, for profit or nonprofit, that offers medical services, including medical care and treatment, medical equipment, pharmaceuticals, or medical supplies. These are the doctors, nurses, pharmacists, aides, therapists, and staff that make up the core of the medical system. Health care providers range in size from individual doctors to large hospitals and medical systems. The other requirement to be covered under the law is that the provider electronically transmits health information, such as for payment or administrative operations.

Health Plans. Health plans are groups that pay or provide the cost for medical care. These offer insurance, medical treatment, or provide group medical services such as health maintenance organizations (HMOs), preferred provider networks (PPOs), employer-sponsored medical plans, Medicare and Medicaid. There are exceptions to this category for food stamp programs, that can cover some medical or pharmaceutical costs, workers' compensation programs that provide wage replacement and medical cost reimbursement, other forms of non-medical insurance, and similar payments that might have an incidental repayment for costs that are health related but which do not primarily serve as health insurance.

Health Care Clearinghouses. Health care clearinghouses are companies that process health information, translating it into the standardized data formats and data sets required by other HIPAA regulations for payment and operational processing. Clearinghouses include billing services, repricing companies, value-added networks, and community health management information systems.

Business Associate. Business associates are companies that have entered into a contract with the covered entity to provide services to the covered entity that use or expose the protected health information of a covered entity. Business associates provide processing, data analysis, utilization review, or billing services for a covered entity. A business associate may extend to additional services to a covered entity such as legal, actuarial, accounting, consulting, data aggregation, management, administrative, accreditation, or financial services, but these services would only make the outside company a business associate if it was providing these services by utilizing protected health information in some manner. If the third party contracting with the covered entity did not have access to any protected health information (or if the access was incidental), then the third party would not have to be treated as a business associate covered by HIPAA.

If a company that is a covered entity or a business associate of a covered entity collects or obtains protected health information (PHI), then that company must protect the privacy and security of the information as provided in the HIPAA regulations. There are eighteen categories of PHI:

1. Names (last name and either first name or first name initial)
2. All geographical identifiers smaller than a state, except for the initial three digits of a zip code if, according to the current publicly available data from the U.S. Bureau of the Census: the geographic unit formed by combining all zip codes with the same three initial digits contains more than 20,000 people; and the initial three digits of a zip code for all such geographic units containing 20,000 or fewer people is changed to 000
3. Dates (other than year) directly related to an individual
4. Phone numbers
5. Fax numbers
6. Email addresses
7. Social Security numbers
8. Medical record numbers
9. Health insurance beneficiary numbers
10. Account numbers

11. Certificate/license numbers
12. Vehicle identifiers (including serial numbers and license plate numbers)
13. Device identifiers and serial numbers
14. Web Uniform Resource Locators (URLs)
15. Internet Protocol (IP) address numbers
16. Biometric identifiers, including finger, retinal and voice prints
17. Full face photographic images and any comparable images
18. Any other unique identifying number, characteristic, or code except the unique code assigned by the investigator to code the data

A covered entity's use of PHI falls into three categories: those actions the covered entity is required to take, those actions the covered entity is permitted to take, and those actions the covered entity authorizes. If the covered entity uses PHI in any other manner, then it will be subject to fines and legal actions.

When disclosing information for purposes other than treatment, payment, and health care operations, there is a general duty to provide the minimum amount of protected health information required to carry out the purpose of the disclosure. There are many exceptions to the minimum necessary rule, however, so it operates more as a reminder of best practices for data management than as a significant limitation of data disclosure.

Required actions.

HIPAA requires the covered entity to provide patients or the patient's personal representative access to the information collected about that person. Other than a very limited exception for the notes of psychologists and therapists, a patient is entitled to a complete set of their own information.

The second requirement under HIPAA is to provide HHS access to protected information when the department is taking an enforcement action or conducting a compliance review. When these investigations take place, a covered entity must provide the requested information to HHS.

Although these first two reasons are the only basis for mandatory reporting under HIPAA, the Privacy Rule permits covered entities to comply with mandatory reporting obligations that are based on state laws or other authority. Such examples typically include instances of child or elder abuse, gunshot and stab wounds, certain communicable and highly infectious diseases, neonatal drug use, and similar public health concerns. HIPAA is not the source of the duty to report these medical conditions, but it is designed to allow the preexisting mandatory reporting to take place.

Permitted actions.

The largest category of information that a covered entity can disclose is for the treatment, payment, and health care operations of a covered entity. This means that a doctor or hospital has the right to communicate with other medical staff, insurance, and billing operations to assure that the intended treatment is provided and that the service providers are paid. A patient cannot, for example, agree to treatment but then deny the covered entity's right to share the necessary health care information with the billing company to issue a billing statement.

Some covered entities prefer to obtain consent in these situations, but consent is not required by law and reflects a misunderstanding of consensual coverage. As noted in the discussion of the GDPR, a company should avoid seeking consent if the refusal to provide consent will be ignored. Instead, a covered entity should seek acknowledgement of its notice. A false characterization of consent can lead to conflicts and potentially to legal issues concerning the validity of the consent in other contexts. On the other hand, a covered entity providing treatment services is required to make a good faith effort to obtain written acknowledgement from patients of receipt of the privacy practices notice.

Where a patient is incapacitated, such as in the event of an accident, the covered entity can use its professional judgment to speak with family members and make disclosures as the treatment requires, in the best judgment of the medical professionals. The patient controls this disclosure, so if a patient had previously informed the covered entity not to provide information to a particular individual, the covered entity would need to respect that instruction. But in general, the consultation with family remains part of the treatment process and remains within the discretion of the covered entity.

As noted in the section on required disclosures, HIPAA mandates the reporting of protected health information to the individual who is the subject of the information. The Privacy Rule goes further by providing that the disclosure of such information is both required and allowed, presumably to encourage the covered entity to provide the greatest amount of information it can ethically disclose.

The Privacy Rule also takes into account that there may be incidental disclosures of protected health information and permits incidental disclosures. Provided a covered entity has taken the necessary and appropriate steps to implement its data security and made efforts to minimize overall data exposure, an incidental disclosure does not automatically trigger a violation of the Privacy Rule.

In addition to the treatment, payment, and health care operations and for disclosures to the patient, there are a number of permitted uses for protected health care information that cannot be stopped by the patient. The obligation to report public health risks under state law fall within the category of permitted disclosures of protected health information under HIPAA. The Privacy Rule identifies twelve areas where the regulations permit covered entities to disclose the information because there are other laws or obligations that require mandatory reporting.

- *Required by Law.* This category may overlap with some of the other categories, but it provides a broad general permission to keep covered entities from violating jurisdictional laws. In some ways, this exception to the Privacy Rule reverses the preemption of the state law and federal law. State laws govern mandatory disclosure.

- *Judicial and Administrative Proceedings.* Covered entities must comply with lawfully conducted judicial or administrative proceedings, including court orders and subpoenas.

- *Law Enforcement Purposes.* In addition to obligations to comply with the law and in judicial proceedings, covered entities may be required in some jurisdictions to identify or locate a suspect, fugitive, material witness, or missing person; to provide information about a victim or suspected victim of a crime; to report a death if there is a suspicion that criminal activity caused the death; to provide evidence of a crime that occurred on the covered entity's premises; and more generally to report a crime. Each jurisdiction will have its own version of these obligations.

- *Serious Threat to Health or Safety.* Covered entities may disclose protected health information as part of its duty to report a serious and imminent threat to a person or the public, as required by the *Tarasoff* decision. The disclosure of a serious threat is permissible both to the potential victim and to law enforcement.
- *Essential Government Functions.* A covered entity can also disclose protected health information for certain essential government functions. As provided by HHS, "such functions include: assuring proper execution of a military mission, conducting intelligence and national security activities that are authorized by law, providing protective services to the President, making medical suitability determinations for U.S. State Department employees, protecting the health and safety of inmates or employees in a correctional institution, and determining eligibility for or conducting enrollment in certain government benefit programs."
- *Public Health Activities.* The FDA and public health authorities have authority to collect certain data pertaining to public health outbreaks and drug distribution. This also extends to certain workplace disclosures covered by the Occupational Safety and Health Administration (OSHA), the Mine Safety and Health Administration (MSHA), and similar state agencies.
- *Victims of Abuse, Neglect or Domestic Violence.* In addition to the mandatory reporting for children and

elder abuse, some laws require reporting of suspected spousal and partner abuse.

- *Workers' Compensation.* Workers' compensation laws often include certain reporting requirements and workplace risk mitigation documentation. To meet these legal and administrative obligations covered entities are permitted to disclose the information required under these systems.
- *Health Oversight Activities.* Health care is a highly regulated industry requiring that covered entities sometimes disclose protected health information to health oversight agencies for audits, investigations, and assessments of the health care system and government benefit programs.
- *Decedents.* Covered entities may disclose protected health information to funeral directors, coroners, or medical examiners to identify a deceased person, determine the cause of death, and perform other functions authorized by law.
- *Cadaveric Organ, Eye, or Tissue Donation.* Covered entities may use or disclose protected health information to facilitate the donation and transplantation of cadaveric organs, eyes, and tissue.
- *Research.* Most research activities require the informed consent of all participants in the research. Nonetheless, there are exceptions in the Privacy Rule that allow for the covered entity to provide protected health information to the research initiative because of the limited use to which the information would be put or because informed

consent has been obtained directly by the researching institution. In addition, there are provisions for the disclosure of de-identified and anonymous data that do not contain PHI because the data set is considered to have been rendered sufficiently anonymous.

Disclosures requiring consent.

Unless the use of the protected information falls into one of the categories listed above, the covered entity must obtain consent in advance of the disclosure of the information. Nonetheless, some consent requirements are more formal than others. Generally, covered entities are permitted to allow the patients' contact information to be available as part of the directory information so that friends and family calling to check on a patient may be appropriately directed to the patient. Hospitals can reasonably rely on an opt-out notice because the practice is so well known. A patient has the right to object to being in the hospital patient directory, but most hospitals will not request consent first.

Similarly, as noted above, if a patient brings a friend, spouse, or other family member into a consultation or treatment room and the patient does not object to the person's presence during consultation or treatment, the consent to the disclosure to that person is deemed to have been given through the conduct of the patient.

Where the covered entity would like to disclose protected health information for purposes other than the treatment, payment, and health care operations, then the covered entity must obtain written consent. The most common such use would be for marketing purposes. Even here there are exceptions. There is no requirement for written consent to marketing if the marketing is for additional treatment services, case management services, or services similar to those provided under the treatment, payment, or health service operations.

If the marketing is for more general purposes or if the use of the PHI is to sell to data brokers for consumer profiling, then express written consent is required. The consent must be sufficiently specific so that the consumer understands the purpose of the consent being requested. The consent requirements are much more exacting than general privacy notices. The result is that health care organizations tend not to use their PHI as a revenue stream in the consumer product markets.

4. *Security Rule*

Unlike the Privacy Rule, the Security Rule extends only to electronic health records held by covered entities (including business associates). The Privacy Rule covers PHI while the Security Rule protects ePHI. It does not cover the obligation to keep physical documents safe from theft or alteration, leaving any such legal obligation to state laws. The Security Rule established the obligation that each covered entity adopts reasonable administrative, technical, and physical safeguards in order to protect ePHI from unauthorized access, use, or disclosure. Covered entities are required to appoint a privacy officer who is responsible for the implementation of the HIPAA obligations.

The Security Rule requires the covered entity to protect the confidentiality, integrity, and availability of the ePHI. This means the duty to secure the information is more than to protect it from hacking and theft. As described more fully in Chapter 6, the obligation of confidentiality requires that the data are free from unauthorized access by anyone either inside or outside the organization. The obligation to maintain data integrity means that there is a verifiable system to establish that the data has not been corrupted due to the materials on which they are stored, altered without authorization, or otherwise changed. Finally, the obligation to maintain the availability requires the covered entity to keep the data in a manner that makes it reasonably retrievable, including the operational copies during the normal course of business and a backup system that can reasonably restore the data in a practical timeframe should the operational copies be destroyed due to malware, natural disaster, or other incident.

Every covered entity must assure that the ePHI remains functional and useful until such time as the covered entity is obligated to remove the records. Record retention laws will provide different retention obligations, depending on the jurisdiction and the type of record. The Security Rule is an affirmative duty to protect the information. Covered entities are even required to anticipate the range of likely criminal threats and take appropriate steps to thwart those attacks.

The general requirements are very straightforward, but the technical requirements become very detailed. There are four core requirements:

(1) Ensure the confidentiality, integrity, and availability of all electronic protected health information the covered entity or business associate creates, receives, maintains, or transmits.

(2) Protect against any reasonably anticipated threats or hazards to the security or integrity of such information.

(3) Protect against any reasonably anticipated uses or disclosures of such information that are not permitted or required under subpart E of this part.

(4) Ensure compliance with this subpart by its workforce.

The Security Rule is designed to be technologically neutral so that as the technology evolves, the implementation of security continues to improve without becoming locked into outdated mandates. The regulation allows the covered entities to take the size, complexity and capabilities of the company into account when developing and operating its security infrastructure, as well as the cost, hardware and software security capabilities. The covered entity must then balance these against "the probability and criticality of potential risks to electronic protected health information." Despite the effort to provide only general guidelines that establish reasonable requirements based on the size and nature of the covered entity, the Security Rule is actually a cumbersome and detailed regulatory framework that companies struggle to apply.

In an era of constant online threats to personal information and the additional threats posed by business risks and natural disasters, the HHS expects strong protection for ePHI even from the smallest of covered entities. Nonetheless, the HHS anticipates that the actual implementation will differ considerably between a small physician group and a major hospital system.

To comply with the Security Rule, a covered entity must meet each of 20 subcategories identified as required. In addition, there are other standards labeled "addressable" which the covered entity should treat as strong recommendations. Together, the required and addressable standards cover all the administrative, technical, and physical requirements of the Security Rule. The addressable standards must be analyzed carefully, and a covered entity should not ignore them unless they are truly inapplicable to the security system put in place. Merely meeting all the required standards may not be sufficient to comply with the Security Rule, and the covered entity will be liable if failure to address one of the addressable standards results in a security incident that discloses ePHI or results in a malware attack that shuts down the enterprise.

Administrative Safeguards.

Although it is the technical safeguards that keep malware from attacking a computer system, the administrative safeguards establish the institutional culture and level of investment in security. The administrative safeguards drive the rest of the security framework.

Risk analysis and security management. The first step in compliance is risk analysis. Comprehensive risk analysis frames the compliance process because it helps the covered entity establish the scope of its ePHI and its risk of any potential security incident. Risk analysis is an ongoing process that should have at least annual reports to continuously update the threat assessment and effectiveness of the security provisions.

The regulations contemplate a four-step process for continuous risk analysis:

- Evaluate the likelihood and impact of potential risks to ePHI.
- Implement appropriate security measures to address the risks identified in the risk analysis.
- Document the chosen security measures and, where required, the rationale for adopting those measures.
- Maintain continuous, reasonable, and appropriate security protections.

Leadership and management. A covered entity must designate a security officer or official who holds the primary responsibility for developing and implementing the policies and procedures for implementation of HIPAA. There should be direct reporting to senior leadership in the covered entity, and senior leadership should be educated and involved in the implementation of all HIPAA compliance. There can be direct consequences to senior leadership for significant HIPAA security incidents.

Workforce education and training. Just as senior leadership must be held accountable in a proper administrative plan, all personnel in a covered entity must be trained to protect confidential information and ePHI. The personnel policies must have clear consequences for failures to protect ePHI and for any misconduct that results in an intentional security incident. Appropriate training must begin at the onboarding of new personnel and continue on a regular basis for all staff. Training should be developed to be appropriate for the role of the employee. Those who regularly utilize ePHI as part of the treatment, payment, or operations of a covered entity require more specialized training than those employees who do not come into contact with any ePHI. Even for staff with no ePHI access, however, every employee who has access to a computer network is a potential target of a phishing attack, so everyone needs some level of training.

Workforce and vendor access management. One of the most effective ways to reduce the chances of a security incident is to restrict access to the data. Both the Privacy Rule and Security Rule implement this approach through the philosophy to limit disclosure of PHI/ePHI to the "minimum necessary" to fulfill the treatment, payment or operational needs of the covered entity. The minimum necessary approach must be incorporated into the personnel and business associate practices to reduce the amount of PHI that may be utilized. This means that employees and business associates should only be able to have access to particular PHI/ePHI when their duties and operational role requires access. These role-based access rules must be updated frequently, and every change in role by an employee should be accompanied by a change in access as appropriate to the change in role. Covered entities should also be mindful to avoid the false assumptions that more senior officials have a need for access to protected information. The role-based access should be focused on the tasks assigned to the individuals rather than the status within the enterprise.

Physical Safeguards.

Physical safeguards focus on the buildings, doors, and workspaces where ePHI is stored and used. These include physical access controls, physical safety from theft and natural disaster. To meet this standard, the covered entity must "implement policies and procedures to limit physical access to its electronic information systems and the facility or facilities in which they are housed, while ensuring that properly authorized access is allowed."

The physical safeguards include steps to limit access to the electronic records and the machines or devices on which those records are stored, to utilize the minimum necessary framework to keep personnel away from ePHI unless they have a specific need to be given privileges to access, the records, and to verify that these steps are in place. The verification will likely require more than strong door locks. It generally will require some type of system to track who has accessed the facility using card readers or similar technology. The standard also recommends that covered entities retain a maintenance record, since the upkeep of the facilities may trigger risks of data loss.

Physical safeguard should include methods of tracking all mobile devices on which ePHI may be kept. Laptop computers, mobile phones, iPads, and similar devices create significant security challenges. At a minimum, a covered entity should have a verifiable audit trail for each of those pieces of equipment. While encryption of data is an addressable standard rather than a requirement, the loss of a device with unencrypted data has become the most easily predicted security incident that exists. The failure to encrypt stored data illustrates the negligence standard of failing to take reasonable steps to safeguard data. Put another way, covered entities must encrypt all stored data on mobile devices or plan to pay significant fines when those devices go missing or stolen.

The ability to track the mobile devices will help reduce the risk of lost ePHI. The ability to remotely delete the ePHI will further mitigate the risk of loss, though it will not assure that the protected information had not already been copied before the device was reported lost and the steps were taken to remotely erase the content.

In addition, to fulfill the obligation that ePHI remains available, the physical safeguards provide standards requiring that the covered entity take appropriate steps to provide backup systems for the ePHI to handle the range of potential risks, including intrusion by hackers and through phishing, physical incidents at the company's facilities such as a fire or water-line break, and to account for larger natural disasters such as wildfires, floods, hurricanes, blizzards, earthquakes, and similar natural disasters.

The scope of the physical safeguards must be scaled to the size of the covered entity so that it is financially and technically appropriate. The physical safeguards can also be scaled to the number of protected records, so that a small physician's group need not implement the same level of redundancy as a national hospital chain. Nonetheless, even the small physician's group must be able to restore all its records in the event of a devastating fire that destroys its office.

Through the use of business associate agreements, the smaller covered entities are able to contract with services that meet the HIPAA standards to provide the physical safeguards needed. These third parties can store encrypted ePHI in a manner that meets the physical and technical requirements, while providing restoration services that will make the data available even in the event of a national disaster or destruction of a local facility.

Technical Safeguards.

The technical safeguards provide an outline within the Security Rule but leave the details to external standards. The rules include access controls, audit controls, transmission controls, and data protections for authentication, integrity, and reliability of the data. The access controls require unique user identifiers and an emergency access procedure.

For the unique user identification, covered entities must provide login systems with unique identifiers and be able to track that information across the many different software tools and systems employed by the company. Unique user identification is part of a broader obligation to assure that the person "seeking access to electronic protected health information is the one claimed." RFID technologies, biometric scanning, multi-authentication technologies and similar approaches help assure that the person identified is the person signing on. In addition, single sign-on software provides a useful solution to both the individuation and the segmented access. Systems that log a user off after a period of inactivity are recommended. More sophisticated systems can also employ proximity sensors and RFID technologies to assure the right person is on the system and that it is not being used by a second person, following a lawful log-on.

The term "system" may also be somewhat misleading. The Security Rule requires that covered entities manage the risk for every piece of equipment that touches the ePHI. This includes the servers, desktop computers, cloud storage solutions, and non-networked devices as well as any cell phones, USB drives, laptops, tablets, readers or other pieces of equipment that might have stored, processed, or transmitted ePHI. For example, covered entities have been fined for failure to adequately dispose of ePHI created on a digital photocopier that stored copies of the documents photocopied and scanned. The hard drives in the copiers were not part of the covered entities' network. Instead, the leased photocopiers were serviced by a vendor without a business associate contract with the covered entity, and thousands of patient records were exposed on these photocopier hard drives.

Covered entities must plan for the disposal of any unnecessary copies of ePHI, including surplus digital copies created incidentally during the transmission and usage process for the data. Similarly, the hardware used in a covered entity must be erased in a manner that assures the ePHI cannot be recovered if the media was ever reused in any other context, either inside the organization or as a result of the decommissioning, lease-transfer, sale or disposal of the equipment.

Another of the technical safeguards requires emergency access procedures. To accomplish this, suggested steps include remote co-location of data and offsite failover facilities. Covered entities also typically use uninterruptible power supplies and backup generators to avoid loss of access.

The technical security requires that the administrative risk assessment is carried out to mitigate risks of all kinds. A data map showing where all ePHI resides provides an essential tool to understand where information is held. Logs and transfer reports then give the covered entity the ability to see how information flows operate in the normal operating procedures. That data flow can be mapped to identify potential vulnerabilities. Tools can be used to catch and create alerts to any anomalous activity. If an employee or intruder tries to copy data that is not normally copied, then the data mapping tool can both observe the copying and create a real-time alert. Permission controls can be used to make such copying impermissible.

Encryption remains a recommended standard under the regulations, though the failure to encrypt data at rest and in transit is increasingly an unreasonable risk. While encryption is addressable rather than required, a covered entity must encrypt ePHI "whenever deemed appropriate." This is a very passive-aggressive way of saying that encryption is required unless the encryption becomes an unreasonable burden on the operational needs for the data in a particular use case.

5. *Enforcement Rule*

Enforcement by the HHS Office for Civil Rights is authorized and regulated under the Enforcement Rule. The Enforcement Rule addresses the investigation, the bases for liability, and the framework for penalties, waivers, hearings, and appeals.

The Office for Civil Rights is authorized to conduct compliance reviews and respond to complaints through its own investigations. Generally, a complaint must be filed within 180 days from the time the person bringing the complaint became aware of the security incident, but the Office can grant extensions when the Office wishes to proceed with the investigation. At any time, the Office can also refer the matter to the Department of Justice for a criminal investigation.

As an outcome to a civil matter, the Office may determine that there has been no violation or, through the collaboration of the covered entity, may develop a plan for voluntary compliance or corrective action. Voluntary compliance and corrective actions may involve fines, but these will be lower than if a formal finding is required. In some instances, however, the covered entity remains unwilling or incapable of taking corrective action, in which case the Office issues a formal finding of violation and assesses its fine. A covered entity may request a hearing regarding the civil penalty. The hearing will be held before an HHS administrative law judge, who decides if the penalties are supported by the evidence developed by the Office for Civil Rights. State attorneys general are also authorized to bring a civil action in federal district court against an individual who violates HIPAA. The state action may occur in addition to the action taken by the Office for Civil Rights or be conducted in collaboration with that office.

Although penalties can start at as little as $100, the amount can be as high as $50,000. Each disclosed record is a separate violation. The regulations provide that the annual cap for fines is $1,500,000. If a situation is allowed to extend beyond a year, then the fine can also be increased accordingly. The fines are based on the level of diligence demonstrated by the covered entity. For those situations where the company did not know of the security incident and the exercise of reasonable diligence would not have disclosed the incident, the situation may be remedied without fines or with fines at the lowest end of the spectrum. The fines will also be lower if the company is very responsive to the Office for Civil Rights upon learning of the security incident and addresses the incident quickly.

Many situations fall into the middle category where the covered entity did not know of the vulnerability or security incident, but it should have known had it exercised reasonable care. In other words, the company was negligent in some aspect of its security. Again, the fines will range significantly. The determination of the fine may depend on the effectiveness the covered entity demonstrates in remedying the situation. The highest fines are reserved for situations where the covered entity is considered to have willfully ignored the vulnerabilities. Where the Office for Civil Rights determines there is willful neglect, the fines begin at $10,000 per incident and may result in criminal charges.

6. *Additional Considerations*

Business Associates.

Throughout the discussions in this chapter, obligations of covered entities have included the same obligations for their business associates, but business associates are a slightly different category of enterprise. The HHS explains the concept:

> A "business associate" is a person or entity that performs certain functions or activities that involve the use or disclosure of protected health information on behalf of, or provides services to, a covered entity.
>
> Examples of Business Associates.
>
> - A third party administrator that assists a health plan with claims processing.
> - A CPA firm whose accounting services to a health care provider involve access to protected health information.
> - An attorney whose legal services to a health plan involve access to protected health information.
> - A consultant that performs utilization reviews for a hospital.
> - A health care clearinghouse that translates a claim from a non-standard format into a standard transaction on behalf of a health care provider and forwards the processed transaction to a payer.
> - An independent medical transcriptionist that provides transcription services to a physician.
> - A pharmacy benefits manager that manages a health plan's pharmacist network.

These business associates are not themselves covered entities, but because they have access to PHI and ePHI they must undertake a contractual obligation to treat the protected information under HIPAA. Other common examples of covered entities are cloud computing companies and data storage companies that store, transmit, process, or recover data for covered entities. These entities do not use PHI or ePHI but their infrastructure would potentially give them access. Even if all data were encrypted, the cloud computing and data storage companies must still follow the legal and contractual obligations as business associates.

The covered entity and the business associate must enter into a written agreement that has terms and provisions to satisfy the Privacy Rule. The agreement must clearly specify the permitted uses of the PHI and otherwise restrict any other use. The covered entity must itself abide with the obligations under the Security Rule to protect the ePHI.

Although the specific steps taken may differ from the covered entity, the security steps must be sufficient to meet the HIPAA standards. For example, if the covered entity uses biometrics to assure sign-on authentication, the business associate may instead use multi-factor authentication. Both are reasonable solutions to the same authentication obligation. The covered entity and its business associate must meet the standard, but they are free to arrange different strategies to do so. When drafting these agreements, the parties should understand the difference between meeting the same obligations and adopting the same technologies.

Like the covered entity, the business associate must comply with the breach notification rules, and generally it must also notify the covered entity. The contract should give the covered entity the right to terminate the agreement if the business associate cannot cure a breach or fulfill its notice obligations. In those situations where the covered entity's business associate has had a security incident and it cannot be cured, nor the contract terminated, then the covered entity must report the situation to the Office for Civil Rights.

Not every contractor for a covered entity is a business associate. HHS gives examples of janitorial services, the U.S. Post Office, banks, credit card companies and other vendors that are providing general services to the covered entity and do not have the right to access PHI. Even though the Post Office transfers letters that contain PHI, the Post Office has no legal right to open those letters. A credit card company has information about the patient and covered entity, including the amount charged for service, but this information is in furtherance of its normal business function. As such, the regulations do not require the credit card company to become a business associate. (The bank information, however, is covered in the next chapter.)

Preemption.

HIPAA creates some interesting issues surrounding preemption. As a comprehensive federal regulation, it generally would preempt the states from legislating and regulating in the same field. Instead, HIPAA provides a basic minimum set of requirements and permits states to engage more stringent regulations. In contrast, if a state law is "contrary" to HIPAA, then that law cannot be enforced, and the laws and regulations of HIPAA govern.

Where it would be impossible for a covered entity to comply with both the state law and the HIPAA Privacy Rule, then such a law is contrary to HIPAA and cannot be enforced. The same is true if the state law presented an obligation to HIPAA. It is for this reason that HIPAA includes provisions that make permitted disclosures to law enforcement, courts, health departments and other agencies required by states. In the absence of the HIPAA permission, these state laws would be preempted.

California provides an example. The California Confidentiality of Medical Information Act (CMIA) has a broader definition of protected information than that found in HIPAA, a broader definition of health care provider, and a private right of action that allows a person to sue for a breach of the CMIA. For example, under CMIA, app developers and other companies that offer software or hardware designed to maintain medical information will be considered providers. Many health care apps do not provide actual health care treatment, meaning that they are covered under CMIA but not HIPAA for purposes of privacy regulations.

C. Genetic Information

Genetic information was first used in medical diagnostics with the tracking of chromosomes to detect Down Syndrome in the early 1950s. The chromosome holds genes, which are made up of deoxyribonucleic acid (DNA). Some of the genes make protein molecules that provide the code for all inheritable traits. Through this process, the DNA molecule produces proteins that contains the genetic code for animals, plants, and other types of organisms. Other DNA molecules do not code for proteins but are still sufficiently unique that they provide a highly accurate identifier of the person from whom the cell sample was taken.

Genes on particular chromosomes are associated with different diseases and mutations. In simple cases a mutation of a gene is directly connected to a specific disease. Often, a disease or trait is linked to dozens or more different genes. As technology has improved, forensic scientists and medical experts can now identify a great many genes that indicate a predisposition for a medical condition, and work is progressing to be able to modify a person's genetic code in a therapeutic manner that will result in correcting genetic mutations.

Beginning in 1984, the U.S. government began supporting a project to map the human genome. The project formally began in 1990 and successfully mapped the human genome in 2003 at a cost of $3 billion. The technology that developed and the information it revealed has opened the floodgates to new products, services, and medical treatments. Today the cost of a mail-in DNA test can run less than $100, though they typically cost as much as $500 for more scientifically accurate results. They can be used by consumers to establish paternity, to trace family history, or for medical investigations on genetic predispositions to medical conditions or predispositions to treatment protocols.

Beginning in 2020, genetic testing companies will become subject to CCPA for California residents and the biometric information collected will be governed by similar states' biometric laws. Depending on the consent requested by the DNA company, however, consumers will likely continue to consent to their genetic information becoming available for deidentified research and for identifiable law enforcement use.

In a number of high-profile cases, law enforcement has uploaded DNA recovered at unsolved crimes and used the familial information to obtain information leading to criminal convictions. Since these commercial databases are not protected by federal law, these agencies have had little restriction on their use.

1. CODIS

When parts of the DNA strand became scientifically replicable in the 1980s, forensic experts were able to utilize samples of DNA from saliva, blood, or hair follicles found at crime scenes and use the matches to identify individuals who were at those crimes. DNA from sperm provided conclusive evidence for many rapes and sexual assaults. In 1987, there were rape and murder convictions in both the U.K. and United States using the sperm left by the perpetrator at the crime scene. Seven years later, in 1994, Congress passed the DNA Identification Act, which authorized the FBI to create and maintain a database of DNA called "The Combined DNA Index System" (CODIS). CODIS is supplemented by federal, state, and local forensics departments. Unlike its presentation on television, CODIS only contains the DNA and reference information. It does not, itself, hold names, Social Security numbers or other personal identifiers of those in the database. Instead, the CODIS software connects the requesting and supplying departments to provide the individual information.

One part of CODIS is the National DNA Index System (NDIS), which became operational in 1998. Under the law, NDIS has a registry of DNA from convicted offenders, arrestees, legal, detainees, forensic [casework], unidentified human remains, missing persons, and relatives of missing persons.

Genes provide an excellent form of identification at crime scenes and provide the definitive analysis of paternity in cases of disputed parentage. Nearly every cell in the human body contains an identical sample of a person's DNA. Law enforcement has been successful sampling DNA from the bite mark on an attack victim, from semen, cigarette butts, and postage stamps. With modern technology, only a few cells are needed to collect a sample, including from a single hair that no longer has a root.

In theory, laboratories uploading to NDIS must remove files if a convicted felon's conviction has been overturned or when an arrestee has had charges dismissed, been acquitted, or had no charges brought within the statutory time period. There is no meaningful audit for the removal of files, however, so this unlawful data may often still be part of the NDIS. The database exceeds 14 million files.

Unlike the commercial services, the DNA Act does not allow for familial searching. Exact matches and matches with certain partial match criteria are the only permissible information that can be retrieved from a CODIS search.

2. *Genetic Information Nondiscrimination Act of 2008 (GINA)*

Given the expansion of use to which law enforcement was putting DNA, Congress recognized that there were inevitably going to be opportunities to exploit DNA for purposes that were inconsistent with the public good. In response, Congress enacted the Genetic Information Nondiscrimination Act of 2008 (GINA). The law does not seek to limit the collection or access of genetic information. Instead, it protects individuals from genetic discrimination in the areas of health insurance and employment. GINA was actually preceded by a 2000 Executive Order which prohibited the discrimination in federal employment based on genetic information.

The law prohibits employers and health insurers from using the results of genetic testing to discriminate based on the information disclosed by the genetic tests. In the most common example, this means that a company cannot refuse to hire a person who has a genetic disposition for cancer in hopes of reducing its health care costs. Similarly, a health insurer cannot list the genetic predispositions as preexisting conditions and exclude health care coverage for diseases that were identified through one's DNA.

GINA is very limited in scope. It does not extend to life insurance, long-term disability care or other forms of insurance. GINA also did not apply in the case of a California school district quarantining a young student because he tested positive for the gene associated with cystic fibrosis. According to the lawsuit information, the student did not actually have the disease, but the school district acted out of fear that he would develop the condition.

The ability of a person to provide a sample of DNA to a consumer testing agency that came from a third party rather than from the person requesting the sample creates significant privacy concerns. An employer would be precluded from conducting such a test or using the information for any adverse decisions regarding an employee as would a health insurance company. In contrast, a person could use a sample to investigate a potential spouse, to explore the medical conditions of acquaintances, or to exploit the information in furtherance of identity theft.

Genetic medical information is the most sensitive aspect of medical information, but unlike a person's medical files, the ability to access a person's genetic information is easy to obtain. Through doctor confidentiality, HIPAA, and state laws, medical records are heavily protected from disclosure and misuse. Because of its easy access, DNA does not yet have the full protection of law but the laws surrounding DNA use and misuse will continue to evolve.

Key Takeaways from This Chapter:

The health care sector requires the strongest privacy protections under U.S. law. Doctor-patient confidentiality continues to be protected under state law, but most other forms of medical privacy are governed by HIPAA.

Despite the strong privacy protections, every state has laws that create a duty for doctors, psychologists, and others to warn of threats to individuals, of health risks, transmission of certain diseases, and other information relevant to law enforcement. The duty to warn incorporated into state laws is a permitted exception under HIPAA to the nondisclosure duties of a covered entity and its business associates.

HIPAA creates a structure that has increased confidentiality at every stage of the treatment, payment and health care operations process. Hospitals, doctors' offices, pharmacies, and other covered entities have improved their systems to reduce inadvertent public disclosures. Patients are better able to receive copies of the medical records in a form that makes them useful to other health care providers. And the enforcement by the HHS Office for Civil Rights has held covered entities accountable for failing to take adequate steps to protect health records.

Things to Know:

HIPAA data security relies on the framework of physical, administrative, and technical protection measures that must be followed to meet the obligations under the Privacy Rule, the Security Rule, and the Enforcement Rule. Together these regulations establish the standards to assure that a covered entity is able to collect, process, store, and distribute its health care data in a manner that assures the integrity of the data while protecting it from theft, destruction, or unauthorized manipulation.

HIPAA does not prescribe a particular set of technical obligations. Instead, the regulations are technology neutral, so that a covered entity can continue to audit and address the needs of the institution as the business changes and the technology changes. The nature of the threats and risks continually evolve as do the needs of the covered entity and the needs of the patients. This process of regular assessments is an essential part of the ongoing process to maintain privacy and security.

Things to Think About:

Given that HIPAA continues to establish the most vigorous model for data privacy and security, could states or other regulators simply establish that the Privacy Rule and Security Rule should be followed for other types of data? What are the benefits and drawbacks to this approach?

How close has the New York SHIELD ACT or CCPA come to adopting a version of the Privacy Rule and the Security Rule?

Even if states are unwilling to adopt the Privacy Rule and the Security Rule as the legal model, should companies that deal with highly sensitive non-medical data use the HIPAA certification as a framework for their voluntary security assessments? What are the benefits and drawbacks to this approach?

CHAPTER 10

Sectoral Privacy: Banks, Financial Institutions, and Lending Activities

Historically, banking, lending, and financial organizations have been some of the most heavily regulated industries in the U.S. These include regulations regarding consumer lending and banking practices. These laws include the Fair Credit Reporting Act, the Gramm-Leach-Bliley Act, the Sarbanes-Oxley Act, and regulations under the Securities Act and Securities and Exchange Act.

In addition, since banks are where the money is stored, they are also the focus of significant criminal activity. As a result, the banking and financial sector is the second most extensively regulated sector for privacy and security. Only health care is more closely regulated. Many of the laws and regulations focused on the financial sector are designed to keep the financial system secure from criminal activity, including both the theft of consumer funds and the use of the financial systems for money laundering in furtherance of criminal and terrorist activities.

The financial regulations are enforced through a combination of agencies, primarily the Consumer Financial Protection Bureau (CFPB) and the FTC. The joint regulation was established when the financial reporting laws were restructured by the Dodd-Frank Act in 2010. The CFPB was created as part of the banking reform efforts in 2010. The Consumer Financial Protection Act requires the establishment of the CFPB to facilitate the centralized collection of, monitoring of, and response to consumer complaints regarding Consumer Financial Products and Services and the CFPB's coordination with the FTC to route complaints to the FTC, where appropriate.

The regulations assign the CFPB authority over banks, thrifts, or federal credit unions and the FTC authority over financial institutions other than the banks, thrifts, and federal credit unions. For example, in recent years, the FTC has brought actions against companies offering credit or making loans for automobile financing, car title loans, payday loans, and financing of consumer electronics. All of these companies are non-bank lenders that are still regulated in their offering of credit to consumers.

The financial industry describes these financial lending institutions as consumer reporting agencies (CRAs). The CFPB began a national review of all CRAs under its jurisdiction to assure the banks and financial institutions had sufficient physical, administrative and technical cybersecurity procedures in place to maintain confidence in the banking system. In the past decade, the regulators have relaxed the privacy notice aspects of the financial institution regulation but increased the data security obligations.

This chapter summarizes and explores the common aspects of privacy and data security law in banking, lending, and finance.

A. Gramm-Leach-Bliley Act (GLBA)

The primary law regulating the obligations of privacy and data security in the financial industry was the Gramm-Leach-Bliley Act of 1999. Much like HIPAA, the GLBA incorporated a Privacy Rule for covered financial institutions and a Safeguards Rule to assure sufficient minimum data security. Under the GLBA, financial institutions must provide annual notices to their customers that explain the information collection and data sharing practices. For certain types of the data sharing, the customers have the right to opt-out of the information sharing and the annual notice must provide a mechanism to do so.

1. *Business Significantly Engaged in Financial Activities*

Coverage under the Privacy Rule is much broader than just for banks. As provided in the Bank Holding Company Act regulations, any business that is "significantly engaged in financial activities" is covered by the regulations. Financial activities will include:

- Lending, exchanging, transferring, investing for others, or safeguarding money or securities.
- Insuring, guaranteeing, or indemnifying against loss, harm, damage, illness, disability, or death, or providing and issuing annuities, and acting as principal, agent, or broker for purposes of the foregoing, in any state.
- Providing financial, investment, or economic advisory services, including advising an investment company (as defined in section 3 of the Investment Company Act of 1940).

- Issuing or selling instruments representing interests in pools of assets permissible for a bank to hold directly.
- Underwriting, dealing in, or making a market in securities.
- Engaging in any activity closely related to banking or managing or controlling banks (domestic and foreign, if operating in the U.S.).

In addition to banks, thrifts, and credit unions, businesses subject to the GLBA will include insurance companies, financial advisors, mortgage lenders, finance companies, mortgage brokers, auto dealers, check cashers, payday lenders, wire transferors, collection agencies, credit counselors and other financial advisers, tax preparers, and providers of real estate settlement services.

Not every IOU is covered by the GLBA. The limitation is that the person or business offering financial activities is not significantly engaged. The FTC helps illustrate the distinctions:

> A storeowner or bartender who "runs a tab" for customers is not considered to be significantly engaged in financial activities, but a retailer that offers credit directly to consumers by issuing its own credit card would be covered. Second, how often does the business engage in a financial activity? A retailer that lets some consumers make payments through an occasional lay-away plan is not "significantly engaged" in a financial activity. In contrast, a business that regularly wires money to and from consumers is significantly engaged in a financial activity.

A financial institution covered by the Privacy Rule is required to provide an annual privacy notice to its customers as well as to some non-customer consumers if the financial institution collects or receives nonpublic personal information. Written in 1999, the nonpublic personal information is a much narrower category of personal information than the information now covered by CCPA, GDPR, HIPAA or the SHIELD Act.

Nonpublic personal information: "Nonpublic personal information" generally is any information that is not publicly available and that:

- a consumer provides to a financial institution to obtain a financial product or service from the institution;
- results from a transaction between the consumer and the institution involving a financial product or service; or
- a financial institution otherwise obtains about a consumer in connection with providing a financial product or service.

The FDIC compliance manual explains that nonpublic information is a narrow category.

> Information is publicly available if an institution has a reasonable basis to believe that the information is lawfully made available to the general public from government records, widely distributed media, or legally required disclosures to the general public. Examples include information in a telephone book or a publicly recorded document, such as a mortgage or security interest filing.

Unlike most state privacy laws, the use of general public records, distributed media, mortgage filings, and other documents eliminate the obligation of these financial institutions to provide a notice. Still, nonpublic personal information does extend to the customer list, since the information that the person is associated with that financial institution is nonpublic information. The nonpublic information also includes the Social Security numbers, credit scores, computer cookies and other data tracking, and any information generated by the financial institution about the consumer.

The regulations only apply to personal transactions rather than business transactions. A consumer is an individual who obtains or has obtained a financial product or service from a financial institution that is to be used primarily for personal, family, or household purposes. A customer, in contrast, is a consumer who has a continuing relationship with the financial institution where the institution provides one or more financial products or services to the consumer. The real distinction is the ongoing relationship between the parties. Consumers may be entitled to privacy notices at the time they interact with the financial institution, but customers are entitled to privacy notices both at the time they first interact with the financial institution and annually thereafter.

2. Annual Privacy Notices

In 1999, the annual privacy notice requirement under GLBA changed the regulatory landscape for national consumer privacy. In the decades following its introduction, the opt-out regulation has had very limited continuing relevance. The content of the privacy notice is largely dictated by regulations and a standardized form published by the regulators for use by the financial institutions. The current model form is formatted into a series of boxes, with most of the information provided in a very superficial manner. At the top are three boxes explaining the why, what, and how of the disclosure. The brackets indicate the information to be filled in by each financial institution.

> Why?—Financial companies choose how they share your personal information. Federal law gives consumers the right to limit some but not all sharing. Federal law also

requires us to tell you how we collect, share, and protect your personal information. Please read this notice carefully to understand what we do.

What?—The types of personal information we collect and share depend on the product or service you have with us. This information can include:

- Social Security number and [income]
- [account balances] and [payment history]
- [credit history] and [credit scores]

How?—All financial companies need to share customers' personal information to run their everyday business. In the section below, we list the reasons financial companies can share their customers' personal information; the reasons [name of financial institution] chooses to share; and whether you can limit this sharing.

The second section of the form includes a table that lists seven generic explanations of data sharing, along with columns to show whether or not the financial institution shares this information with affiliates or other third parties and a column to indicate whether the customer can opt out of the sharing. Beginning in 2014, the CFPB revised its rules to allow financial institutions to provide the annual privacy notice disclosure by merely posting the annual notice on its web site.

The forms simplify the reporting considerably, informing the customer that control over their nonpublic personal information is limited to nonaffiliates and the marketing by affiliates. There are no opt-out rights for direct marketing or for the operational needs of the financial institutions.

The form notes that state laws may be much more restrictive. The tension between the GLBA and the obligations under CCPA and

GDPR will become very significant for those financial institutions that do not receive federal preemption. While the banks, thrifts, and federal credit unions are usually exempt from the state privacy laws, the other financial institutions will need to provide data privacy in a manner that recognizes both the state and federal approach to privacy.

3. *Safeguards Rule*

In contrast with the diminishing role for the GLBA Privacy Rule, the Safeguards Rule was substantially updated in 2019 to increase the expectations of information security across the wide array of financial institutions subject to the regulations. As with many other regulatory regimes, the Safeguards Rule requires a financial institution to "develop, implement, and maintain a comprehensive information security program that consists of the administrative, technical, and physical safeguards the financial institution uses to access, collect, distribute, process, protect, store, use, transmit, dispose of, or otherwise handle customer information."

Each financial institution must develop a written security plan appropriate to the size and complexity of the institution that is reasonably designed to ensure the security and confidentiality of customer information. The security plan must protect the consumer information from unauthorized access, improper use, destruction, or other degradation that could result in substantial harm or inconvenience to any customer. The Safeguards Rule focuses on "reasonably foreseeable internal and external risks to the security, confidentiality, and integrity of customer information that could result in the unauthorized disclosure, misuse, alteration, destruction, or other compromise of such information." To protect from these risks, each financial institution's written plan must include provisions on these three areas:

1. Employee training and management;

2. Information systems, including network and software design, as well as information processing, storage, transmission, and disposal; and

3. Detecting, preventing, and responding to attacks, intrusions, or other systems failures.

The Safeguards Rule identifies the ongoing obligations to create an appropriate security plan:

> The financial institution must then design and implement safeguards to control the risks identified through the risk assessment, and must regularly test or otherwise monitor the effectiveness of the safeguards' key controls, systems, and procedures.
>
> The financial institution is also required to evaluate and adjust its information security program in light of the results of this testing and monitoring, as well as any material changes in its operations or business arrangements, or any other circumstances that it knows or has reason to know may have a material impact on its information security program. The financial institution must also designate an employee or employees to coordinate the information security program.
>
> Finally, the Safeguards Rule requires financial institutions to take reasonable steps to select and retain service providers that are capable of maintaining appropriate safeguards for customer information and require those service providers by contract to implement and maintain such safeguards.

Covered financial institutions are required to have a comprehensive written security program detailing the administrative, technical, and physical steps needed to provide the reasonable security required. Each is required to identify a qualified individual to serve as administrator for security officer such as a Chief Information Security Officer (CISO) and a more senior executive responsible for the oversight of the CISO.

The regulations provide, however, a small carve-out for institutions with fewer than 5,000 consumer records. While these smaller companies still fall within the rule, they are excused from the mandatory written risk assessment; continuous monitoring or annual penetration testing and biannual vulnerability assessment; written incident response plan; and annual written report by the CISO.

The requirements to meet the administrative, technical, and physical obligations are less detailed than those specified under HIPAA, which is appropriate considering the broad range of different businesses that fall within the federal definition of financial institution. The regulators also wished to avoid creating a check-the-box security system that could be easily adopted but then not followed. Financial institutions can look to the practices under HIPAA, the SHIELD Act, and other national published standards to meet the requirements under the updated Safeguards Rule.

Although the updated Safeguards Rule is not technically a checklist, it describes the steps needed for comprehensive security in a very useful manner. It can be read as a primer on data security, including a detailed response plan. The updated Safeguards Rule requires much more specific compliance.

The various financial regulators, including the CFPB and FTC, are reviewing the efforts of the financial institutions to implement the updated safeguards, adopt the required written plans, appoint the required personnel, and institutionalize the testing and assessment protocols under the plan. Given the broad range of companies that may be considered financial institutions, the GLBA revisions will substantially improve data security across the country.

B. Fair Credit Reporting Act (FCRA)

The Fair Credit Reporting Act (FCRA) was passed as the first federal law to regulate the use of personal information by businesses. Although it was enacted in 1970, it has been updated significantly to keep it at the forefront of consumer protection for credit reporting. The FCRA was introduced in Chapter 4 because it plays an important role in protecting potential employees and current employees from the misuse of their financial information in the context of employment decisions, but the FCRA reaches well beyond this role. In addition to the rights under the FCRA, many states supplement the law with additional state law protections, providing additional consumer protections.

The primary purpose of the FCRA is to protect consumers regarding the information supplied to Equifax, Experian, and TransUnion—the three major consumer credit reporting agencies—and the information provided by these three agencies to businesses for credit, employment, and other uses. In addition to the three consumer credit reporting agencies, the FCRA also regulates certain aspects of information disclosed by data brokers, employment screening companies, housing screening companies, and other reporting agencies. Most of these companies also fall within the financial institution definition of the GLBA, requiring that they follow the Privacy Rule and Safeguards Rule.

The FCRA goes well beyond mere privacy protection. It provides affirmative protections for consumers about how a person's personal information is reported. These rights include the right to receive a copy of the information collected by the credit agency, the right to dispute incomplete and inaccurate information, and the right to delete unverifiable information and out of date negative information. Consumers also have the right to receive a free credit score, to obtain a free copy of their report each year from each of the three reporting agencies, and the right to be notified in every instance where a company takes an adverse action based on the information in the consumer report.

The FCRA is also central to efforts to limit identity theft. The law provides that anyone has the right to place a "security freeze" on his or her account. This prohibits the consumer reporting agency from issuing any information or credit report without the express authorization of the account holder. The security freeze makes it harder for identity thieves to use the information they have gathered to open new accounts for obtaining credit or making unauthorized purchases. Consumers can instead choose to put fraud alerts on the accounts, which requires businesses to take additional steps to verify the identity of the consumer but does not actually freeze the reporting of the credit bureau.

The FCRA provides how a credit report can be used and where its use is prohibited. The permitted uses include the following:

- Applications for credit, insurance, and rentals for personal, family or household purposes.
- Renewal or updating of accounts by companies with existing relationships with the consumer.
- Pre-employment and employment decisions, hiring, promotion, reassignment or retention, when the employer has obtained consent from the applicant or employee.
- Professional licensure.
- Court orders, including grand jury subpoenas.
- Consumer transactions where there is a legitimate business need to complete the transaction.
- Child support payment determinations.
- Law enforcement access in limited cases for terrorism and counterintelligence investigations.

This list provides the exclusive purposes for which a credit report can be used. Although some of these categories might be considered rather broad, it goes a long way to restrict the use of the information. The credit reporting agencies cannot sell the information to companies to financially vet and prescreen their customers.

The FCRA does not include certain basic information in the restrictions on data sharing, including name, address, and contact information. It also allows credit card companies to purchase lists of consumers who are pre-qualified for credit cards.

In addition, while the FCRA gives consumers the legal right to review and correct their credit reports, there are many studies and investigations suggesting that as many as 75% of all credit reports have some errors in them. If a credit reporting agency does not accept the evidence that there is an error in the report, it can continue to use the disputed information. As a result, the FCRA continues to have a mixed impact on the actual consumer experience.

C. Regulations Under the Securities Act and the Securities and Exchange Act

As data privacy and cybersecurity have become increasingly important to the operations of both small and large businesses, the importance of the security of a company's data has become increasingly material to its investors. Since 1933, there has been federal legislation to protect investors from fraud, material misrepresentations, and lack of information related to publicly traded securities. These laws began with the Securities Act of 1933 and the Securities and Exchange Act of 1934. There had already been some state laws, and even today federal laws on securities regulation are supplemented by state laws. Nearly every securities law is implemented through additional regulations that carry additional obligations at both the state and federal level.

Broadly speaking, the national system of securities regulation is separated into the federal model that emphasizes the disclosure of all material information regarding publicly traded companies and the state approach which includes protecting residents from unfair securities offerings. A company that registers federally is then exempt from the state filing obligations.

At the federal regulatory level, the government requires that the issuing company provide full and accurate disclosure of all material information for the prospective purchaser of the securities. This means that for a stock to be publicly traded, it must first file a prospectus that contains financial information and information about the management and operations of the enterprise that is sufficiently detailed to allow a reasonable investor to make an informed decision regarding the decision whether or not to invest in that stock. Once a company is publicly traded, it must file certain quarterly and annual reports, as well as report on certain changes in its ownership or operations.

For companies that are owned by a smaller group of investors, the federal registration system does not typically apply. Instead, the securities are likely to be regulated under state law. State laws often require that companies selling securities do not take advantage of the buyers through state regulations regarding the financial valuation of the companies.

In practice, there are many gradations between a small company owned by its key ownership and a large, publicly traded company. States require a balance of disclosure as well, and there are categories of offerings that can allow a company to file federally without being a fully registered public company. These distinctions are beyond the scope of this introduction.

For the purposes of data privacy and securities regulations, the regulatory focus has been on the duties of publicly traded companies. The Securities and Exchange Commission (SEC or Commission) has stated that "cybersecurity risks pose grave threats to investors, our capital markets, and our country. . . . It is critical that public companies take all required actions to inform investors about material cybersecurity risks and incidents in a timely fashion, including those companies that are subject to material cybersecurity risks but may not yet have been the target of a cyber-attack."

The regulations include duties of the publicly traded companies to disclose their data security profile in their formal reporting documents and to put "internal accounting controls" in place to protect against fraud and misuse of financial and other data. Finally, the SEC has raised concerns about insider trading and the actual or perceived misuse of confidential, inside information that corporate leaders gain during cybersecurity incidents.

1. Enterprise-Wide Risk Management

The SEC has become very focused on cybersecurity. In its 2018 guidance, it made clear that it evaluates "how the board of directors engages with management on cybersecurity issues allow[s] investors to assess how a board of directors is discharging its risk oversight responsibility in this increasingly important area." As a result of this direct oversight, the SEC has become an additional voice in requiring comprehensive administrative, technical, and physical security measures for all publicly traded companies.

This effort does not have the same force of law as does HIPAA or GLBA. Companies that provide financial services are covered by the GLBA and other specific regulations that require specific security measures. For those outside of those regulations, the SEC has merely "encouraged adoption" of comprehensive policies for cybersecurity. The SEC does have some regulatory authority under the framework of disclosure controls to insist that cybersecurity is part of the disclosure control process.

The SEC further notes that issuers are required to "devise and maintain a system of internal accounting controls sufficient to provide reasonable assurances that transactions are executed with, or that access to company assets is permitted only with, management's general or specific authorization." These systems are at risk of breach as part of a security incident, providing additional authority for the SEC to mandate security measures.

2. *Duties to Disclose Cybersecurity Risks*

Since 2011, the SEC has required companies to provide public information on cybersecurity risk and security incidents. The SEC acknowledged that data security was not listed in the text of the legislation, but since significant cybersecurity risks and known security incidents were material to the investors regarding the financial status of the company and its managerial operations, reporting companies were required to provide meaningful information.

Public companies generally resisted the obligation to report on cybersecurity risks, with most providing only the vaguest of disclosures. Some companies believed the background risks of cybersecurity were everywhere, so that it was not a material factor for any particular company. Other companies asserted that providing any form of detailed information would only assist criminal actors in their efforts to hack the public companies.

The SEC responded with additional guidance in 2018 to make clear that this obligation continues to be a priority of the Commission. The SEC pointed to the quarterly and annual reports, in which companies must "make disclosure regarding their business and operations, risk factors, legal proceedings, management's discussion and analysis of financial condition and results of operations ("MD&A"), financial statements, disclosure controls and procedures, and corporate governance." The SEC guidance has established that "material cybersecurity risks and incidents that trigger disclosure obligations."

The SEC went on to remind companies that the laws require that "registration statements must disclose all material facts required to be stated therein or necessary to make the statements therein not misleading." The failure to include the known cybersecurity risks and security incidents would make the other statements about the company inaccurate and could give rise to liability under the regulations as well as to shareholders.

> The Commission considers omitted information to be material if there is a substantial likelihood that a reasonable investor would consider the information important in making an investment decision or that disclosure of the omitted information would have been viewed by the reasonable investor as having significantly altered the total mix of information available.
>
> In determining their disclosure obligations regarding cybersecurity risks and incidents, companies generally weigh, among other things, the potential materiality of any identified risk and, in the case of incidents, the importance of any compromised information and of the impact of the incident on the company's operations. The materiality of cybersecurity risks or incidents depends upon their nature, extent, and potential magnitude, particularly as they relate to any compromised information or the business and scope of company operations.

The SEC noted that the materiality of a security incident is not measured merely by the size of the data breach. As noted in Chapter

6, there are many costs associated with a security incident beyond the cost of forensic investigations, customer notification, and enhanced security. A breach that results in a significant loss of customers can cripple a company, and that is information that the shareholders or potential shareholders have a right to know. The SEC agrees:

> The materiality of cybersecurity risks and incidents also depends on the range of harm that such incidents could cause. This includes harm to a company's reputation, financial performance, and customer and vendor relationships, as well as the possibility of litigation or regulatory investigations or actions, including regulatory actions by state and federal governmental authorities and non-U.S. authorities.

One type of information that public companies must disclose is "risk factors" that make potential investment in a company's securities speculative or risky. The SEC suggests that companies treat cybersecurity risk as one of the risk factors, if that is an accurate description for the company. The SEC provided a series of factors that could elevate the risk for a company:

- the occurrence of prior cybersecurity incidents, including their severity and frequency;
- the probability of the occurrence and potential magnitude of cybersecurity incidents;
- the adequacy of preventative actions taken to reduce cybersecurity risks and the associated costs, including, if appropriate, discussing the limits of the company's ability to prevent or mitigate certain cybersecurity risks;
- the aspects of the company's business and operations that give rise to material cybersecurity

risks and the potential costs and consequences of such risks, including industry-specific risks and third party supplier and service provider risks;

- the costs associated with maintaining cybersecurity protections, including, if applicable, insurance coverage relating to cybersecurity incidents or payments to service providers;
- the potential for reputational harm;
- existing or pending laws and regulations that may affect the requirements to which companies are subject relating to cybersecurity and the associated costs to companies; and
- litigation, regulatory investigation, and remediation costs associated with cybersecurity incidents.

In meeting their disclosure obligations, companies may need to disclose previous or ongoing cybersecurity incidents or other past events in order to place discussions of these risks in the appropriate context.

Cybersecurity risks could also play a role in the discussion of management's discussion and analysis of financial condition and results of operations for the company. The disclosure regulations require the management's discussion and analysis to cover cybersecurity if it materially affects the company's "products, services, relationships with customers or suppliers, or competitive conditions." The regulations also require disclosure of "the costs and other consequences of cybersecurity incidents, and the risks of potential cybersecurity incidents," In addition, the company must discuss the financial burden associated with both the cost of security compliance and the cost of a security incident if those costs become material to the financial statements.

Finally, the SEC noted that the duty to provide material, accurate information also includes the duty to correct any prior information that was not accurate. The SEC stated that security incidents often take considerable time to investigate, and the scope of many incidents is found to increase as the investigation proceeds. Publicly traded companies, therefore, have an ongoing duty to correct earlier statements if they materially misstated the situation, even if the company acted reasonably in disclosing the information at the time of the disclosure. The duty to disclose cybersecurity risks and security incidents remains an ongoing obligation.

3. Challenges of Insider Trading

Another important additional consideration is that officers, directors and other insiders are prohibited from insider trading, by using material, nonpublic information to trade the securities of their company to make a profit or avoid a loss in the securities. The SEC has stated that the knowledge of a cybersecurity incident or other material risk of a security incident could be the basis for a claim of insider trading. The SEC has explained that

> Public companies should have policies and procedures in place to (1) guard against directors, officers, and other corporate insiders taking advantage of the period between the company's discovery of a cybersecurity incident and public disclosure of the incident to trade on material nonpublic information about the incident, and (2) help ensure that the company makes timely disclosure of any related material nonpublic information.

The SEC noted that companies should have statements and procedures to identify the risk of insider trading while in the midst of cybersecurity incidents. It has encouraged companies to adopt preventative measures to avoid both actual insider trading and the avoidance of the appearance for insider trading. As publicly traded companies recognize the need for these steps, the risk of inappropriate trading during cyber incidents can be reduced.

The avoidance of insider trading when the senior executives are aware of cybersecurity incidents can be very challenging because some security incidents take a long time to investigate and the information often changes as the forensic evidence helps draw a more complete picture of the intrusion. Companies are often quick to publicly announce that a modestly sized breach occurred that did not disclose the most sensitive of information. During the investigations, the evidence becomes clearer that the scope of the incident was larger, and the nature of the information accessed was much more sensitive. If a corporate insider makes a stock trade after the first announcement but prior to the final disclosure, there is certainly an appearance of insider trading. If the corporate insider used information about the investigation to make the trade, then there would be actual insider trading, which is illegal under the state and federal securities laws.

D. Sarbanes-Oxley Act of 2002

The complement to the SEC's heightened data privacy and cybersecurity protection for publicly traded companies can be found in the Sarbanes-Oxley Act (SOX) of 2002, which was adopted in the wake of massive accounting scandals involving publicly traded companies. The original goal of SOX was to stop the misuse of accounting information, particularly as it applied to the documents supplied by publicly traded companies. As a result, SOX applies both to publicly traded companies and to accounting firms. The law has even greater influence. Because of its mandates for accounting firms, the law has influenced the general practice of accountancy, which has then reshaped business practices in every other sector of the economy.

Although SOX was enacted to protect against financial tampering, the law was written with the understanding that financial records are just another form of data. All data must be protected from tampering, destruction, or manipulation. As a result, SOX has emerged as an important security regulation even though it has no explicit privacy component. Because it covers all publicly traded companies, it provides a strong regulatory basis for the SEC to demand that all reporting and data information systems are sufficiently robust to protect all information from security incidents.

SOX requires that all publicly traded companies report to the SEC regarding their implementation and reporting of internal accounting controls. These internal accounting controls, in turn, include protections for all financial and other information collected by the company to assure that there are adequate protections from any tampering, manipulation, interference, or destruction of the information used by the company. Although the 2002 law does not describe unauthorized access in the same language as the Safeguards Rule or other more recent legislation, its required internal accounting controls provide the same types of security obligations from internal and external misuse or threat.

SOX implements its audit control requirements for cybersecurity under two primary provisions. The first is section 404 regarding "management assessment of internal controls." Internal controls are described as "the policies and procedures that financial institutions establish to reduce risks and ensure they meet operating, reporting, and compliance objectives," which are essentially the administrative procedures required under the HIPAA Privacy Rule and other regulatory regimes.

The Federal Deposit Insurance Corporation (FDIC) has developed a comprehensive guide for Internal Routine and Controls. As explained by the FDIC, "internal control programs should be designed to ensure organizations operate effectively, safeguard assets, produce reliable financial records, and comply with applicable laws and regulations." The FDIC organizes the internal controls into five elements:

- Control environments,
- Risk assessments,
- Control activities,
- Information and communication, and
- Monitoring.

Although these procedures were originally contemplated to reduce the risk of fraud in financial institutions and publicly traded companies, the same efforts to reduce fraud and theft apply to reduce privacy violations, hacking, unauthorized use of data, and other cybersecurity incidents.

Under section 404, public companies must provide an Internal Control Report as part of the company's annual financial report. The company must have an internal control structure that is "adequate" to protect the company from the foreseeable internal and external risks. The term adequate should not be considered a low standard. Like HIPAA and GLBA, the SOX requirements establish comprehensive obligations to provide sufficient administrative, technical, and physical security to assure that protected information is secure. In addition, the management of the company must describe its operations in the annual report and report any issues or shortcomings with the protections and systems employed by the company.

In addition, the public accounting firm serving as the external auditor for the company must provide its certification or attestation regarding the accuracy of the company management's statements that internal accounting controls are in place, operational and effective. Although the primary focus is on financial systems, all related cybersecurity issues are also covered. The auditor will require all information, including disclosure of cybersecurity risks and incidents to provide its comprehensive audit and report.

The second SOX provision is section 302, regarding "corporate responsibility for financial reports." To assure that a publicly traded company takes its obligations to have appropriate security, the law requires the chief executive officer (CEO) and the chief financial officer (CFO) of the company to certify that all records submitted to the SEC by the company are complete and accurate.

There are penalties for failing to fulfill the corporate obligations, including fines, loss of the right to be listed on a public stock exchange, or the invalidation of Directors and Officers (D&O) insurance policies. The failure of the CEO or CFO to submit accurate information can also result in direct, personal liability. Willful violations of the act can result in fines of up to $5 million and up to 20 years in jail.

Through the obligations under SOX, publicly traded companies and public accounting firms provide another important sector for increased data privacy and cybersecurity regulation. SEC regulation through SOX and the securities laws helps expand the umbrella of regulatory protection so that companies of almost any significant size are obligated by one or more laws to provide some level of data protection and cybersecurity.

Key Takeaways from This Chapter:

The financial industry is among the most heavily regulated industries and one of the first to have widespread data privacy protection. As concerns about cybersecurity increased in the past decade, many federal agencies have expanded the regulatory obligations to provide robust cybersecurity and to increase corporate transparency about cybersecurity issues.

The GLBA provides only modest consumer protection since it is an opt-out privacy regulation that has many exemptions for use of customer data for non-marketing purposes. For financial institutions outside the core group of banks, thrifts, and credit unions, state privacy laws will not be preempted, and these will often provide more robust consumer privacy protection.

In addition to the GLBA, the FCRA provides significant consumer privacy protection regarding the use of reported information and the ability of consumers to acquire, monitor, and correct their credit reports. These efforts have improved the protections for the general public.

The GLBA Safeguards Rule illustrates a sharp contrast with the Privacy Rule. The Safeguards Rule mandates that financial institutions undertake significant data security obligations. The federal regulatory approach to data security of financial institutions has obligated these companies to undergo very significant security improvements.

In addition, the regulations under federal securities laws have also increased the obligation to improve data security and to report significant events such as data breaches in a candid and timely manner. These regulations have improved the overall data security profile of the financial services industry while highlighting the constant challenge for maintaining data integrity and protection.

Things to Know:

The nature of federal financial regulation has focused primarily on stability and accuracy rather than consumer protection. SOX was enacted to assure that fraudulent activity by either insiders or by third parties would be detected early, before it could grow to destroy a company. The protections to improve auditing and detect fraud also cover steps needed to detect data breaches. Both SOX and GLBA were enacted before data breach incidents had grown to be a significant business risk, but the regulations authorized under these laws have enabled federal regulators to help improve data security as part of the broader effort to protect from financial fraud.

Each of the banking models adopts a similar approach to the health care models, requiring companies have the appropriate range of administrative, technical, and physical safeguards needed to protect the data stored and used. These regulations allow for the particular strategies to be appropriate to the size and complexity of the enterprise while requiring that all the components for an appropriate data security strategy is created and followed.

Things to Think About:

As noted in Chapter 2, the third party doctrine allows the government to review bank records using a subpoena rather than a search warrant. In contrast, the banking laws require that financial institutions and public companies adopt strong measures to protect the information they collect regarding their customers from misuse. Does the third party doctrine continue to make sense in light of the reasonable expectation Congress has established for financial records?

Many of the regulations for financial privacy are based on laws that were intended to improve financial integrity of the banking system and greater accountability. To what extent does Congress give regulators latitude to evolve regulations for associated purposes? Should Congress be more responsible for the changes made via regulation?

The adoption of the GDPR, CCPA, and SHIELD Act to large segments of American business has likely shifted the regulation of consumer privacy from a sectoral approach to a more general approach, but each of these laws differs from the others and impacts different companies. What will be the next stage of consumer privacy regulation? Will it expand the sectoral approach to privacy or the more general approach of consumer protection?

CHAPTER 11

Final Considerations on Privacy

Although this book is a short and happy guide to privacy and cybersecurity, it introduces a dizzying array of concepts, laws, regulations, policies, and practices. Nonetheless, there are important general themes that help government, business, and individuals address the rapid changes to privacy policy in the United States and across the globe.

A. Returning to the Big Picture

The concept of privacy has been part of Western law and culture since ancient times. Samuel Warren and Louis Brandeis worked diligently in their 1890 law review article, "The Right to Privacy," to establish that the right of privacy was not new, just enforced using a variety of labels. They pointed to the leading torts treatise by Judge Thomas Cooley that "the right to one's person may be said to be a right of complete immunity: to be let alone."

At the constitutional level, the right of privacy is an essential part of the First Amendment's protection for speech, religion, and association; the Fourth Amendment's protection against unwarranted searches and seizures; the Fifth Amendment's right against self-incrimination; and the Ninth Amendment's reservation of rights to the people. Privacy underlies the decisional autonomy individuals have over their marital choices, sexual practices, and means of worship.

Governmental restrictions.

Despite the fundamental nature of privacy, the right has been met with mixed regard by legislatures and courts. In the case of the government, for example, it may be that the constitutional protections against the government are often challenged by elected and appointed officials who do not wish to have their power restricted. This is not out of malice. These elected officials and government employees want to fulfill their professional duties. Law enforcement wants to collect the information needed to arrest and convict criminals. Even if the laws represent good public policy, constitutional restrictions and statutory limitations make this work harder for the law enforcement officer. Warrant requirements protect society from abuse of power, but few individual officers believe that they would abuse their authority if given the ability to exercise their own judgment.

Where constitutional protections were not recognized by the courts, Congress and state legislatures stepped in to establish restrictions on the use of invasive technology to surveil suspects in criminal cases. Wiretap laws and laws restricting the recording of private conversations were passed to restrict the government's ability to eavesdrop on suspects. The Supreme Court recognized the modern smart phone has become the twenty-first century equivalent of the home for purposes of a search, requiring a warrant supported by probable cause.

Common law and sectoral privacy.

The initial hesitancy to expand privacy laws also helps to explain the sectoral approach to privacy adopted in the United States throughout the twentieth century. The earliest cases enforcing privacy rights were those categorized as rights of publicity cases. Requiring business to pay for the exploitation of a person's privacy or publicity right was a simple extension of requiring that a company pay for the exploitation of a person's labor or their intellectual property. It took more than another century before public policy began to recognize the value of the information about the individual, the consumer, as a separate and valuable commodity.

Today we recognize the tremendous economic benefit companies gain by utilizing the private information of their customers. Nonetheless, there have been no significant efforts to shift the economic benefits from the companies to the individuals. The most recent laws are beginning to empower customers to refuse to let their private information be commercialized, but the laws have not yet suggested a property right or compensation model for the exploitation of a consumer's personal information.

Instead, the sectoral approach to privacy emerged in response to the areas in society where the violations of a person's privacy could result in the greatest harm. The doctor-patient relationship had always been protected by confidentiality, and those social norms were expanded upon with state laws and through HIPAA. HIPAA emerged as the most comprehensive regulatory regime for personal privacy and led the way for federal regulation of data security as well.

In the financial sector, the regulations began with the FCRA and the use of credit reports for unintended purposes. GLBA expanded the role for privacy information as well, but to a much less significant extent than in health care.

The potential for harm also led to specific laws aimed at protecting the privacy of children under the age of thirteen. Through COPPA, the FTC has expanded its regulation regarding advertising, mandatory disclosures, and parental consent. The FTC has also begun to increase significantly the size of fines and the intensity of enforcement action to make these privacy regulations meaningful and effective.

Data security.

The need for comprehensive data security overlaps with the need to maintain the privacy of sensitive information collected by government and business. There are many other reasons government agencies and businesses need to have confidence that the information they collect is valid, reliable, and stable. The value of the information collected disappears if the information is unreliable. Decisions based on unreliable data also become unreliable.

In the context of privacy, there is a special obligation to keep information collected secure. If a government agency or business is obligated not to share or sell personal information, then it also has an obligation not to let third parties gain access to the information accidentally. In the health care and financial sectors, among others, federal law mandates that there is robust security to assure that the privacy protections are not undermined through the carelessness of the companies holding the information or through the criminal conduct of third parties.

In addition, the FTC and various states require data security as a necessity to meet any information privacy obligations, including both COPPA requirements and adherence to a company's own information privacy policy. Information is not private if it is free for anyone to peruse or copy.

In the next two sections of this chapter, this book provides some suggestions on how to follow these rules and lessons to protect the privacy of oneself and one's customers and employees.

B. Running a Data Secure Business

The FTC has published very useful guides instructing small businesses on how to manage a secure business to avoid violating the privacy rights of customers and to avoid the various attacks and scams that could harm the small business. Together with the lessons from this book, a business owner should be able to operate a secure and productive business. As noted in many of the data security regulations, one size does not fit all. Some business operations rely on data analytics much more heavily than others and some business models incorporate sharing information much more actively than others.

While there are many differences among businesses, there are fundamentals essential for every business. These eight key lessons for small business are simple, and they provide an outline that will help most businesses improve customer privacy and data security without sacrificing the use of information helpful to the company. Although these key lessons are simple to outline, they require diligence to maintain:

- *Be transparent about privacy practices.* If the company sells or shares customer information, disclose that clearly. Most consumers don't object most of the time.
- *Only make promises that the company can keep.* Some information sharing is outside the control of the business, so do not over-promise the company's ability to restrict disclosure of private information.

- *Avoid collecting information that is not used.* The company is responsible for the data security of all personal information it collects, both from third parties and from misuse within the business. If information is not collected, it cannot be lost, stolen, or misused.
- *Institute appropriate administrative, technical, and physical data security systems.* The data security used for each business must be appropriate for the size of the company, but all companies need physical security, appropriate policies, training, audits, and assessments. At a minimum, this includes always installing security updates and planning on financing updates and upgrades to key software tools.
- *Provide employees both their rights as consumers and with the protections for employees.* Legal protections provided to employees are in addition to the protections afforded to all consumers. Even the smallest company needs a clear, written employee manual and needs to follow it.
- *Work closely with the PCI security, staying current on all security updates.* Small businesses are often targeted around credit card payment systems. Keeping the pay terminals and other payment systems up-to-date will significantly reduce exposure to theft and loss.
- *Manage vendors and contractors carefully.* Small businesses rely on their contracts with service providers to enable them to compete. But these contracts come with risks for privacy and security. Companies must be diligent in picking the companies

with which to do business and focused on the contractual terms of these relationships.

- *Do not implement any policy you would not want to see on the front page of the local newspaper.* The best advice for small business is to approach its business model and its customers as a tight-knit community. If there is a practice that would embarrass its owners when made public, then the owners should choose another approach. Small business is the financial and social backbone of America, so the business owners should always stand proud in how they adopt and implement policies.

These eight rules provide companies a useful strategy for protecting the privacy of the business customers, maintaining trust between the customer and the company, and minimizing the risk of data breach or other liability. While nothing is foolproof, these rules create an approach that should minimize risk. Each of these is discussed below.

1. Be Transparent About Privacy Practices

Some companies collect no personal information from their customers. They operate on a purely cash basis and have few records. Other companies investigate the profile of each customer to tailor particular recommendations based on that customer's prior purchases through the company and through information gathered from third parties. Most companies operate somewhere in between. Corporate websites track the advertising used to find the landing page and use trackers to understand each customer's use of the website. Physical stores use cameras to observe movements in the store.

To the extent that information is collected and identified with an individual consumer, the business should include that in its posted privacy policy. Most customers barely glance at these disclosures, so companies rarely get in trouble by including too much information. On the other hand, if something goes wrong and the company did not disclose that it collected the data that was later stolen, there can be many negative consequences.

This also requires that companies understand how their technologies work. A company may hire a third party service provider as web host. The web host may be collecting data for its own use that the company does not utilize, but the customer is still having personal information gathered and sold because of the small business.

Companies must also implement do-not-track technology and make customers' profiles available to them, at least where the law requires these additional steps.

2. Only Make Promises That the Company Can Keep

Some companies tried to publish very simple privacy statements: "We never disclose your personal information." But that statement is unlikely to be true, since governments have rights to information in certain criminal matters, companies are subject to subpoenas in civil litigation, and other regulatory demands may arise. Companies may also share customer information with their service providers, cloud storage companies, online shopping cart services, and other vendors that enable the small business to operate effectively online. In addition, companies often change their marketing strategies as they evolve.

A company must be sure that any promises it makes about use of information is consistent with the use to which the company's vendors and partners have access and make use of the information. The types of information collected may also vary significantly depending on the nature of the engagement. For companies that have a presence on Facebook, Instagram, Twitter, or other online services, the online service company will have its own privacy policy and relationship with the customer. Statements in the privacy policy should recognize that information collected by the company through social media will be subject to the social media site policies as well.

As a result, most companies are collecting and sharing far more information than they realize. It is very important to know what is being collected and shared. Once a company knows what information it has, it can make reasonable promises about the use of that information.

3. Avoid Collecting Information That Is Not Used

Accurate data are extremely helpful for decision making. Consumer patterns and preferences, changes in tastes and attitudes, demographic shifts, pricing information, and much other information can be learned from the management of certain data points about the business. When the information is important to business decisions, companies should make efforts to keep the information up to date and accurate.

In contrast, companies have the ability to collect considerable amounts of information that does not help decision making. This is particularly true for the personally identifiable information about customers.

The single best way for a small business to avoid liability regarding customer information is to avoid collecting the customer's personal information. Many businesses do very well by minimizing the customer information collected and keeping all tracking information separate from personally identifiable information. Unless there is a present business purpose for collecting certain types of information, do not collect the information.

Once data are collected, the data must be stored, maintained, and updated. There is a cost for man-hours and for technology to collect information. When a business case develops for tracking a particular kind of information, then that data should be tracked. But collecting data with the thought that there might someday be a business use is very insufficient.

Consumer data become stale quite quickly. Emails and addresses change, customers age, product lines evolve, and the information that can be learned becomes inaccurate. Companies that collect data often find they are making decisions based on outdated information or information that becomes misleading because of the aging of the data.

4. *Institute Appropriate Administrative, Technical, and Physical Data Security Systems*

Every business must develop and adopt the appropriate set of safeguards necessary to protect the company. For many small businesses, they run everything from a single desktop computer or single server. The loss of the central business computer could mean the loss of all orders, inventory tracking, customer lists, and personnel records. If it were to crash without backups or become infected with malware, the loss of central business computer would become the point of failure for all business operations. Whether the company runs on a single computer or operates in a complex cloud-based infrastructure, the company must manage its infrastructure to eliminate the possibility that a single point of failure could shut down the business.

Physical safeguards must include locked print files and/or encrypted storage of key documents; controlled and limited access to sensitive files; regular backups of all computer records that are tested to be sure they will restore properly; and physical protection of information so that trade secrets, customer lists, supplier lists and other key information cannot be copied by unauthorized employees or third parties. As companies become larger and more sophisticated, there must be additional physical safeguards to the information stored, but locked files and resilient, working backups are the starting point for all businesses.

The technical measures will include, at a minimum, the use of firewalls, encryption, and strong passphrases to avoid simple attacks. Access to various computer systems should not be given to all employees. Instead, each employee should have access only to those computers, programs, and networks related to the person's job duties. Administrative access should be even more carefully limited. For slightly larger organizations, networks should be separated so public facing systems never can be used to breach the corporate, financial, operational, employee, or customer data.

As the company grows in scope, regular audits and assessment of the technical measures should be used to improve the tracking of data flows, the control of information, and the adherence to regular software updates and patches. The company should never let software become out of date. When faced with the financial challenges of investing in new software and hardware tools, the company should always choose to be up to date or to stop using a particular tool. The choice to keep outdated software and hardware will invite hackers, malware, and business disruption.

The administrative safeguards are just as critical. If a company has employees, it must have employment policies. As discussed in earlier chapters, the employer can establish the company's ownership of computer systems and disclose how it monitors the workforce to assure compliance with state and federal law, minimize theft, and improve customer satisfaction. Computer usage policies, and workplace monitoring policies are included along with sick leave, health and safety, benefits, and other important policies for the employees. The employees must be trained and updated on each of the physical and technical safeguards regularly to assure that passwords and authentication steps remain secure, and that good data hygiene is being followed.

The administrative safeguards will also include policies on how data security is maintained. One person within the company should be identified as primarily responsible for all privacy and data security issues, even if that person is also responsible for many other aspects of the business operations. For larger companies, that position will become a full-time job, but for small companies, it should still be highlighted as a priority among the designated employee's duties.

The administrative policies should detail how the owners or key management of the business takes responsibility for privacy and data security. If the company is large enough to have a board of directors that holds regular meetings, then the board of directors should receive periodic updates on the privacy and data security measures. The administrative procedures should include training for all employees on how to identify attempts to breach the computer systems, including threats from phishing, malware, and weak passwords.

The cost and scale of the technical measures will vary dramatically depending on the operations of the business and the size of the company. As companies grow and evolve, they must regularly update their security to meet the current needs of the business and the nature of the ever-evolving threat.

5. Provide Employees with Both Their Rights as Consumers and with Their Protections as Employees

Employees have all the rights of customers and the protections as employees. Small employers rely very heavily on their key employees. Customers all judge a business based on the last interaction they had with an employee. If the employees are committed to the employer, they will usually go the extra mile for the customer. Strong business support for employees, when combined with training and a customer-centric business model, will generally turn into high quality customer service and high customer satisfaction. While this virtuous cycle seems self-evident, it is all too common that businesses make poor choices regarding the working conditions for their employees.

Even the smallest company needs a clear, written employee manual and needs to follow it. In addition to the protections that employees have under the FCRA and other laws, employers can improve the employee satisfaction by making the protection of employee records a priority and minimizing the disclosure of employee information to unauthorized personnel. At a minimum, companies should keep employee records separately from other business records. The employee records may have protected health information that requires additional security.

Employee handbooks and other documents should make clear that the policies apply to both full-time and part-time employees. Where certain provisions apply differently for part-time employees rather than full-time employees, those differences should be clearly explained.

Employee handbooks do not apply to independent contractors, since these are not employees. A contractual addendum related to data privacy and the use of the computer systems for the company should be included in all hiring of independent contractors.

6. Work Closely with the PCI Security, Staying Current on All Security Updates

Most small businesses operate by taking funds in person and online through credit cards and other payment systems. While a few check-only offices remain, those are increasingly rare and a testament to customer disregard. At the same time, payment systems are a focus for thieves, since they are the most direct opportunity to steal money from a company.

The PCI banking consortium has developed the PCI DSS as a business-friendly tool for data security compliance for financial transactions. Businesses that take credit cards are required to comply with the PCI DSS. Nonetheless, companies will sometimes buy used equipment or skip mandatory updates. These cost-shaving efforts can put the entire business at risk. Companies should be diligent on staying up to date with the PCI DSS.

7. Manage Vendors and Contractors Carefully

No business is an island. Companies often lease their property, outsource their cleaning services, utilize service providers for websites, cloud storage, computer processing, conduct financial transactions through banks, and hire independent contractors. Product supply chains may include dozens of companies for manufacturing, assembly, and transport. Each of these vendors and contractors is a business ally and a potential source for data breach risks. The risks will flow from one of three general insecurities: the inadequacy of the vendor's software hygiene, the inconsistency in policies for shared data access, and the misuse of protected, private information.

Inadequate vendor hygiene.

Hackers often look to outside contracts for a backdoor into the protected systems of networks. For example, the 2013 Target breach was triggered by a heating and air conditioning vendor that was used as a conduit for a hacker to install malware into the Target system. Computer consultants often need to adjust firewalls to conduct audits or other activities, and the result is a compromised system. Companies need to be very diligent to assure that systems remain secure after a vendor completes its work.

Contracts with any vendors who require network access with the business should include warranties that the vendor has met current state and federal regulations related to its own security, that is does not know of any ongoing data security incidents with its systems, and that it will indemnify the company for any data losses directly caused by its access to the company's system.

Admittedly, these are not necessarily contractual provisions that all vendors will be willing to sign, but they highlight the risks of letting a company into the computer systems of the small business. Such arrangements should be entered cautiously and only with vendors that have strong industry reputations.

Inconsistent privacy protection policies.

When a small business signs up with an online service provider to hosts its website, provide shopping cart tools, and manage its online presence, the small business agrees to the terms and conditions of that agreement, including the privacy policies of the online host. The privacy policies of the online host can vary significantly from one company to another. If the small business offers its customers a tracking-free customer experience, it will only be able to meet that promise if the online host also commits to operating without any customer tracking.

Every visitor to the small business website is also a visitor to a site of the online hosting service. Whether or not the small business utilizes the data tracking built into the software, the online service provider may be tracking IP addresses, movement across its multiple sites, engagement with ad service providers, and many other interactions. The small business cannot provide more privacy than it has contracted with its online service provider.

Most banks donottrack the customers of their businesses using point of purchase devices. Other financial transaction intermediaries, however, are not restricted by law. These companies may collect information regarding the transactions as well. Like the online services providers, the contract with the financial intermediary must be carefully reviewed to understand what data are being used during the transactions.

Misuse of protected, private information.

In addition to the challenge created for small businesses which contract with large vendors for standardized services, many small businesses also rely on independent contractors and so-called "gig workers" to provide flexible staffing. The independent contractors might be hired for specific projects, like the graphic artists creating a company's artwork and logos, or they might be temporary workers updating websites, designing products, or otherwise working on a fixed-price basis with the company. Because they are not regular employees, the contractual terms of the employee handbook do not apply to independent contractors.

Although there should be a contractual addendum for independent contractors that restrict their use of confidential information and private information, such agreements are not that common. In addition, the ability to enforce the provisions of a restrictive contract against independent contractors are very difficult. To the greatest extent possible, companies should avoid giving independent contractors access to confidential information or to protected customer information.

The risks of misuse of the information is also present with employees and larger vendors, but the company has many avenues of recourse to deal with misuse of information by employees, and the ability to bring breach of contract actions against larger vendors.

8. Do Not Implement Any Policy You Would Not Want to See on the Front Page of the Local Newspaper

This last rule is a general matter of sound advice for all business practices. Data privacy and cybersecurity are very complex areas of law and business practice. Clever attorneys and slick business operators can take advantage of the public by saying one thing and doing another. If an approach feels altogether too clever, it probably is and should be avoided. Small business owners should ask themselves if they are proud of each policy the company implements and if a particular policy would be an embarrassment, then the company should adopt a different strategy.

Some small businesses pride themselves on the privacy protections they give to their customers, while others do not treat privacy as important. There are many companies that are highly profitable even though they promote the lack of privacy or even treat the lack of privacy as a transparency feature. More than privacy, truthfulness and transparency are essential for the success of a small business.

This rule is particularly important when a company makes a significant change in its privacy policy. If a company reverses a longstanding policy and starts to monetize customers, then it has an obligation to provide ample notice to the customers and offer a method of opting out of the policy change or deleting their account. So long as this is done, the change in policy will not usually be newsworthy. If instead, a company makes a rapid change in policy and traps customers into the new policy, then there is much more likely to be a negative reaction by the public.

The successful small business is the pride of its community. The business should operate all its policies to make its community remain proud. In the context of the Fourth Amendment, the

Supreme Court explained that the test for constitutional protection is based upon a reasonable expectation of privacy. The same is true for customer relations with business. The expectation of a corporation's reasonable behavior represents the trust between a company and its patrons. It is when a company violates this expectation that the public becomes upset. Customers expect the companies on which they rely to operate in a reasonable manner with regard to all its policies, including the policies on privacy and data security. Successful companies never breach this trust; the best companies manage to somehow exceed their customers' expectations.

C. Protecting Yourself at Work and at Home

Consumer attitudes towards privacy vary dramatically from person to person and from situation to situation. As a regular shopper, a person might appreciate that a retailer knows which products and brands are preferred and appreciate the customer service offered through tracking and behavioral advertising. The same person might find that behavioral advertising used by a company rarely visited feels creepy, as if the company is stalking the customer by placing ads across multiple websites. Both are examples of behavioral advertising in which the ad is triggered by the online conduct of the consumer, but in the first example, the company that tied the ads to customer behavior is appreciated and in the second example, the company's ads were unwanted.

Health information provides another typical example. Most people appreciate the strong health privacy protection established by HIPAA. They do not want their doctors sharing any information about their medical histories and they do not want employers or insurance companies to make adverse decisions based on the medical files. At the same time, millions of individuals participate in social media sites and support groups for various illnesses and conditions, finding support by sharing their personal stories and medical challenges with others.

Both these examples illustrate that privacy is both personal and contextual. What is appropriate to share in one context may not feel appropriate in another context. As a result, any guidance on personal privacy will be relevant in some situations but unhelpful for others. Nonetheless, there are some basic considerations that may prove helpful.

- *Prioritize where privacy matters the most.* Some people are most concerned about government surveillance, while others are more concerned about their employers' access to personal information or to the use of personal information by corporate advertisers. While good privacy practices can reduce exposure to more than one area of surveillance, some choices make tracking easier than others.
- *Select vendors and technologies based on your own level of privacy concerns.* Privacy protection is a feature of smartphones, web browsers, payment providers, and communications apps. For consumers who prioritize privacy, they should select among the vendors that have made online anonymity and privacy protections a priority. In many cases, companies will offer an advertising-based version of a product and a more expensive version of the product without advertising and data tracking. Again, the consumer has the choice to pay for additional privacy. If an app requests more access to a smartphone than it should need to provide the service, uninstall the app.
- *Be sure to implement the privacy protections available.* Many products, websites, and apps have

privacy settings that can increase the privacy for the user, but often these are not turned on by default. Each user must take the additional time and effort to turn on these settings.

- *Read the privacy policies or analysis of the privacy policies.* Most privacy policies are long, complex, and vague. For popular products and services, there are often published reviews of the privacy policies and settings to help cut quickly through the language of the policy. Consumers should read the policy or read the review to know what they are getting with each product and service.
- *Privacy protections will be breached, so only share content that can be public.* While there are online health care, education, and financial transactions that are increasingly essential, most information posted online is shared as part of social media or other forms of engagement. Since even the most diligent companies have experienced data breaches (and few companies are that diligent), the public should assume that anything posted or shared electronically might become public. Intimate photos and explicit personal details can do a great deal of harm if disseminated widely without authorization. The only guarantee that a photo will not be shared is to avoid taking the photo.
- *Assume personal profiles will be screened by employers.* Most employers look at the public social media profiles of employment candidates, and many candidates are online friends with people already employed by the potential employer. As a result, both the public facing information and often much

of the nonpublic facing information might be available to the employer. Candidates should assume that employers are checking to see if the behavior of potential employees meets the corporate culture desired. Photos of drinking or drug use and statements breaching confidentiality or badmouthing other employers will make it much more difficult for candidates to land new positions. Increasingly, high school and college students maintain both a real pseudonymous social media presence and a clean, public presence moderated for grandparents and employers as a way to manage the unwanted lurkers on social media.

- *Be on the lookout for phishing and other attacks.* Both at home and at work, people are inundated with fraudulent content. Avoid clicking on links in emails unless the sender is well known. If a bank or other company sends information, log in directly rather than clicking the link to the email. If an email seems odd when sent by a friend or colleague, a person should always verify the legitimacy of the email before clicking on a link or sharing the information.
- *Be mindful of unauthorized access at home and at work.* For most people, the friends and family they love and trust are their primary source of support and protection. Nonetheless, there are far too many people who are victims of fraud, violence, and abuse. Anyone who has even the slightest concerns over the trustworthiness of a family member or close friend should be careful to protect their passwords, secure their computers and devices, and take the

same types of steps as do businesses to ensure that no one can get into their accounts. There are apps that let a person hide smartphone apps and accounts so that the phone can be shared without opening the personal accounts to another. Many examples of identity theft, fraud, and abusive postings come because the attackers had access to the computers and phones of the victims.

- *Use good data hygiene.* Personal data hygiene includes the use of strong passwords; never sharing passwords; encrypting data; avoiding untrustworthy websites; erasing all data on any equipment before selling or disposing it; not using public networks for sensitive information; and limiting the disclosure of Social Security numbers, drivers' license numbers, and account numbers. Good data hygiene includes the physical as well as the electronic, so the information in a person's wallet or purse should also be curated to avoid carrying a social security card.

For each person, some of the suggestions may prove more important than others. The goal of these suggestions is to provide each person the power to control how much or how little they would like to be private or to be public.

D. What the Future Holds

Privacy laws have changed considerably in the past five years, and the changes are likely to continue. As governments outside the United States demand higher levels of privacy and security protection, states are also likely to continue to make the same demands. The dizzying array of laws and regulations makes it harder than ever for companies to be fully compliant with all the laws, and the confusion is discouraging the public from caring.

The introduction of GDPR was supposed to increase consumer privacy and consumer control over their data. Instead, it resulted in a barrage of annoying pop-up messages disclosing cookies but offering little meaningful change in corporate behavior or consumer control. The failure of GDPR to matter to the United States public makes it harder for the regulations to make a difference for consumer privacy.

Looking only slightly further into the distance, the expansion of artificial intelligence tools and expanded access to data analytics could significantly exacerbate the challenge of privacy. Both government surveillance and behavioral advertising relies on the interactions between the subject of the surveillance and opportunities to track the behavior. As the efficiency of artificial intelligence continues to increase, the technology will expand in its ability to track individuals as they use online services and operate in the off-line world. Today, all online media consumption can be monitored and used to infer social and economic profiles, personal tastes, and behaviors. Small improvements in the technology will allow the media to be personalized and edited for each individual consumer as it is being produced. Behavioral ads will be augmented with behavioral product placement.

Just as Justice Harlan wrote that the Fourth Amendment is grounded on a reasonable expectation of privacy, it is likely that changes in technology will alter what the public accepts as reasonable. The development of radio and flash photography led to the legal publication of "The Right to Privacy." The improvements in the power of the cell phone led to constitutional protections limiting the ability of police to search phones without a warrant. The use of artificial intelligence to perfect facial and other biometric recognition have the potential to drive courts and legislatures to find new forms of legal protections.

Technology will continue to make it easier for governments, corporations, and individuals to track and follow individuals. Technology will also offer tools to protect consumers from being tracked. It will take more time, but laws and regulations will also help balance these interests, as law makers learn from the public what the public considers reasonable and updates the laws to reflect the emerging consensus.

Key Takeaways from This Chapter:

For both businesses and individuals, there are simple steps that can be followed to improve privacy and data security. There is no "correct" level of privacy. Instead, both the individual and the business must make intentional decisions regarding the extent to which privacy is a priority and then take the steps to achieve that level of privacy.

Small business enterprises must make extra efforts to be transparent regarding their privacy policies. Businesses need to adopt policies that customers can understand and rely upon. Companies must utilize appropriate security measures to be sure that the privacy policies will stand up to hacking, phishing, malware and other attacks.

All individuals must also make choices about their own expectations of privacy. Privacy is a feature of the products, services, and experiences that consumers select. Although the consumer does not have total control over their information, consumers do have an important role to play in shaping the privacy protections they receive.

Things to Know:

Privacy and data security go hand in hand. Just like a corporation or the government, each person must use good data hygiene to protect their own information and the information on all the networks they use.

Technologies are regularly changing, making the choice of phone, computer, browser, and networked devices more important than ever. To maximize privacy, consumers must insist on robust privacy settings and strong data security. These features will only become a priority if the public makes privacy and security a requirement for all purchasing decisions.

The reasonable expectation of privacy will continue to evolve as attitudes shift and new technologies become ubiquitous. The reasonable expectation of privacy is important for business relations as much as for government's Fourth Amendment limitations because the public expectations help inform the business-customer relationship.

Things to Think About:

Is there a way to make a privacy policy simpler and less driven by changes in technology and expectations?

What would a comprehensive privacy regime look like? As the rules change, which parties are benefitted from the changes and which parties are better off with the status quo?

What will United States privacy policy be ten years from now, and what events will shape the change in the policy?

Bibliography

Chapter 1

4 WILLIAM BLACKSTONE, COMMENTARIES ON THE LAWS OF ENGLAND Book 4, Ch. 13, (1769) (eavesdropping).

Irwin R. Kramer, *The Birth of Privacy Law: A Century Since Warren and Brandeis*, 39 CATH. U. L. REV. 703 (1990).

John A. Robertson, *Decisional Authority over Embryos and Control of IVF Technology*, 28 JURIMETRICS J. 285 (1988).

Paul M. Secunda, *The (Neglected) Importance of Being Lawrence: The Constitutionalization of Public Employee Rights to Decisional Non-Interference in Private Affairs*, 40 U.C. DAVIS L. REV. 85 (2006).

Daniel J. Solove, *A Brief History of Information Privacy Law* in PROSKAUER ON PRIVACY, PLI (2006).

Daniel J. Solove, A TAXONOMY OF PRIVACY, 154 U. PA. L. REV. 477 (2006).

Chapter 2

Samuel Dash, Richard F. Schwartz & Robert E. Knowlton, The Eavesdroppers (1959).

Susan Freiwald, *Online Surveillance: Remembering the Lessons of the Wiretap Act*, 56 Ala. L. Rev. 9 (2004).

Yale Kamisar, *The Wiretapping-Eavesdropping Problem: A Professor's View*, 44 Minn. L. Rev. 891 (1960).

Orin S. Kerr, *The Curious History of Fourth Amendment Searches*, 2012 S. Ct. Rev. 67 (2012).

Neil Richards, *The Third-Party Doctrine and the Future of the Cloud*, 94 Wash. U.L. Rev. 1441 (2017).

Chapter 3

Denis O'Brien, *Right of Privacy*, 2 COLUM. L. REV. 437 (1902).

Dorothy J. Glancy, *The Invention of the Right to Privacy*, 21 ARIZ. L. REV. 1 (1979).

Samuel Warren & Louis Brandeis, *The Right to Privacy*, 4 HARV. L. REV. 193 (1890).

William L. Prosser, *Privacy*, 48 CALIF. L. REV. 383 (1960).

Chapter 4

Ifeoma Ajunwa *et. al.*, *Limitless Worker Surveillance*, 105 CAL. L. REV. 735 (2017).

Matthew T. Bodie *et. al.*, *The Law and Policy of People Analytics*, 88 U. COLO. L. REV. 961 (2017).

Matthew W. Finkin, *Employee Privacy, American Values, and the Law*, 72 CHI.-KENT L. REV. 221 (1996).

Bob E. Lype, *Employment Law and New Technologies: Emerging Trends Affecting Employers*, 47 TENN. B.J. 20 (2011).

Chapter 5

Daniel J. Solove & Woodrow Hartzog, *The FTC and the New Common Law of Privacy*, 114 COL. L. REV. 583 (2014).

Jane E. Kirtley & Scott Memmel, *Rewriting the "Book of the Machine": Regulatory and Liability Issues for the Internet of Things*, 19 MINN. J.L. SCI. & TECH. 455, 498 (2018).

Michal S. Gal & Niva Elkin-Koren, *Algorithmic Consumers*, 30 HARV. J.L. & TECH. 309 (2017).

Stuart L. Pardau & Blake Edwards, *The FTC, the Unfairness Doctrine, and Privacy by Design: New Legal Frontiers in Cybersecurity*, 12 J. BUS. & TECH. L. 227 (2017).

Tal Z. Zarsky, *Incompatible: The GDPR in the Age of Big Data*, 47 SETON HALL L. REV. 995 (2017).

Chapter 6

JASON ANDRESS, THE BASICS OF INFORMATION SECURITY: UNDERSTANDING THE FUNDAMENTALS OF INFOSEC IN THEORY AND PRACTICE (2014).

DAVID KIM & MICHAEL G. SOLOMON, FUNDAMENTALS OF INFORMATION SYSTEMS SECURITY (2016).

Jeff Kosseff, *Defining Cybersecurity Law*, 103 IOWA L. REV. 985 (2018).

Lawrence J. Trautman, *Managing Cyberthreat*, 33 SANTA CLARA HIGH TECH. L.J. 230 (2017).

JOHN R. VACCA, COMPUTER AND INFORMATION SECURITY HANDBOOK (2ND ED. 2013).

MICHAEL E. WHITMAN & HERBERT J. MATTORD, PRINCIPLES OF INFORMATION SECURITY (6TH ED. 2017).

Chapter 7

DOUGLAS J. LANDOLL, INFORMATION SECURITY POLICIES, PROCEDURES, AND STANDARDS: A PRACTITIONER'S REFERENCE (2016).

MARK RHODES-OUSLEY, INFORMATION SECURITY: THE COMPLETE REFERENCE (2ND ED. 2013).

Daniel J. Solove & Danielle Keats Citron, *Risk and Anxiety: A Theory of Data-Breach Harms*, 96 TEX. L. REV. 737 (2018).

LIISA THOMAS, THOMAS ON DATA BREACH: A PRACTICAL GUIDE TO HANDLING DATA BREACH NOTIFICATIONS WORLDWIDE (2016 ED.)

Chapter 8

Carolina Alonso, *This Little Piggy Went to Wall Street: Privacy Law When A Toy Becomes Your Child's Banker*, 1 GEO. L. TECH. REV. 458 (2017).

Natalie M. Banta, *Minors and Digital Asset Succession*, 104 IOWA L. REV. 1699 (2019).

Eldar Haber, *Toying with Privacy: Regulating the Internet of Toys*, 80 OHIO ST. L.J. 399 (2019).

Stacey B. Steinberg, *Sharenting: Children's Privacy in the Age of Social Media*, 66 EMORY L.J. 839 (2017).

Chapter 9

REBECCA HEROLD & KEVIN BEAVER, THE PRACTICAL GUIDE TO HIPAA PRIVACY AND SECURITY COMPLIANCE (2ND ED. 2014).

SEAN MURPHY, HEALTHCARE INFORMATION SECURITY AND PRIVACY (2015).

BERNARD PETER ROBICHAU, HEALTHCARE INFORMATION PRIVACY AND SECURITY: REGULATORY COMPLIANCE AND DATA SECURITY IN THE AGE OF ELECTRONIC HEALTH RECORDS (2014).

LAURIE RINEHART-THOMPSON, INTRODUCTION TO HEALTH INFORMATION PRIVACY AND SECURITY (2013).

SHEBA VINE AND JULIE SHEPPARD, FIRST HEALTHCARE COMPLIANCE HIPAA PRIVACY AND SECURITY (2019).

Chapter 10

Douglas W. Arner *et. al.*, *Fintech, Regtech, and the Reconceptualization of Financial Regulation*, 37 NW. J. INT'L L. & BUS. 371 (2017).

Chris Brummer & Yesha Yadav, *Fintech and the Innovation Trilemma*, 107 GEO. L.J. 235 (2019).

BURTON ROSENBERG, HANDBOOK OF FINANCIAL CRYPTOGRAPHY AND SECURITY (2010).

Katherine E. Ruiz Díaz, *Pre-Paid Payment Cards in A Post-Schrems World: A Case Study on the Effects of the Privacy Shield Principles*, 9 U. PUERTO RICO BUS. L.J. 86 (2018).

Cheng-Yun Tsang, *From Industry Sandbox to Supervisory Control Box: Rethinking the Role of Regulators in the Era of Fintech*, 2019 U. ILL. J.L. TECH. & POL'Y 355 (2019).